'Policing The P

Written and Researched
By Alf Tunstall
and
Jeff Cowdell

THREE COUNTIES PUBLISHING (Books) LIMITED

Published by

TCP BOOKS

Three Counties Publishing (Books) Limited

P.O. Box 435 Leek, Staffordshire England, ST13 5TB
telephone 01538 380910 fax 01538 382204
e-mail: tcpbooksltd@aol.com

ISBN 0-9535239-9-3

Typeset by Clerment Ferrand International, Leek, Staffordshire, ST13 5TB
and Printed by J.H.Brookes Printers, Hanley, Stoke-on-Trent, Staffordshire, England

Best wishes to Mark
October 2002

CONTENTS

Contents

ACKNOWLEDGEMENTS

We would like to thank the following for their help and assistance in compiling this book. Sergeant Alan Walker Curator, and Mr. David Baldwin Assistant Curator of the Staffordshire Police Museum. Mrs. Beard and her staff at the City of Stoke-on-Trent Archives and Library Department. The staff at the Stoke-on-Trent City Museum.

Mr. Harry Steele formally Assistant Chief Constable of Stoke-on-Trent.

The Editor of the Evening Sentinel Newspaper Stoke-on-Trent, and Mr. Stewart Robinson Librarian at the Sentinel. The Tyne and Wear Archives Service. Mr. John Mason of the Norfolk Police Museum. We would also like to thank the following retired members of the former City force for their help. Mr. Jim Kelly, Mr. Gerry Herbert, Mr. & Mrs. Tony Lea, Mrs. Doreen Whitehurst. We must also thank the following for the use of photographs. Mr. Neil Bradley, Mr. E. Bateman, Mr. Bill Bates, Mr. John Ackerley, Mr. M. Griffin, Mrs. A. Gleves, Mrs. M. Hollings, Mr. Ray Reardon, Mr. Peter Saunders, Mr. Jack Wild of Halifax. Mr. Colin Jackson of Wakefield, P.C. Ian Thorton and Mr. Noel Smith of Wallasey.

I would also like to thank my friend Robert, who taught me to use a computer in place of my old and trusted typewriter.

If we have forgotten to mention anyone then we do apologize.

The first seeds for a book giving the history of policing in North Staffordshire, were sown by the late Inspector Ralph Gribble, who unfortunately died before he was able to complete his research. Some of the notes made by the late Inspector Gribble have been of tremendous use to us in compiling this book, and for which we are entirely grateful.

The Coat of Arms on the cover of this book, is used by kind permission of the Lord Mayor and Council of the City of Stoke-on-Trent.

FOREWORD

I am delighted to be able to write a foreword for this significant piece of work about the various Police Forces which have policed the Stoke-on-Trent area.

In my case I was helped by having read Alf Tunstall's earlier book on the history of policing in the Borough of Newcastle-under-Lyme, together with a book written by Frank Bunn who describes "his experiences as Chief Constable" in part of his book. This present document should be seen as an historical treasure because it tells us so much about the social history of North Staffordshire over the last 150 years. Some things do not change. Difficulties with increases in manpower and the number off different things that police officers have been expected to do have always appeared over the years. I regret to say that an 81% detection rate is now rather harder to achieve than it was in 1942.

I congratulate Alf Tunstall and Jeff Cowdell for the amount of research that has gone into producing this volume and I am sure that anyone interested in policing or North Staffordshire or both will, as I did, find it fascinating reading.

J. W. Giffard Q.P.M., B.A. (Hons.),
Chief Constable of Staffordshire.

INTRODUCTION

Prior to 1829 the only form of police in England was the Parish Constable system, members of the community appointed each year by the Local Justices. In that year Sir Robert Peel, the then Home Secretary, formed the Metropolitan Police force responsible for the policing of London, the first paid professional police force.

The New Police, as they were known, soon became so successful in the capital that the criminals soon began to move out to the smaller provincial towns. To combat this growing problem, some of these towns decided to set up police forces of their own. The first town within the northern area of Staffordshire to set up its own police force was Newcastle-under-Lyme Borough, which did so in 1834, just months prior to the Government passing the Municipal Corporation Act of 1835. This compelled all boroughs to set up a watch committee, appoint head constables, and other constables.

The possible reason for Hanley not doing this, was because at that time, Hanley was not a borough, and did not become a borough until 1857, and a county borough until 1888.

The first paid professional policeman to walk the streets of Hanley, which was in 1843, were members of the Staffordshire County Police force, formed the previous year in 1842, who became responsible for the policing of Hanley.

It was in September, 1870, that the then Borough of Hanley set up its own watch committee, and police force.

In 1910 upon the federation taking place of the six pottery towns of Burslem, Fenton, Hanley, Longton, Tunstall, and Stoke-upon-Trent, the Borough of Hanley Police force became a part of the Stoke-on Trent County Borough Police.

A. Tunstall.

CHAPTER I.

THE EARLY YEARS 1843 - 1879.

Hanley was to see its first professional policemen on its streets in 1843, when a few members of the Staffordshire County Constabulary which had only just been formed, were stationed in the town under Superintendent William Lance. The total strength of the County Constabulary at that time was 187 officers and men, however, it is not known how many of these men were stationed in the Hanley Division. Only one of the original Hanley Watchmen was taken into the new county force. 12 years later the total strength of the county force was 282. In 1864, the County had a total of 29 men under Superintendent Samuel Coles stationed in the division, but not all of these men would have been stationed in the town of Hanley itself, because the division took in Brown Edge, Bucknall, Etruria, Milton, Norton, Tinkersclough, and Washerwall. At the time of the County ceasing to be responsible for the policing of Hanley in 1870, on the formation of the new Hanley Borough force, it had 31 officers stationed in the division.

SETTING UP OF THE NEW BOROUGH FORCE 1870.

The seeds for the establishment of the Hanley Borough force were first sown at a meeting of the General Purpose Committee of the Council on the 2nd July, 1870, when the Committee came to the unanimous decision to recommend to the full council that they establish their own police force for the Borough. All the members of the council were. However, not in favour of a separate force, and one of them pointed out that it would mean an increase in the rates. He said that there were only 31 men stationed in the town at present. If they set up their own force they would require 44 men if they were receive the government grant. There must be one police officer to every 1,000 of the population. Another councillor referred to Newcastle-under-Lyme, who he said paid less rate than Hanley, and managed their own force, and that force was held up in admiration by the local people (but what this councillor failed to say was that the Newcastle force at this time was not receiving a government grant due to inefficient numbers of men in the force. A vote was later taken in favour of the setting up of a separate police force for the borough.

The first meeting of the newly formed Watch Committee took place at the end of July, 1870. The main priority of this meeting was to find a suitable person to fill the office of Chief Constable for the force. Adverts were placed in various newspapers and as a result 47 persons applied for the position, and from these applicants, on the 10th September, 1870, the Watch Committee interviewed the following four persons, who were short listed;-

Mr. Alexander, Chief Constable of Newcastle-under-Lyme.

Mr. White, Huddersfield.

Mr. Bamford. Ashton-under-Lyne.

Mr. Lindsey, Chester.

Mr. Stanford Alexander, Chief Constable of Hanley 1870 to 1872. Seen here on right of photograph in top hat. Photograph taken when Chief Constable of Leominster.

Mr. Ted Hadley

MR. STANFORD ALEXANDER, CHIEF CONSTABLE 1870 - 1873.

The successful applicant was Mr. Stanford Alexander, who was to be paid £150 per year, with free accommodation. With the appointment of the Chief Constable the new borough force came into being

TERRIFYING INCIDENT AT A SCHOOL 1871

In the afternoon of July, 1871, the children at Shelton School, were alarmed when a man rushed into the school with a long knife, and threatened to cut the children's throats. All the children ran out of the school terrified, some to get assistance. When the police arrived the man had left the scene. It is reported that the man was known, and was believed to be a lunatic from a nearby town, however, it was not reported what action if any was taken against that man.

THE FIRST GOVERNMENT INSPECTION OF THE FORCE *1871*.

In 1871, the first inspection of the force was carried out by Colonel Cobbe, H.M.Inspector of Constabulary for the Midland Counties. There were 31 men on parade, and Colonel Cobbe, said, I am very pleased with what I have seen, and I shall report very favourably on the force.

Although, the Government Inspector may have certified the force efficient, a few of the residents of the town did not seem to agree with him from the following letter which appeared in the local newspaper.

Sir,

Hanley at the present time is infested with beggars, codgers, and impostors, who pursue their calling without the slightest check or interference from the police. This change which is for the worst has taken place almost immediately after the formation of the Borough police force.

COMPLAINTS AGAINST MR. ALEXANDER *1871*.

It would seem from the beginning that the Hanley force was not run as efficiently as it should have been. Too much authority seems to have been left in the hands of the Chief Constable, and too little supervision applied by the Watch Committee.

The force was less than 8 months old when Councillor Bebbington was making the following allegations against Mr. Alexander;-

(1)   That he did by improper, and illegal means obtained money, and valuables from a Mr. William Pepworth, and his wife.

(2)   That he caused to be obtained a fictitious warrant to obtain the above articles.

(3)   That the warrant was obtained by the Chief Constable for his own pecuniary advantage.

Councillor Bebbington also said that it was common knowledge in the town that the Chief Constable had a Mrs. Hodgkinson brought into the police office, and obtained £1 from her by threats.

Mr. Alexander later said that this £1 was a lawful debt that was owed by Mrs. Hodgkinson, and that he had only helped a local tradesmen recover what was due to him.

Councillor Bebbington made the following statement to the Council; I bring these charges before this committee, not as a vendetta against the Chief Constable, but as a public duty, and I think the members of the Watch Committee should know what is going on.

Members of the Watch Committee interviewed the Chief Constable, and must have been more than satisfied with his explanation, because in March 1872, they gave him a pay increase of £15 per year. This was after Mr. Alexander asked the Committee for permission to apply for another police post. He was told that the Committee did not want to lose his services.

In April, 1871, three little urchins, none of them whom were over 6 years of age, were alleged to have started a fire in a furniture dealers premises in Tontine Passage, causing damage amounting to £55, by throwing lighted matches into straw. The court took no action because of their age.

During the year 1871 a total of 63 persons were charged with assaults on police. This was an increase of 2 on the previous year.

FURTHER PROBLEMS FOR MR. ALEXANDER 1872

In October, 1872, Thomas Edward Watson, a Metropolitan Police officer, who was in Hanley to collect a prisoner to convey back to London, appeared before the police court on a charge of being drunk and disorderly in the police station. The case, however, was thrown out by the magistrates. Watson then made a complaint against Superintendent Alexander, and his wife. He alleged that Mrs. Alexander had spoken to him in a derisory, and objectionable manner, and that when he himself objected, he was assaulted by Superintendent Alexander, and thrown out of the office. When he protested he was arrested and put in a cell. The relieving officer who was present in the police station at the time, stated that Watson was not drunk.

A few days after the incident Alderman Stephenson suggested that a special meeting of the Watch Committee be called, but before this meeting could take place, a public meeting was held in the town at which the Mayor officiated. The Mayor was told that the majority of people in the town had no confidence in Mr. Alexander the Chief Constable.

The meeting asked that the Chief Constable and all the other officers which included the two inspectors, who had given perjured evidence should be dismissed by the Watch Committee, as they felt that the proper administration of justice in this Borough could not take place under the present set up.

Mr. Alexander was called before the meeting of the Watch Committee at the beginning of November to answer the following charges, and questions that were put to him. He was told that they did not think it was proper that Mrs. Alexander should be in the police office at all, and was to be kept out in future. The Chief Constable said that his wife would be only too pleased to keep out of the office, but it meant that if he was called out, and there was no one else available, the office would have to be locked. He was instructed to keep a man on a local beat so that he could be called upon if need be.

Mr. Alexander was also informed that the Watch Committee thought that there were a large number of irregularities in the management of the force, and that a sub committee of the Watch Committee under the Chairmanship of the Mayor would carry out a thorough investigation into the working of the force.

From what this committee found out, it would appear that the Watson affair was only the tip of the iceberg.

When the force books were examined, it was found that £40 which had been paid to the Chief Constable, by the management of the theatre, had not been paid into the Superannuation Fund, but had been divided equally among the men. Mr. Alexander replied that he had never received any instructions as to what he must do with the money.

The Watch Committee said that in future the payment of gratuities would not be left in the hands of the Chief Constable, but would be decided by the Committee. Members of the Watch Committee had also received a number of complaints from people in the town that they had not received any allowances when they attended court as witnesses. The Chief Constable replied that the money was at the police station should they wish to collect it.

RESIGNATION OF MR. ALEXANDER 1872.

It was quite obvious that the Watch Committee were not happy with things, and a special meeting of the Watch Committee was held on the 14th December, 1872. It was to this meeting that Mr. Alexander tendered his resignation.

A replacement to Mr. Alexander had to be found, and adverts were placed in a number of newspapers. As a result 22 applications for the post were received of which the following 5 persons were interviewed. They were;-

Inspector Joseph Bamford, Ashton-under-Lyne Borough Police.

Inspector W. Bottom, Stalybridge Borough Police.

Superintendent W. Hernaman, Lichfield City Police.

Inspector Ramsdon White, Huddersfield Borough Police.

Inspector George Williams Salford City Police.

MR. GEORGE WILLIAMS, CHIEF CONSTABLE 1873 - 1875,

Inspector Geo. Williams was appointed the Boroughs second Chief Constable. He was 32 years of age, and took up his new duties on the 11th January, 1873.

The new Chief Constable, however, refused to occupy the official residence that had been used by his predecessor. This was a flat above the police station. Alderman Pidduck commented, I don't blame him, its horrible accommodation. Mr. Williams was to be allowed £45 per year, to pay for rent for his new home. Mr. Pidduck remarked to fellow members of the Watch Committee, I think we will get on in harmony with the new Chief Constable. The Chief Constable was now receiving £210 per annum, which also included the £45 per year rent allowance.

At the end of February of that year, the former Chief Constable Mr. Alexander applied to the Watch Committee for a refund of his superannuation deductions amounting to £18 12s 5d. After the Town Clerk had taken legal advice, he had to inform Mr. Alexander that the money could only be returned in exceptional circumstances, and they did not exist in this case.

In May, the Chief Constable suggested to the Watch Committee, that a competent person should be appointed to look after the books, forms, etc. This man would reside at the police station, and he or his wife would also be responsible for the general upkeep, and cleanliness of the station. He would be paid as a 3rd class sergeant, i.e. £1 7s 0d per week.

A Mr. Evans, of Swan Street was at this time supplying the prisoners meals at 4d each.

At the 1873 Brewster Sessions the magistrates made the following statement; Hanley is in an unfavourable position compared with other towns of similar size. There is one public house to every 132 of the population, which is above the national average. Last year 90 persons were charged before the court with being drunk and incapable, and 208 with being drunk and disorderly.

GOVERNMENT INSPECTION 1873

Her Majesty's Inspector of Constabulary Colonel Cobbe, inspected the force in 1873. The following were on parade;

1 Chief Constable.   2 Inspectors.   3 Sergeants.   30 Constables.   1 Vacancy.   Total establishment 38 men . Four constables who had previously served with the Salford Police had recently transferred to Hanley.

Her Majesty's Inspector said, I am pleased with all I have seen. I would like to make one suggestion. I would like to see the Chief Constable being able to deal with minor disciplinary offences and fine up to one days pay.

ELECTION DISTURBANCES *1874.*

1874 was to see a Parliamentary Election held, and most elections in those far off days resulted in general mayhem, and disorder. The Watch Committee instructed the Chief Constable to take all necessary precautions to keep the peace. Police reinforcements from Birmingham, and Newcastle-under-Lyme were brought into the town. A number of special constables were also sworn in for the day. Officers, and men from the 22nd Regiment of Infantry stationed at Hulme Barracks, Manchester, were also stationed in the area on standby.

All went off well until the night of Thursday 12th February, 1874, when the results of the General Election were declared, then ugly scenes took place in Hanley. A number of drunken and ill-disposed persons tried to force their way into the Town Hall with intent of destroying the ballot papers, in order that there may be another election. When this proved unsuccessful, the crowd then tried to attack the police office to release the prisoners who had been taken into custody earlier that day.

The situation was finally brought under control by the local forces and special constables, with the assistance of the County constabulary from surrounding pottery divisions.

Mr. Williams the Chief Constable was later able to report to the Watch Committee, that the cost of the damage on the night amounted to £30, and that no one was seriously injured.

The Watch Committee requested the Chief Constable to obtain helmets, and cutlasses for the members of the force. They also said that metal shutters and bars be fixed to the windows of the police station, and that the door be clad in metal. The committee ordered that the few members who were still off duty as a result of injuries received in the riot, were to be paid in full, and their medical expenses would also be paid. During the disturbances, the military, although on standby nearby, were never called upon to assist.

The Watch Committee later sent a letter of thanks to Captain Congrave, the Chief Constable of Staffordshire, and the Chief Constables of Birmingham, and Newcastle-under Lyme.

CHIEF CONSTABLE'S REPORT *1874.*

The Chief Constable's report to the Watch Committee in 1874 showed that 2,005 persons had appeared before the magistrates, of this number 833 had been arrested , and 1172 summoned. Of these 1666 were male, and 339 female. 473 of them were unable to read or write. There were 55 ale houses, 184 beer houses, and 59 outdoor beer houses situated within the Borough. During the year 75 houses had been found insecure, 9 shops insecure, and 10 warehouses insecure. 9 constables had appeared before him for neglect of duty.

At the last meeting of the Watch Committee for the year 1874, the Committee decided that in future the Hanley men were to receive the same rate of pay as the County force.

RESIGNATION OF MR. WILLIAMS 1875.

In June, 1875, after only 18 months as Chief Constable, Mr. Williams tendered his resignation, to take up a similar post as Chief Constable of Wigan Borough Police.

The Mayor said, " We are sorry to see you go. You have always carried out your duties in the most efficient , and polite manner.

MR. HERBERT WINDLE, CHIEF CONSTABLE 1875 - 1901.

The Watch Committee decided not to advertise for a replacement to Mr. Williams, but to offer the post to Inspector Herbert Windle, already serving in the force. Mr. Windle had originally joined the Hanley Borough force on its formation in 1870, having transferred from Chesterfield Borough Police, with the rank of inspector.

Mr. Windle's promotion to Chief Constable took effect from the 25th June, 1875. He was to be paid a salary of £200 per annum, rising to £225 after 3 years.

The year 1875, had opened with the two inspectors being granted an increase in pay.

Mr. Herbert Windle Chief Constable of Hanley 1875 to 1901

Mrs. Audrey Gleves.

People in the town were complaining to the police and members of the council regarding the number of boys, who were about the streets, throwing stones, and breaking windows. The Chief Constable was requested to employ a constable in plain clothes to try and put a stop to the problem. P.C. Dennis was to be allowed £6 per year in lieu of uniform.

Inspector Lloyd Leaves to become Chief Constable.

In 1878, Inspector William Lloyd, left the force on being appointed Chief Constable of Louth Borough Police, in Lincolnshire. He had originally joined Newcastle-under-Lyme Borough Police in 1866, as a constable, later transferring with Stanford Alexander, when he was appointed the Chief Constable of Hanley Borough on it's formation in 1870. He was later promoted sergeant then inspector.

William Lloyd died in 1886, aged 50 years.

PROMOTIONS *1879*

Sergeant Proffitt left the force in February, 1879, on transfer to Warrington Borough, Lancashire, as inspector. Constable Bailey was promoted sergeant to fill the vacancy, and was also appointed engineer in charge of the fire engine.

At this time the force was paying the following prices for its uniform;-

Inspector's tunics	… …	£2 9s 0d	*each*	(£2.45p)
" *dress trousers*	… …	£1 1s 0d	*per pair*	(£1.5p)
" *undress trousers*	… …	19s 6d	*per pair*	(.95p)
" *serge tunics*	… …	£1 0s 0d	*each*	
Sergeant's tunics	… …	£1 11s 0d	*each*	(£1.60p)
Constable's tunics	… …	£1 5s 0d	*each*	(£1.25p)
Helmets	… …	7s 6d	*each*	(.35p)
Capes	… …	£1 0s 6d	*each*	
Inspector's capes	… …	£1 11s 6d	*each*	(£1.65p)

CONSTABLES IN TROUBLE *1879.*

Police constable Castle appeared before the Watch Committee in August, 1879, to answer the following charges:-

(1)   That he did assault P.C. Maycock in Market Square, Hanley on the 18th July.

(2)   That on the 21st July, he did parade up and down outside P.C. Maycock's house for up to half a hour, and did use indecent language likely to cause a breach of the peace. Castle was fined 5s (25p). He resigned in September the following year.

P.C. Thompson also appeared before the same Committee charged with taking part in an illegal lottery, for a gold grand in the Roebuck beer house. He was dismissed from the force.

A Victorian Helmet Badge of the Hanley Borough Police

Author's Collection

CHAPTER II

A NEW DECADE 1880 - 1889

FURTHER DISCIPLINE PROBLEMS 1880.

The year 1880 seems to have been a busy one for members of the force and the Watch Committee, who received a number of complaints from a variety of people.

A special meeting of the Watch Committee was held in August, that year to deal with a number of disciplinary offences committed by members of the force, mostly involving drunkenness. At the end of the meeting 5 constables had been dismissed from the force, and 2 fined.

In the following months Abraham Davies wrote a letter to the committee making the following complaints about the police:-

He said the police had taken £1 2s 0d from him when he was arrested and did not give him a receipt. Also that they had failed to return a knife to him on his release from custody. After an inquiry the committee came to the conclusion that the allegations were unfounded, and no action was taken.

CONVEYANCE OF PRISONERS 1880.

From the beginning of the year the Watch Committee decided to pay for prisoners to be conveyed from the police station to the railway station by carriage. This was due to the council having received numerous complaints regarding prisoners being marched through the streets of the town in shackles.

EARLY TRAFFIC PROBLEMS 1880.

In September of this year, complaints were being received about carters driving on the wrong side of the road. The Watch Committee had a number of placards made, and put up in the main street of the town, cautioning persons against committing this offence, and warning them that action would be taken against offenders.

Serious Assault on P. C. Lewis 1880.

On the night of the 16th October, 1880, an assault of a most savage nature took place upon Police constable Lewis, in Marsh Street, Hanley, which resulted in the following persons Eileen Freeman, William Freeman, Patrick Conroy, James Burke, John Hammond, John Brown, Catherine Brown, Mary Ann Orde, all appearing before the Borough magistrates on a charge of causing grievous bodily harm upon Constable Lewis.

The facts were presented to the court including the evidence of Constable Lewis, who said " I was on duty in Marsh Street, when I saw James Freeman, who was not in court, drag a woman, who he knew to be his wife, along Marsh Street, and into Black Horse Lane, and then began to hit her. I then took hold of Freeman, and attempted to arrest him. His brother William then came to his assistance, and they both knocked me to the ground and began kicking me, soon a crowd had gathered, and they all began to hit, and kick me while I was on the floor. Inspector Wall, and Constable Johnson later came to my assistance"

The hearing before the magistrates lasted from 2.pm until 7.pm, and P.C. Lewis was allowed to give evidence sitting down, due to the injuries he had sustained in the assault.

Doctor Spanton who attended to Lewis, was to tell the court that when he first saw him, he was partly stunned, and did not seem to know what had happened. At the moment P.C. Lewis is in constant pain, he has abrasions to his chest, and his finding it painful to breath. He has a very severe cut to his lip, cuts, and bruising to his face, head, and several injuries to the back of his ear. He had also had some of his whiskers pulled out.

The case against Catherine Brown, and Mary Ann Orde, was dismissed, all other defendants were remanded to the next Quarter Sessions, where William Freeman, and John Brown were sentenced to 9 months imprisonment, and the rest 6 months imprisonment. James Freeman was to avoid arrest until May, when he was then sentenced to 12 months imprisonment. All defendants had previous convictions for drunkenness, and assault.

These were some the first defendants to appear at the Borough Quarter Sessions, as Hanley was not given the authority to appoint a Recorder, and hold it's own Quarter Sessions until October, 1880. Mr. J.B. Brindley was appointed the first Recorder, and the first sessions took place in January the following year.

Police constable Lewis was to receive a gratuity of £5 5s 0d., and a letter of commendation from a grateful Watch Committee for his actions on the night.

At the meeting of the Watch Committee in April, 1881, they were informed that P.C. Lewis was still off sick. Councillor George Bradford suggested that Lewis should be sent to the convalescent home at Southport, and that he would meet the costs, which were 4 guineas.

Less than a year later Lewis was to resign from the force due to his injuries received. The police surgeon reported that he had been permanently maimed, and would not be able to discharge his duties properly. He was awarded £40 from the superannuation fund which assisted him to emigrate to Canada.

SERIOUS ALLEGATIONS AGAINST POLICE CONSTABLE JOHNSON 1880.

Serious allegations were made against a Police constable Johnson at the Borough police court on Tuesday, November, 12th 1880, by a man named John Mulligan, a potter, after being found guilty of being drunk in the police office on the previous night. On the conclusion of the case, the defendant produced from his pocket, a muffler saturated in blood, pointed to an ugly cut on the side of his head, and asked the Bench if they allowed policeman to ill-use prisoners as he had been ill-used in the cells. The magistrates then asked the prisoner if the officer he was complaining about was P.C. Johnson, to which Mulligan replied, Yes.

The magistrates then ordered Johnson to be sent for, and on his arrival at the court, was formally charged with having assaulted Mulligan, to which he pleaded not guilty.

The complainant was then sworn, and gave evidence to the effect that he had been locked in the cell for about one hour, he was thirsty, and kicked on the cell door to attract the attention of the officer so that he could request a drink of water. Johnson then came to him, and after opening the cell door, made an insulting remark, then struck him a violent blow on the side of the head with the empty metal water can, causing the wound he now had. He was not given any water.

The following morning P.C. Rabbit came to his cell, and the complainant asked him for warm water to bath his head, and told him what Johnson had done to him.

P.C. Rabbit was then called to give evidence, and did admit that Mullingan had informed him that P.C. Johnson had hit him. P.C. Rabbit was censured by the Bench, when he said that he had not informed the Chief Constable of the complaint.

In answer to questions put by P.C. Johnson, the complainant denied that he attempted to wrestle with him, or bite him in the cells.

William Stanford, a lad who had been confined in the adjoining cell, said that he had heard complainant ask for water, he then heard the knock of a tin can, and then Mulligan began to cry. He had not heard any wrestling in the cell.

A woman who had been with the prisoner, when he was locked up, and Sergeant Jones, who was on duty in the police station when Mulligan was brought in both said that he did not have a cut to his head, and that his muffler was not covered in blood.

P.C. Weston who was with Johnson when he went to answer the banging on the cell door, said that Johnson supplied the prisoner with water on him requesting it, but instead of him taking hold of the water can, he grasped Johnson, and a struggle took place. Johnson fought his way out of the cell, and the door was closed. Weston also stated that he was not aware that the prisoner had received any injury.

The Mayor who was on the Bench said that it was the duty of the magistrates to protect the police, but they must also protect the public from acts of excess violence by the police. We will have the case sifted to the end, and if the charge is substantiated I will certainly object to Johnson remaining in the police.

Mr. Windle, the Chief Constable, said, I had not heard of this matter until this man made his statement in the box this morning. So far as I am concerned I have always endeavoured to protect the prisoners under my charge.

The Mayor said, I can corroborate this, I do not believe Mr. Windle could be guilty of committing, or sanctioning any cruel action. The case was then adjourned until Friday, when a full bench of magistrates heard the case. Mulligan who was charged with assaulting P.C. Johnson, was represented by a Mr. Swords, and Johnson by a Mr. Ayre.. P.C. Johnson then gave evidence that he was attacked in the cells by the prisoner, before he struck him. After an adjournment of 40 minutes, the Bench returned, and announced that both cases would be dismissed.

CONTINGENCY PLANS AGAINST ELECTION PROBLEMS 1880.

A parliamentary election was held 1880, and the council not wanting a repetition of the riots that had taken place at the previous election, decided to reinforce the local police. Thirty extra officers from Wolverhampton, Macclesfield, Newcastle-under-Lyme, and Staffordshire County Police forces, also Special Constables performed duty in the town. The Chief Constable afterwards reported that all had been quiet on the day of the election.

Hanley officers later travelled to Wolverhampton, and Macclesfield to assist at elections there.

The Watch Committee later received a bill for £36 13s 11d from the County to cover the cost for the loan of their officers.

FURTHER PROBLEMS WITH DISCIPLINE 1881.

The new year did not star well for Police constable Dovey. He failed to report for duty on the first day of the year, and was not seen again until the 18th January, when he was found in a drunken state at his lodgings by Inspector Vickers, and a sergeant. Action was also taken against him for not delivering up his uniform. He was fined by the court, and dismissed from the force.

GOVERNMENT INSPECTION 1881.

In March, 1881, Colonel Cobbe, H.M.Inspector of Constabulary for the Midland Counties, requested the Watch Committee to increase the strength of the force, but did not stipulate a number. A few months later the strength of the force was increased by three men, one of whom was to be a sergeant. This sergeant was to have sole responsibility for summons and warrants dealt with by the force.

The Chief Constable was to make his own selection, and P.C. Williams was promoted to sergeant, and placed in charge of this new department.

HELMETS AND INSIGNIA 1881.

It would appear from records that helmets were back in use again, less than a year after being replaced by caps. A number of helmets were purchased at 7s 6d each.

It was at the Watch Committee meeting in May, 1881, that the committee decided that a badge be procured for the constable's helmets. The badge was to be of German silver, with the Borough arms therein. The cost of the die was £3 8s 9d, and 48 badges were purchased at 1s 5d each.

Also on the agenda was a report relating to the employment of the Borough policemen as firemen, but no action was taken.

The Chief Constable was found an additional job, he was appointed Inspector of Hackney Carriages for the Borough.

Councillor Ringland was complaining to the Watch Committee, that the Chief Constable had the impudence to send him a summons for alleged obstruction outside his shop in Stafford Street. He was informed by members of the Watch Committee, that they had received a great number of complaints about shopkeepers displaying their goods outside their shops, and they had instructed the Chief Constable to try and put a stop to the problem.

P. C. SAVES PRISONER FROM DROWNING 1882.

In January, 1882, P.C. Wallbanks was awarded 2 guineas (£2 10p) gratuity by the Watch Committee, after he had rescued a man from drowning in the canal. This man had just escaped from P.C. Wallbanks's custody.

DRILL INSTRUCTION AND FIRE DUTIES *1882.*

The Chief Constable was instructed by the Watch Committee to have all members of the force drilled for at least 2 hours, one night each week for the next month.. It is not recorded if this was military foot drill, or fire brigade drill.

It was a part of the Chief Constable's duty at this time to make sure that all fire plugs in the town were kept in a proper working order, each plug to be tested at least once every year, and a report was to be submitted to the Watch Committee.

At this time boy delinquents were being sent to the Werrington Industrial School (still open today as a detention centre), and girls delinquents were sent to the Saint Margaret's School, in London.

The Chief Constable was instructed to have as many men as possible on duty on Sundays in the vicinity of the recreation ground, as a deterrent against playing of pitch and toss by disorderly persons, who frequented the ground for that purpose on a Sunday.

STRENGTH OF THE FORCE *1882.*

The strength of the force in 1882 is shown as follows:-

April.	July.
1 Chief Constable.	1 Chief Constable.
2 Inspectors.	2 Inspectors.
5 Sergeants.	6 Sergeants.
33 Constables.	34 Constables.
41 Total.	43 Total.
	1 Constable short. Vacancy.

In the same year, the Chief Constable requested that the Watch Committee provide 20 additional cutlasses for use by the men.

THE SALVATION ARMY 1882.

Both the Chief Constable, and the Council were receiving numerous complaints at this time relating to the Salvation Army. The main complaint seems to be in relation to their band playing in the town on Sunday morning during the hours of worship.

The Chief Constable said that he had spoken to both Gypsy Smith, and the local Captain in charge at Hanley. The Town Clerk was instructed to write to General Booth in London, telling him that he must stop the annoyance.

IMPROVED WORKING CONDITIONS 1883.

The year 1883 started with the constables and sergeants submitting a request to the Watch Committee, asking that their hours of duty be reduced from 9 hours per day to 8 hours. At the same time the inspectors requested that their hours be fixed like every other force. The Chief Constable was asked to write to a number of other forces to establish what hours their men worked. It is not reported as to whether the actual hours were reduced, but a small number of improvements were made in relation to the working conditions.

The constables were to be allowed to finish night duty at 5.am between the months of May, and September. Constables would also be allowed 4 hours off duty every 6 weeks, without loss of pay. Inspectors were to be allowed 7 days leave per year, with pay. Officers off sick would have 1/- per day deducted from their pay. Twenty two crimes were reported as having been committed in the town during February, 1883, of which 17 were detected. The following month 40 crimes were reported, and 40 persons arrested.

POLICE PREMISES 1883.

As well as the main police station in the town, policemen also operated from two other police houses, one situated in Ashford Street, Shelton, and the other in Bold Street, Northwood. Later accommodation was found in the Etruria area, and a constable stationed there. Each of these sub stations were equipped with a hand pump in case of fire.

Both the Chief Constable, and the H.M.Inspector were complaining about the unsatisfactory conditions of the cells at the police station.

FATAL ROAD ACCIDENT 1883.

June, 1883, was to see the first fatal road accident involving a steam tram, when a 2 year old girl was knocked down by a one in Hope Street. The steam trams had been operating in the town for just under a year.

POLICE CONSTABLE COMMENDED 1883.

Police constable Humphries was awarded £1 by the Watch Committee, for his courageous conduct in Vine Street, on the 14th July, 1883. It is not known what the circumstances relating to the incident were.

POLICE CONSTABLE BEAUMONT.

Police constable Beaumont was appointed to the force in 1883, to replace Sergeant Cook in the office as clerk. His pay was to be 27s 6d per week. This was increased two months later to 30s per week. Beaumont was to become somewhat of a problem to the Chief Constable, and the Watch Committee, for 18 months later, Mr. Windle had to report to them that he had been under the influence of drink on the 16th and 17th March, 1885, when on duty in the office. Also it had been found that he was in arrears with his book keeping.

The Watch Committee after some deliberation agreed that Beaumont be allowed to keep his position, providing he gave the Committee a written undertaking not to do the same again. The Chief Constable was to report to the Watch Committee three months later on the matter. However, six months later in September, 1885, the Chief Constable had to report to the Watch Committee that P.C. Beaumont had left the police office without his knowledge or permission the previous day, and in consequence he had suspended him from duty. The Chief Constable was instructed to tell Beaumont to hand in his resignation as an alternative to dismissal.

George Taylor formally a constable with Halifax Borough Police was appointed as Constable Clerk at the end of 1885, in replacement to Beaumont. He was paid 30s (£1.50p) per week with free uniform. His hours would be 8.am to 8.pm.

In 1883, the detective officer P.C. William Dennis was promoted to sergeant.

SERIOUS EXPLOSION 1883.

On October, 18th 1883, an explosion occurred at the shop of W. Henry, Ironmonger, situated in Piccadilly. Two men in the shop were severally burned. The owner of the shop was summoned for keeping gun powder in an unauthorised place.

Less than three weeks later , four young men were severally injured by a further explosion in Heales Square. Three of the injured had to be taken to the infirmary.

The Council must have been alarmed by these explosions, because a few weeks later, Inspectors Vickers, and Wall were both appointed Inspectors under the Explosives Act. They were ordered to inspect each month, all premises where gunpowder was stored.

In December, 1883, Inspector Vickers, unsuccessfully applied for the post of Chief Constable of Bedford Borough Police.

The Chief Constable was instructed to take action under the Borough By Laws against the owners of shops that exposed their goods for sale outside their premises.

GOVERNMENT INSPECTION AND CRIME STATISTICS 1884.

On the 27th March, 1884, the force was inspected by Colonel Cobbe, Her Majesty's Inspector of Constabulary. At that time the Chief Constable held the following appointments:-

Superintendent of the Fire Brigade.

Inspector of Weights and Measures.

Inspector of Common Lodging Houses.

Inspector of Hackney Carriages.

Inspector under the Explosive Act.

In the month of the inspection 26 crimes were reported; 26 persons arrested; 25 crimes cleared up. What today's Chief Constables would give for a detection rate like that.

At this time waterproof coats were supplied to both sergeants Dennis, and Williams.

Pay Increase for the Chief Constable 1884.

Mr. Windle was to have his reward for all the extra duties that had been forced upon him. His pay was to be increased from £225 per year to £270 per year. However, at the end of October, 1884, the Watch Committee was to receive a letter from the Home Office, stating that the Secretary of State could not approve all the increase of pay to the Chief Constable, and suggested the following:- That the Chief Constable be paid £250 per year, plus £20 allowance in lieu of accommodation. This was approved, but meant that the Government Grant would only be on the £250.

Further Problems with Discipline

Police constable Nightingale was up before the local magistrates, charged with absenting himself from duty without lawful authority between the 9th and 12th August, 1884. He was fined £1 by the magistrates, and then dismissed from the force by the Watch Committee.

The Watch Committee suggested to Mr. Windle that preference should be given to constables who were recovering from sickness, or who were in a weak state, when men were selected for duty in the cells as gaolers.

1885.

At the start of the year 1885, Sergeant Keats requested permission to keep a cow, saying his wife would be able to sell the milk. Records do not show whether permission was granted to the sergeant.

Mrs.Sinclare.

Photograph of Sergeant Keats and his wife taken in the 1890's. Keats served in the Hanley Borough force from 1870 to 1896 when he retired on pension.

SUICIDAL WOMAN 1885.

In June, 1885, a woman by the name of Emily Jones, living in Bryan Street, Hanley, appeared before the Magistrates Court, charged with attempting suicide. It was said that she had thrown herself in front of a steam tram in Hope Street. Only a few months earlier she had attempted to throw herself into the canal. The magistrates were informed that the woman had a drink problem. She was committed to the lunatic asylum.

NEW POLICE HEADQUARTERS AND GOVERNMENT INSPECTION 1885.

In January, 1885, the Watch Committee ordered that for the next three months, the prisoner's food was to be purchased from Halls Temperance Hotel, Tontine Street.

At the end of January, 1885, the Chief Constable was given instructions to remove the whole of the police force from the old Town Hall (now the site of the present Lloyds Bank), to the Town Hall, Albion Square, which had just been constructed.

At the annual inspection of the force in March the same year, the Government Inspector Colonel Cobbe, reported most favourably on the new accommodation. He said it is a great improvement on the old building, something that the council should be very proud of, and an envy of most other towns in the Midlands. I am especially pleased with the cell accommodation. The Inspector also recommended that the constable's capes, and overcoats be lined.

Members of the Watch Committee then asked the Inspector if he would make representation to the Home Secretary with a view of enabling the Council to obtain the grant in respect of the additions made to the Chief Constable's pay. This he promised to do.

Ex-Police constable George Johnson met Colonel Cobbe, on his visit, asking him if he could be granted an allowance from the Superannuation Fund, or the Council could make him a gift. P.C. Johnson had been forced to resign from the force in December, 1884. It is not recorded whether he received anything from them.

Two months later the new police station was connected to a telephone system, and allocated the telephone number 8. The Chief Constable, however, had to wait until, 1897, until his private house was connected to the telephone system.

The total cost of the running of the force for the year was £3,956 0s 2d.

The council would later receive half the cost back from the Central Government, if the force was certified as efficient by the H.M.I.

UNIFORM AND HEADGEAR 1885.

The Chief Constable was instructed to obtain a number of sample helmets with white metal fittings, and submit same to the Watch Committee for approval. The Committee selected a helmet with a spike on top. Members of the force were also told at this time, that if they were in possession of war medal, they should wear them only on special occasions, but for ordinary street duty, they were only to wear the medal ribbons.

Staffordshire Police.

Hanley Borough Police circa 1885, the new spiked helmets were issued at this time.

The cost of the uniform for the entire force was £140 15s 3d., and the following individual costs were being paid in 1885:-

Inspector's tunics … … … …   *£ 2 9s 0d   each.*

" "   dress trousers … …   *£ 1 1s 0d   per pair.*

" "   undress trousers …   *19s 0d   "   "*

	helmets	10s 6d	each
Sergeant's tunics		£ 1 8s 3d	"
" " dress trousers		13s 3d	per pair
" " undress trousers ...		12s 6d	" "
" " helmets		7s 6d	each.
Constable's tunics		£ 1 5s 3d	"
" " dress trousers		13s 3d	per pair.
" " undress trousers ...		12s 6d	" "
" " helmets		7s 6d	each
Cloth waterproof capes		£ 1 0s 6d	"

NEW APPOINTMENTS TO THE FORCE   1885.

With effect from June, 1885, Mr. Windle was instructed to submit all applications for appointments in the force, along with their recommendations to the Watch Committee.

James Evans was appointed Probationary Constable. It was the first time an appointment made, was referred as to being on Probation.

A Mr. Brock sent a letter and the sum of £2 to the Watch Committee, asking that he be distributed between the men who attended a fire at his premises in Broad Street. The Committee agreed, but instructed the Chief Constable to tell the men that they must not expect to receive gratuities from all fires.

The Tramway Company made an application to the Watch Committee for the loan of two constables during the Wakes Week. The Committee agreed providing the Tramway Company paid all cost.

The Borough accountant reported that the sum of £8 19s 0d had been paid out in sick pay the previous year, and that £3 3s 0d had been paid to the infirmary.

POLICE ASSAILANTS IMPRISONED   1885.

At the Borough Police Court, on Monday, 5th September, 1885, William Ritch, a carter, was charged with having been drunk while in charge of a horse, and trap, with assaulting Police constables Collier, and Frost, and also with wilfully damaging the windows of the police cell. It was stated that on Saturday evening the defendant, who was drunk. Was driving a horse, and trap in Trinity Street as the Salvation Mission procession came along Marsh Street. He was requested to pull up until the procession had passed, but he refused, and on the officer climbing onto the conveyance in order to stop it, the defendant struck Collier with a whip, kicked him several times, and bit his arm. He also assaulted Frost by striking him with the whip. Eventually the defendant was driven to the police station, and locked up. While detained in the police cells, he broke three panes of glass in the window. The magistrates committed the defendant to prison for a month with hard labour.

At the same court John Smith, collier, was charged with having been drunk and disorderly, and assaulting Police constable Tunnicliffe, on Saturday night. The officer had arrested the defendant for being drunk and disorderly, and on the way to the police station, he had struck the constable several times. Defendant was committed to prison for a month with hard labour.

ALLEGATIONS AGAINST SERGEANT WILLIAMS   1885.

A letter was received from the Chief Constable of Cheshire County Police. It was relating to Sergeant Williams, who was alleged to have taken certain articles from the Arclid Union.   Mr. Windle was instructed to confer with the Chief Constable of Cheshire, and suspend Sergeant Williams from duty in the meantime.

At the September meeting of the Watch Committee, the Chief Constable reported that he had interviewed Inspectors Vickers, and Wall, Sergeant Dennis, also Police constables Beaumont, Barker, and Rabbit. Also that he had spoken to Mrs. Griffiths.

The Watch Committee also interviewed Sergeant Dennis, the detective officer, Sergeant Williams, also read statements. After a short deliberation, the Watch Committee said, We find no just cause to continue Sergeant William's suspension, and we reinstate him .

ELECTION CONTINGENCY PLANS   *1885.*

The Chief Constable was instructed by the Watch Committee to obtain what help he thought would be necessary for the forthcoming 1885 Elections, also loaning of constables to other towns during the election period. He was to make his own arrangements.

Twenty men were loaned from the Nottingham, Borough force, at a cost of £13 13s 0d. All passed off satisfactory on the day of the election

Some days later Hanley officers travelled as far as Caernarvon to assist with the policing of elections in that county.

INSPECTION OF CANAL BOATS   *1886.*

At the first Watch Committee meeting held in 1886, the Committee were asked by the Council to appoint one of more members of the force to act as inspectors responsible for the inspection of the canal boats.

The Chief Constable, and members of the Watch Committee then decided to contact a number of other forces, 42 in all, to find out what the situation was in their areas. After studying the replies, the Watch Committee then decided that it was not a duty that should be carried out by members of the police force. They then informed the Sanitary Committee to make alternative arrangements.

POLICE CONSTABLE INJURED CLEANING WINDOWS   *1886.*

Police constable Barker fell and broke his leg while cleaning the windows at the police station. He was allowed full pay while off sick.

FURTHER ELECTION DUTIES *1886.*

A number of officer were sent to Nottingham on mutual aid to assist them with the Parliamentary Elections of this year. The Watch Committee later received a cheque to the value of £7 11s 6d from the Nottingham Council for their assistance.

POLICE BAND 1886.

Members of the force made representation through the Chief Constable to the Watch Committee for permission to form a police band. Mr. Windle said that the majority of the men were in favour of this.

Alderman Cooke replied, that he did not think that the force was large enough to form a band, and the matter was dropped.

A letter was received by the Watch Committee, complaining about the amount of bad language that was being used by pigeon flyers in the Northwood area. The Chief Constable was instructed to put a stop to it.

ANNUAL GOVERNMENT INSPECTION   1886.

The annual Government Inspection of the force was carried out in April, 1886, by Colonel Cobbe, who made the following suggestions to the Watch Committee all of which were adopted, with the exception of the last one:-

Inspectors to be issued with mackintosh coats instead of waterproof capes.

Chief Constable's pay to be increased to £275 per year.

Strength of the force to be increased.

Pay increases to members of the force.

Police Reserve of twenty men to be formed.

Later in the year the Inspectors got their mackintosh coats, and the Chief Constable was supplied with a uniform overcoat. Four extra men were added to the force, one of them being a sergeant.

The uniform clothing for the year was purchased from John Hammond & Co, of Newcastle at a cost of £217 8s 3d.

ALLEGED ASSAULT BY POLICE CONSTABLES 1886.

Police constables Clowes, Barratt, and Williams were reported to the Watch Committee in July, and duly appeared before them to answer the charge of assault on Charles Delany.

It was alleged that the constables were called to the Tontine Vaults to eject Delany, and in doing so did physically assault him. The charge against the officers was dismissed.

PRISON VAN AND AMBULANCE 1886.

The Watch Committee were paying a Mr. Mills £1 10s 0d per week for conveying prisoners to Stoke station. The Committee ever mindful of the ratepayers coppers made the decision to purchase a van of their own. The van was a dual purpose vehicle, in addition to being used as a prison van, it was also used as an ambulance. A stable was built at the rear of the Town Hall, and a horse kept for the purpose of pulling the van when required. The horse also had to be available for fire brigade duties.

By this time boys were being sent to the Liverpool Industrial School by the Borough Justices, instead of Werrington. The cost per boys, per week was 21/-.

The Watch Committee made its usual yearly contribution of three guineas to the North Staffordshire Infirmary. Police constable Turner was awarded the sum of £3 3s 0d for bravery, what the brave deed was is not recorded.

PROMOTION OF SERGEANT TAYLOR 1887.

Police constable Taylor the clerk was promoted to sergeant, and his pay increased to 31/- per week.. The promotion, and pay increase were to take effect from May 1887.

A Mr. Bickley applied to the Watch Committee for a licence to keep gunpowder at his shop in Broad Street. But after reading the police report, which said that the premises were not a sufficient distance from the highway to allow Mr. Bickley to store up to 200lbs of the powder. The Watch Committee refused to grant the licence, and Mr. Bickley, stated that he would appeal to the Stipendiary Magistrate.

REWARDS AND GRATUITIES *1887.*

At this period of time, it seems to have been the practice to allow the police officers to keep all or part of reward monies that was paid to them. P.C. Frost was allowed to keep 2/- given to him by the R.S.P.C.A. for giving evidence in a cruelty case.

Sergeants Williams, and Dennis were allowed to keep the sum of £1 0s 0d each from the War Office, for arresting deserters from the army. Sergeant Dennis was also awarded £5 from the Inland Revenue, for the information he gave to them concerning a drinking club in Stafford Street.

P.C. Woodings received £2 from the Royal Navy for apprehending a deserter. Another constable received 10/- reward from the Gas Company for the arrest of a youth found committing damage to a gas lamp.

It is noted from records of the time that it was usual for the War Office to give a reward of £1 for the apprehension of a deserter from the army, but at the same time, the Admiralty seemed to be paying £2 for the capture of deserters from the Royal Navy.

JUBILEE CELEBRATIONS *1887.*

Six members of the force were sent to Newcastle-under-Lyme to assist the force there with the Queen Victoria's Jubilee celebrations in 1887.

Members of the force sent a petition to the Watch Committee, requesting two days extra leave of absence to allow them to take part in jubilee celebrations, this was granted. Twelve months later the men were granted an extra two days holiday per year, as a permanent entitlement

DISAPPEARANCE AND DISMISSAL OF INSPECTOR WALL *1887.*

Mr. Windle reported to the July, 1887, meeting of the Watch Committee, that Inspector Wall had been absent from duty for the previous seven days. His uniform had been returned to the station. He informed them that he had made enquiries in the town which revealed that Wall's furniture had been sold by auction, and he believed that Wall had left the Country. Wall was dismissed from the force in his absence, which left a vacancy to be filled.

The sergeants were instructed to send in their applications in their own handwriting.

The Chief Constable was to convey to all applicants, that if they canvassed any members of the Committee, or Councillor, they would be disqualified.

Five sergeants submitted applications, and the successful applicant was Sergeant Bailey, and Constable John Bellfield was promoted to sergeant.

The promotions were to take effect from 13th September, 1887

Photograph of Daniel Bailey. Mr. Bailey joined the force in 1872. Promoted to sergeant in 1882, and inspector in 1887, retired 31st. of July 1898.

Photograph loaned by family.

1888

The year 1888, opened with the Watch Committee deciding that in the future, police officers would no longer pay local rates on their houses. The Chief Constable was also instructed to draw up a list of accommodation in use by the men, and submit same to the next Watch Committee meeting. When they had read, and studied the report, they decided that the men should be better distributed about the Borough. .

The Borough Surveyor was instructed to replace the wooden beds, and fittings within the cells, with iron ones.

During the Wakes Holidays, the School Board agreed to keep all the school play grounds open until 9.pm at night, to enable the children to play in them.

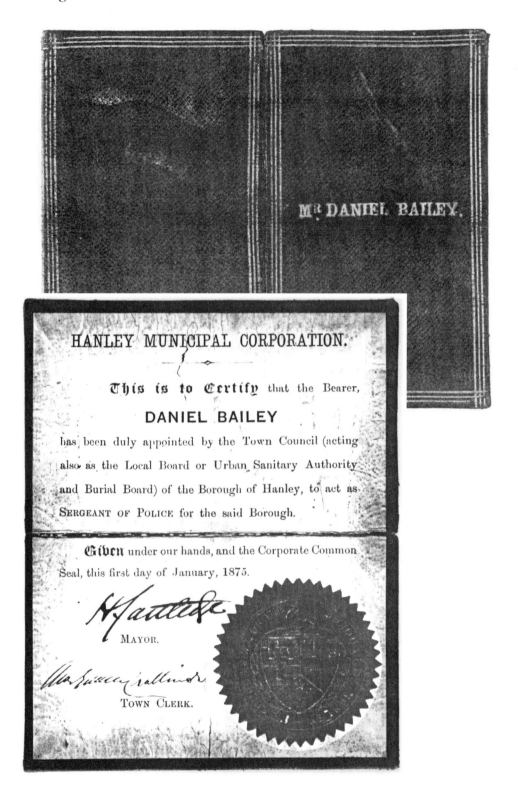

PHONE No. 132

COUNTY BOROUGH OF HANLEY.

Town Clerk's Office,
Hanley,

ARTHUR CHALLINOR,
TOWN CLERK.

29th June 1898

Dear Sir,

Underneath I send you copy of a resolution adopted by the Council of this Borough at its last meeting.

Yours faithfully,

[signature]

Town Clerk.

Mr. Inspector Daniel Bailey.

W A T C H Committee 17th May 18 98

Confirmed by COUNCIL 22nd June 1898.

RESOLVED :- That Inspector Daniel Bailey, having completed 26 years' approved service in the Hanley Police Force, be allowed to retire therefrom on the 31st July next, and receive a pension for life out of the Police Pension Fund, of an annual sum equal to $\frac{31\text{ths}}{50}$ of his annual pay with an addition of $\frac{3}{50}$ths of his annual pay for every completed year of approved service above 25 years; so, however, that the pension shall not exceed two-thirds of his annual pay.

Details loaned by family.

Details of Daniel Bailey. Left his warrant card and above his pension letter
Mr. Bailey joined the force in 1872, he retired as an Inspector on 31st. of July 1898.

CIVIL ACTION AGAINST THE POLICE   1889.

Mr. Windle reported to members of the Watch Committee, that a Mrs. Emily Smith had taken out a County Court action against himself, and two constables. Mrs. Smith claiming that she had been arrested by the two constables, for going round the town with a begging letter. The Town Clerk was instructed to engage counsel to defend the case. The claimant was awarded 1/- plus costs.

During the new year the Chief Constable purchased 1 dozen rugs for the use of the prisoners when confined in the cells.

Two additional constables were appointed to the force in September, 1889. They were appointed at the insistence of Earl Granville to do duty at his Iron Works, in Etruria. The Earl agreeing to pay all the costs that would arise. The cost to Earl Granville was £120 per year. The site was also to be visited from time to time by the patrolling constables, and sergeants.

Certificate of service of Joseph Gough, who served in Hanley Borough Police 1880 to 1887.

Loaned by family.

Both inspectors, who at the time were responsible for the inspection of weights and measures in the town, sent in a petition, with the Chief Constable's approval, asking that a person not a member of the police force be employed to carry out this duty. Some months later the Chief Constable was reporting to the Watch Committee that he was unable to supervise the policing of the town properly, because the two inspectors were being taken away from the street duty. He said, "I have too many duties, and too few men". After some debate, the Watch Committee decided that the police would continue to be responsible for the inspection of weights and measures in the Borough, but an additional inspector would be appointed.

Advertisements were placed in local newspapers to fill the vacancy, and sixteen applications were received, including four from sergeants serving in the Hanley Borough force. The Watch Committee decided that only Hanley officers would be considered for the post, and on 26th March, 1890, Sergeant Dennis was promoted to inspector.

A number of placards were made, and displayed about the town cautioning persons against stone throwing, chalking on walls, and kicking footballs about the street, and warning that action would be taken against them.

Ministers from the Hanley Free Churches met the Watch Committee, and Chief Constable, complaining about the amount of drunkenness, gambling, and immorality that was taking place in the town. Both the members of the Watch Committee, and the Chief Constable said that they were exaggerating the facts, but Mr. Windle was instructed to investigate the complaint.

From the beginning of the year, the force had decided that it would charge a fee of £1 per year to persons who wished to deposit keys or cash in the police safe, and that the depositor was to be informed that it was at their own risk.

CHAPTER *III*

FURTHER DEVELOPMENT OF THE FORCE

COMPLAINTS AGAINST POLICE CONSTABLE 1890.

A letter was received by the Watch Committee in June, 1890, stating that Police constable Stevenson had been borrowing various sums of money from different publicans in the town. The Chief Constable was told to report on Stevenson's financial possessions at the next meeting of the Committee. It was later reported that Stevenson owed £25 8s 0d. He was called before the Watch Committee, and reduced from 1st Class to 3rd Class constable, and instructed to pay off his debts at 5/- per week. Stevenson told the Committee that he was not able to pay of the debt at 5/- per week, but he could afford 3/-. The Watch

Mrs. Audrey Gleves.

Hanley Borough Police Chief Constable Herbert Windle seated centre
This photograph was taken in front of the pavilion in Hanley park in the late 1890's.

Committee agreed to this.

In October, the Watch Committee were to receive another list of debts he owed to various business-men in the town. This time he was told that he must resign from the force at the end of the month. Constable Stevenson made an application to the Watch Committee to have his superannuation, or por-tion of it returned, he was informed that under the regulations, that would be impossible.

A new ambulance was purchased at this time at a cost of £50. It was also in 1890 that the members of the force were given first aid training by the St. John's Ambulance Association. All members of the force who passed the first aid examination, were issued with a certificate, and allowed to wear a badge on their arm to indicate that they were qualified in first aid. Badges shown on photograph.

VIOLENT ASSAULT ON INSPECTOR BY P. C. WILLIAMS 1890.

A Hanley Borough Discipline Report dated the 4th January, 1890, John Williams a constable in the Hanley Borough Police appeared before the Borough Magistrates on Monday last charged with neglect of duty, and assault.

It was said that Williams went on duty at 10.pm., but the patrol sergeant was not able to find him at any of his allotted points, and had to search for him.

At 12 midnight he found him in a state of intoxication, and took him to the police office. Sergeant Bellfield was then instructed to fetch the Chief Constable. Williams then asked permission to sit down behind the counter, which was granted by Inspector Vickers. Suddenly Williams became abusive to the Inspector, who did not answer him. A few minutes later, Williams suddenly jumped up and seized Inspector Vickers by the neck, however he was overpowered by two constables who were in the office at the time, and placed in the cells.

P.C. Williams had 5 years service. He was fined £1., plus costs, and dismissed from the force.

The men petitioned the Watch Committee asking for 8 hour shifts. This was agreed to, and would take effect from the 1st January, 1891.

Newcastle-under-Lyme Corporation borrowed a number of constables, to do duty in the town on the day of the opening of the New Municipal Buildings in the town. They were later charged 6d per man, per hour.

STRENGTH OF THE FORCE *1890.*

At the close of 1890 the Hanley Borough Police force was made up as follows:-

    1 Chief Constable;

    2 Inspectors;

    7 Sergeants;

    38 Constables;

    Total of 48 men. 1 constable to every 37 acres, and 1 constable to every 1,007 population.

Staffordshire Police.

The Chief Constable of Hanley Mr. H. Windle seated centre and flanked by his two inspectors,
with his six burly sergeants at the rear. Photo circa 1890's

SERGEANT TAYLOR APPOINTED CHIEF CONSTABLE OF NEWCASTLE-UNDER-LYME 1891.

At the beginning of the new year, Sergeant Taylor, the police clerk, asked for an increase in pay, but this was not granted. Sergeant Taylor left the force on the 31st May that year, to take up the appointment as Chief Constable of Newcastle-under-Lyme Borough Police.

Police constable Bloor was selected to fill the vacancy. His pay was to be 30/- per week. The Chief Constable suggested that a junior clerk be employed in the police office at 10/- per week.

Major Leggett, the Governor of H.M.Prison, Stafford reported to the Chief Constable, that P.C. Bloor had been conversing with a prisoner, and giving him tobacco.

Bloor was cautioned, and the Committee instructed that in future, all members of the force were to wear uniform when escorting prisoners to prison.

COURAGEOUS ACT BY P. C. TURNER 1891.

In June, 1891, the following letter was received by the Chief Constable, from Mr. W. D. Phillips, the General Manager of the North Staffordshire Railway Company.

"As the train for Stafford due here at 12.45 today, was running into the station, when a woman in charge of your officer, threw herself in front of the engine. Police constable Thomas Turner, of Hanley, made a most plucky , and determined effort to save her, at very great risk to his own life, and limbs. Luckily the train passed over the woman without hurting her, and the officer escaped with trifling bruises. I write this to draw your special attention to the gallant conduct of Turner, which deserves your highest praise."

Constable Turner was awarded a gratuity of £5 5s 0d by the Watch Committee, and it was also suggested that he be allowed to wear some kind of badge. A number of Merit Badges were then purchased, and the first recipient was Police constable Turner.

Constable Turner had only been a member of the force a few weeks, when this incident occurred. He was to bee dismissed about 18 months later.

A member of the Watch Committee at this time suggested that a form be sent out to all persons desiring to join the police force. Mr. Windle was asked to prepare one.

SERGEANT HARRY HARDY GLOVER AND WIFE 1891.

In April, 1891, Harry Hardy Glover, was appointed as a constable to the force, and in later years promoted to the rank of sergeant. Not a great deal is known about him, only that he was the son of a former Town Constable of Fenton. He resided in John Street, Hanley, at the rear of the police station, together with his wife Selina, and their 8 children. His wife was somewhat of a character, but obviously of great assistance to the working of the force. She acted as police matron, duties of which included providing mugs of cocoa, and a wedge of bread and margarine to the prisoners, and cooked the meals for the officers. She also acted as mortuary attendant, and at Christmas time, before the advent of police-women, she would be used to follow potential pick-pockets round the market place, and shops. Selina was paid monthly, and when her money arrived she would buy a jug of ale, and lie on the horsehair sofa and yodel loudly. A barrel of beer was apparently kept in the rear of the house, provided free of charge by Parker's Brewery, Burslem, for the

Mrs. Audrey Gleves.

Mrs. Selina Glover wife of P.C.Glover who was police matron at Hanley in the 1890's.P.C. Glover and his wife lived in John street which was at the back of the police station.

policemen to call in and have a drink. This practise was later put a stop to when Chief Constable Roger Carter was appointed.

Her granddaughter Mrs. Audrey Gleave, a former member of the Woman Auxiliary Police Corps in Staffordshire Police, has been kind enough to provide this information relating to her grandparents.

DETECTIVE CONSTABLE HIGGINS COMMENDED 1892.

Detective constable Higgins was awarded three guineas (£3 15p) by the Watch Committee for the arrest of Hubert Holden, a notorious thief and house breaker.

The Chief Constable was instructed to offer a suitable reward for the detection of offenders in all cases of damage to property, where the offenders cannot be found after due diligence has been used by the police.

Members of the force sent a letter to the Watch Committee in the January of 1892, asking for a pay increase. Mr. Windle was instructed to write to all other local forces, and obtain from them information as to what they paid their men. In June, all members of the force were to receive a 2/- (10p) per week rise. This would bring the starting pay of a constable from 21/- to 23/-, and the top rate from 27/- to 29/- per week. The Chief Constables pay increased from £275 to £285 per year.

There seemed to be a great variation in the estimate received for the uniforms for the year 1892. They varied from £102 17s 9d to £288 13s 4d. The order was placed with James Smith and Co, of Derby, at a cost of £237 0s 9d.

GOVERNMENT INSPECTION BY NEW H.M.INSPECTOR 1892.

The force was inspected by the Hon C.G. Legge, Her Majesty's Inspector of Constabulary for the Midland Counties. It was his first inspection of the Hanley force since his appointment in January, in succession to Colonel Cobbe, who had retired.

The new Inspector told the Watch Committee that there must be an increase in the strength of the force, due to the increase in the population of the Borough. Later in the year the force was increased by three men.

Mr. Windle asked the Watch Committee that a deaf and dumb interpreter be engage in certain cases held before the police court. This was agreed to.

SERGEANT IN TROUBLE 1892.

Sergeant Humphries was called before the Watch Committee in September, 1892, to explain his refusal to pay a fine inflicted on him by the Chief Constable, also his insubordination to him. The sergeant was ordered to pay the fine, and to apologize to the Chief Constable. He was also reprimanded by the Mayor.

Members of the force were still receiving small amounts of money, as gifts for various acts as follows:-

P. C. France received 2s 6d from Mrs. Palsea for attending to her husband, who had attempted suicide, by cutting his throat.

Sergeant Jones, and P. C. Wooding each received 2s 6d from Mr. Stubbs for attending his son's funeral.

Sergeant Jones received 1/- from Mr. Morris, the manager of the Gas Company for attending to one of his workmen who was injured in the Market Square.

P. C. Sherwin was to be awarded the sum of 2/- from Mr. Munroe for bringing lemonade to the Town Hall.

Stray cattle were causing Hanley Police problems, and the following came into operation. All stray cattle would in future be impounded in a pound in the cattle market. The keys were to be kept with a Mr. Hayes, at 41, Bethesda Street. Mr. Hayes was to be paid 1/- (5p) each time he was called out at night to unlock the site.

EXTRA DUTIES 1893.

In January, 1893, the Chief Constable was authorized to formulate a scheme in which about 10 men, who were off duty could be utilized for about 2 hours extra duty on a Saturday nights. Nine months later four sergeants, and eight constables appeared before a meeting of the Watch Committee, requesting to be relieved of the extra duty enforced on them on a Saturday night. Mr. Windle was requested to confer with his inspectors, to try and formulate a better scheme, if possible for police supervision of the town on a Saturday night.

Inspector Vickers sent a letter to the Watch Committee asking that the £10 per year bonus he received for his duty as Inspector of Weights and Measures could be added to his pay, so that it will be added to his superannuation when he claims it. This request was refused.

All three inspectors had other duties besides their normal police supervision duties. As stated Inspector Vickers, the senior inspector, deputized as Chief Constable in his absence, in addition to his duty with Weights and Measures.

Inspector Bailey was in charge of the Police Fire Brigade, and attended all fires in the Borough.

Inspector Dennis was responsible for the inspection of fire hydrants in the town.

Members of the Borough Council wrote the Chief Constable, calling his attention to the way some of the heavy carts were being driven in the town. Drivers were not keeping to their left, and some of them were being driven negligently. Also small boys were employed to drive horses, some of which were dangerous, and the boys were unable to manage them, and should not have been in the charge of young boys.

Mr. Thomas Turner, who had been dismissed from the force in January of that year, wrote a letter to the Watch Committee in September, asking them to reconsider their decision. If it were not possible to reinstate him, could the committee find him another job, or refund his superannuation contributions. He was informed that none of his requests were possible.

George Cook the boy clerk employed in the police office had his pay increased from 10s 5d per week to 15/-.

With effect from the 9th May, 1893, the men employed as Additional constables, were withdrawn from the Shelton Iron Works.

MOUNTED POLICEMEN 1893.

The Watch Committee records show that the Chief Constable sent a letter to a Mr. Hudd, thanking him for the loan of horses for Mounted Police duty in the town during the colliers strike, and disturbances that had taken place.

It was quite common during that period for police forces, to either borrow, or hire the use of horses for mounted police purposes. Very few forces had their own Mounted Police Sections, as do modern day police forces.

Police constable Owen was called before the Watch Committee, and congratulated for the meritious arrest of a dangerous criminal named Norman Cooper. He was given the usual reward of £5 5s 0d., to which the Mayor added a similar amount. No doubt he returned a very happy man, as this amount would have presented seven weeks pay .

Mr. Windle was instructed at this time to obtain samples of waterproof leggings for members of the force.

The Watch Committee obviously decided to make as much use of the police while they were out on patrol during this period, as they were instructed to turn off the water supply to the fountain in Market Square each night.

PROBLEMS WITH STRIKING PICKETS *1893.*

A special meeting of the Watch Committee was held on the 3rd March, 1893, to investigate a complaint made by Councillor Harvey Jones, and a Mr. Bridgewood. Both men complained of the behaviour of Inspector Vickers, whom Bridgewood alleged had pushed against him, and followed him about. Bridge-wood admitted to the Committee that he had, with over 100 other persons been following about, a number of 'Blacklegs' (Union members working during strike), trying to induce them to abstain from their employment. The Chief Constable explained that in consequence of what had taken place, between the masters, and men, at the Eagle Works. It had been necessary for him, almost daily to provide escorts for the protection of some of the employees, who were being intimidated, on leaving work by crowds of people, including Councillor Harvey Jones.

Mr. Windle stated that it was possible that legal proceedings would be considered against the ringleaders. Councillor Jones stated that he had not interfered with the police in any way.

Members of the Watch Committee said that they had the utmost confidence in both the Chief Constable, and Inspector Vickers, and the meeting was closed.

1894

At the first Watch Committee meeting held in 1894, a letter was read out from the management of the Shelton Iron and Steel Company Ltd, asking that a Mr. F. Halfpenny, one their employees be sworn in as a special constable, for the purpose of acting as such at the factory. The outcome of this request is not known. However, Halfpenny was sworn in as a constable to be paid at private cost by the ironworks in September, 1897.

In May, 1894, George Cook, the assistant boy clerk in the police office had his pay increased from 15/-

(75p) per week to 18/- (90p). Also at the same time the Chief Constable had his pay increased from £280 to £300 per annum.

POLICE CONSTABLE APPEARS BEFORE THE COURT *1894.*

Police constable John Biddle appeared before the Police Court on the 20th April, 1894, charged with being drunk on duty, and with neglect of duty.

Evidence was given by Sergeant Humphreys to show that on visiting the constable on his beat, he noticed that he had consumed alcohol. When Biddle was taken to the police office, he said, " I will not go home, until I have seen either a doctor, or the Chief Constable". He was then locked up in a cell. Under oath the defendant said he was quite sober. Inspector Dennis, who took the charge, said that the prisoner was either drunk or stupefied. Biddle was a willing officer, and he had previously had no reason to complain of him.

He was fined 10/- (50p), and costs, and suspended until he had appeared before the Watch Committee.

At a subsequent special meeting of the Watch Committee , it was decided to dismiss the constable.

When Biddle was asked if he had anything to say. He said, "I think I have been unjustly treated. The fact that Mr. Hammersley, who presided over the meeting, and Mr. Hampton, were also two of the three magistrates who tried the case in the first place, seems a little unfair." Biddle had been a member of the force since October, 1889.

The Chief Constable reported to the Watch Committee at their meeting in June, 1894, that Police sergeant Higgins, the plain cloths officer, had received a letter from a solicitor at Fenton. This letter was threatening proceedings against him for detaining persons who he had suspected of stealing wear from a pottery factory.

The Town Clerk was told to take what action he thought necessary in defence of the police.

The same officer later sent in a letter to the Watch Committee, requesting an increase of pay. From the 24th June, 1894, the Committee saw fit to grant him an increase of £6 per year.

At the same Watch Committee meeting , they requested that the Town Clerk take action in the County Court against the Staffordshire Football Association, for the recovering of 9/- (45p) due to the council for the services of the police at their football ground. This action was later withdrawn.

At the same time constables, and sergeants were granted two extra days holiday each year. There is no record of the inspectors receiving the same concession.

Sergeant Bloor received the sum of £3 6s 0d (£3 30p) from the Library Committee, for his attendance in the boys reading room, and keeping order.

In July, 1894, a letter was received from the Home Secretary, instructing that in future, all girls sent to Reformatory, or Industrial Schools, must be accompanied by a female escort. The female searchers would be allowed 1/- (5p) every time they were called upon to examine prisoners.

PROPOSED SEPARATE BOROUGH POLICE FORCE FOR LONGTON 1894.

Members of the Watch Committee met a deputation of Longton Councillors, who were seeking information with regards to the provisions, and workings of a separate police force for the Borough of Longton. However, after consultation, Longton decided against forming its own separate Borough force, and continued to be policed by the Staffordshire Constabulary, until 1910.

The Secretary of the Hanley Hairdressers Association sent a letter to the Watch Committee at this time, asking them to take proceedings against hairdressers who continue to open on Sundays.

DISMISSAL OF POLICE CONSTABLE EMERY 1894.

Police constable Emery was ordered to appear before the Watch Committee, to answer certain allegation made by him. He had made a complaint to members of the Watch Committee that men had been removed from certain beats in consequence of them reporting licensed premises being open during prohibited hours. Emery was unable to substantiate his allegations, and was himself found guilty of being under the influence of drink while on duty. He was ordered to resign, the Mayor saying that his continuation in the force, would be of detriment to its discipline.

JUVENILE CRIME 1895.

During 1895, the Watch Committee received correspondence from the Home Office, in which they pointed out that Hanley was in the unenviable position of having more boys under the age of 16 years committed to prison, than any other town in the county.

It was suggested that they try, and make more efficient means of preventing youths becoming criminals.

The Chief Constable was asked to report at each Committee Meeting, the numbers, and ages of all boys sent to prison.

The Watch Committee must have been feeling benevolent during the first week of the New Year, because they decided to send P.C. Barker to the Police Convalescent Home, at Southport for three weeks. They paid the £2 10s 0d (£2 50p) plus travelling expenses, and said that he was to receive full pay for the three weeks he was at the home. It is not recorded what Barker's problems were to need convalescence.

The contract for the 1895 issue of uniform, was awarded to James Smith & Co, of Derby, at a cost of £169 14s 0d. However, this was not before the Council had satisfied themselves that the working conditions of their employees was satisfactory. They had sent a letter to the company, inquiring into the working conditions, and as a result received the following reply:-

"We beg to inform you that our work is carried out under the factory system. Our hands earn better wages than they would under union conditions, and they work a 54 hour week."

Sergeant Bloor made an application at this time to the Watch Committee for promotion to inspector, but this was refused. He was, however, promoted to inspector several months later.

COMPLAINT OF ALLEGED ASSAULT AGAINST POLICE CONSTABLE 1895.

Police constable Day appeared before the Watch Committee to answer a charge of assault made against him. It was alleged that he had assaulted a man who he had taken into custody for bathing in the canal at Etruria.

After hearing the evidence of several witnesses, and considering the case, the Committee came to the conclusion that Constable Day had used a little more force than was necessary, having lost his temper. He was severally reprimanded by the Watch Committee.

The Mayor, and the Chief Constable went personally to examine a property situated at 176, Etruria Road, Hanley, belonging to a Mr. George Kent, before they granting him a pawnbroker's licence, for the purpose of operating his business from that address.

1896

At the beginning of 1896, four sergeants, and 33 constables signed, and forwarded a petition to the Watch Committee, asking them to cancel the extra duty that they had been required to perform on Saturday nights. The Committee passed on the petition to Mr. Windle, advising him to use his own discretion on the matter.

Arthur Lawrence was appointed as a boy clerk in the police office at 8/- (40p) per week.

Death of Inspector Dennis   1897.

The New Year was only a few days old, when members of the force were to learn of the death of Inspector Dennis, who had been in the force since 1874, and had held his present rank since 1891.

His wife was awarded a gratuity of £206 11s 10d from the superannuation fund.

The vacancy for an inspector, caused by the death of Mr. Dennis was to remain unfilled for over twelve months.

The First C.I.D. 1897

A Watch Committee meeting was held in January, 1897, to consider the setting up of a small Detective department within the Borough force. The Chief Constable was instructed to select a sufficient number of men to set up this department.

The Council at this time received a letter from the Tied House Tenants League, complaining that publicans were suffering from short measures, of ale, beers, and stout that was being supplied to them by the breweries. They asked the Council if they would make some effort to check this evil. This letter was passed onto Inspectors Vickers, the Weights and Measures Officer to investigate the problem.

All members of the force were granted three days extra leave with pay, to celebrate the 60 long and glorious years of Her Majesty Queen Victoria's reign.

Industrial Dispute 1897

In the September, of 1897, an industrial dispute culminating in a strike of sanitary pressers took place at the works of Messrs. Johnson Bros Ltd. Councillor Harvey Jones again appeared before the Watch Committee, as he had done so four years previously. This time he questioned the right of members of the police force ordering people who were walking about the streets, to move out of the area.

Mr. T. Slater, who also attended the meeting on behalf of Johnson Bros, stated that beer was being served out to people who had congregated in the streets adjacent to the factory, and that such, was not conducive to the keeping of the peace.

Some days later the strike was over, and the Chief Constable received a letter from the management of

Johnson Bros, thanking him, and the men under his command for the tact shown throughout the difficult time.

SUMMER UNIFORM 1897

Alderman Cooke, and Councillor Huntbatch, suggested at the September, 1897, Watch Committee meeting, that members of the police force be issued with a light weight helmet, and a serge jacket, with two outside breast pockets for summer wear. The men, however, had to wait two years until they were to receive their new light weight uniform jackets, and helmets. The helmets were to cost 6s 7d (35p) each.

For a few years prior to this caps had been worn during the summer months, by officers on day duty.

A quantity of new leather day belts were also purchased at the time for issue to the men.

Members of the Watch Committee received a letter making allegations that licensees in the town were offering sweats, cakes, toys, and other gifts to children under the age of 13 years, to induce them to purchase liquor for consumption off the premises.

Authors collection.

P.C. No.12 of the Hanley Borough Police. Photograph taken between 1900 and 1910 in summer uniform. This light-weight uniform and helmet were introduced in 1900. Note helmet badge, it is the centre of the large star pattern helmet plate.

The letter was passed onto the Chief Constable for him to instruct his men to report all such cases to him, in order that he could place a report on the matter before the next Committee meeting.

PROMOTIONS, AND ENLARGEMENT OF THE C.I.D 1898.

In March, 1897, Inspector Bailey informed the Watch Committee that it was his intention to retire from the force the following month, having completed 26 years service. The Watch Committee instructed Mr. Windle to place advertisements in the police newspapers for an inspector. However, at the next meeting of the Watch Committee, a petition signed by 14 members of the Town Council was read, asking that an inspector be appointed out of the Hanley Borough force. At the end of the meeting, it was decided that only Hanley men would be called for interview. As a result with effect from August of that year, Sergeant Thomas Humphries, was appointed Uniform Inspector, and Sergeant Thomas Higgins, was appointed Detective Inspector, to take charge of the enlarged Detective Department.

Members of public were complaining about the rowdyism in Hanley Park especially in the vicinity of the pavilion. Mr. Windle was asked if it would be possible to supervise the park more effectively.

Inspector Vickers made application to the Watch Committee in February, 1898, asking that the £10 per year he received as the Weights and Measures Inspector be increased to £15, and added to his salary for superannuation purposes. The Committee did not see fit to increase his pay, but did agree to add the £10 to his annual salary, so that when the time came for retirement, he would then receive the extra superannuation.

COMMENDABLE ACTS BY POLICE OFFICERS 1898.

Three members of the force were to be recipients of gratuities for outstanding police work during the year.

In the month of March, Sergeant Higgins was awarded £3 3s 0d for the smart arrest of a man who had stolen £200 from his employer, most of the money was recovered. Higgins was later promoted to the rank of inspector, and placed in charge of the Detective Department.

Police constable Bloxham was awarded the sum of one guinea for the brave arrest of a dangerous criminal, after a violent struggle at Bucknall Railway Station.

Before the year was out another member of the force Police constable Bowler received an award of £2 2s 0d, for his courageous conduct in rescuing a woman from drowning in the canal at Northwood.

P. C. Bowler was later off sick for a period of three weeks, due to his immersion in the water. The Watch Committee, at the Chief Constable's request, agreed that Bowler should receive full pay while off sick.

One Annie Jones was arrested in Hanley for uttering counterfeit coins, and was later sentenced to 5 years imprisonment at the Staffordshire Assizes.

FURTHER CHANGES IN THE FORCE *1899.*

At the September, of 1898 meeting of the Watch Committee had received notification that Sergeant Belfield intended to retire three months later, and in fact retired on the last day of that year. He did not enjoy a very long retirement, as he died on the 8th October, 1899. His widow was awarded the sum of £15 from the Superannuation Fund.

After his retirement the Watch Committee decided to advertise his vacancy, and as a result 61 applications were received for the post, from these a short list of four were called for interview. They were:-

Thomas TOBIN,	Bootle Borough Police.
W. C. SLEDGE,	Burnley Borough Police.
J. H. GALLOWAY,	Doncaster Borough Police.
D. W. SIMPSON,	Neath Borough Police.

Each man was to be allowed third class return rail fare, plus 10/6d (55p) for refreshments. The day before the interviews took place, a letter was received from Constable Galloway, of Doncaster, informing the Committee that he would not be attending, as he had obtained another position.

Constable Simpson from Neath was the successful applicant, his appointment to take effect from April, 1899. He had previously served in the Cumberland and Westmorland Constabulary.

Thomas Tobin was offered an appointment as sergeant in 6 months time, when Sergeant Wallbanks was due to retire, if he was still interested. Tobin was to take up this appointment, of which more will be read later.

Arthur Edwards the boy clerk was to see an increase in pay, from 10/- (50p) per week to 12/- (60p) per week. Also Inspector Higgins, the Detective officer, was to receive an allowance of £8 per year in lieu of uniform.

POLICE REGULATIONS *1899.*

In April, 1899, new Hand Books were printed, and issued to every member of the force. They replaced the previous issue which had been in use over 15 years. One of the regulations in relation to duties to be carried out by the night shift reads as follow:-

"Any constable omitting to call up another residing on his beat, for early duty, will subject himself to a fine." No alarm clocks in those far off days.

Police constable Scrivens was awarded the sum of £2 2s 0d by the Watch Committee form apprehending a number of offenders in the Bucknall area of the town, who were later convicted of sheep stealing. A few weeks later the Hanley Butchers Association sent P.C. Scrivens a cheque for £2 13s 0d as a reward, however, the Watch Committee refused to allow Scrivens to accept the gift. He resigned from the force a few weeks later, no doubt in disgust.

Inspector Vickers suggested to the members of the Watch Committee that members of the force would cease to pay contributions to the Superannuation Fund after 26 years service. He believed this was done in some other forces. The Committee said that they would look into it, and after a number of replies were received from other Watch Committees throughout the country, they decided to implement the following:-

" With effect from the first day of the New Year. That the Chief Constable be allowed 2s 6d per week, and Inspector Vickers be allowed 1s 3d per week to complement their deductions to the pension fund. Both men had completed over 26 years service in the force.

A BENT COPPER *1899.*

In August, 1899 Mr. Windle reported to the Watch Committee, that Police constable Price who had been acting as warrants officer since Sergeant Williams had retired earlier in the year had absconded on the 31st July, and that an amount of money had gone missing. He was dismissed from the force in his absence, and the Chief Constable was instructed to obtain a warrant for his arrest. Price had been a member of the force for about 8 years

At the next meeting of the Watch Committee, the Rev Norcliffe-Dalton made a claim of £2 13s 0d against the Committee. It was for money he had paid to P.C. Price for a summons issued to him by the Gas Company.

No record can be found as to whether Price was traced and dealt with.

CALLED TO ARMS 1899.

Three members of the force, who were Army Reservists, were called back to their respective regiments for service in South Africa. The Watch Committee was to allow each man three months leave of absence, and their wives were to receive 1/- per day.

When the reservists had not returned to the police duty at the end of the three months, the Watch Committee sought help from the Home Office, and received the following reply:-

"We have received a number of inquiries from both County and Borough Police forces that have members, who belong to the Army Reserve. We intend to adopt the following scale, as regards the Police of the Metropolis. Officer who leaves a wife, and family, 12/- per week plus 2/- per week to each child under 15. Unmarried men who have contributed towards the support of their parents, an allowance not exceeding 8/- per week, should be paid. These arrangements are subject to confirmation".

Before the year was out the force was increased by two men.

Shelton Iron and Steel Company made application to the Watch Committee again, to appoint special constables.

Hanley Borough Police, Kings Crown Helmet Badge. Taken into use 1901 - 1910

Author's Collection

CHAPTER *IV*

A NEW CENTURY, A NEW CHIEF CONSTABLE.

The New Year started off reasonably well as Mr. Windle reported to the Watch Committee that he had placed 20 extra men on duty on the 31st January, 1899, for the New Year celebrations, as it was not only a new year, but a new century. Most of the men were stationed in the town centre. The Chief Constable said there was a lot of noise, with about 60 to 70 persons taking part in a snake dance down Trinity Street, but very little damage occurred, apart from a few windows broken, and only three persons arrested.

It was decided at the first Watch Committee meeting in January, at the suggestion of Mr. Windle that a typewriter be purchased for use in the police office.

LONG SERVING INSPECTOR VICKERS RETIRES 1900.

Inspector Vickers retired from the force as from the 20th February, 1900, after having completed 34 years service. He had spent his entire service in Hanley, having joined the Staffordshire Constabulary in January, 1866, and was posted to Hanley Division a month later. On the formation of the Hanley Borough Police force in 1870, he transferred to that force.

Although retiring from the police force, his connections with the Borough did not finish, as he remained in their employment as a civilian Inspector of Weights and Measures, for which he received an income of 25/- per week.

NEW PAY SCALES 1900.

Members of the force were no doubt happy to be told that their pay was to be increased from the 1st April, 1900. However, to compliment this generous offer, the Watch Committee decided to abolish Good Conduct, and Long Service pay. Also the allowance paid to members to help with their rates. The 7d per week boot allowance would remain.

TALE OF THE ELECTION RIOTS.

The following is an article relating to an interview with Ex-Inspector Jervis Vickers, Hanley Borough Police:

Compared with the lot of those whose duty it was to take part in the suppression of the exciting election riots in Hanley of 1874, when the force armed with rifles were ordered out to disperse the mob, the life of the present day policeman is comparatively hum-drum. One of the policemen who heard the declaration of the election of the late Mr. Robert Heath (the father of the present member) as the Conservative representative of the old Parliamentary Borough of Stoke-on-Trent, and saw the windows of the old Town Hall, in Fountain Square smashed by the mob, has recently retired from public life. His name is Mr.Jervis Vickers, better known until a year ago as Chief Inspector of the Hanley Borough Force.

The ex-Inspector recalled "A policeman's lot is not a happy one." Mr.Vickers spoke with authority, for he was connected with the force from January,1866, when he joined the Staffordshire Constabulary as a constable. At the end of the months he was sent to Hanley, where there were then 13 men, as against 59 at the present time. In September,1870, the Town Council inaugurated a separate Police Force for the borough, and Mr.Vickers, with four other PCs, was transferred from the County to that force, as first-class constable at the princely salary of 17s 6d a week. Within four months he was promoted to the rank of sergeant. Eight years later the subject of our sketch had climbed into an inspector's room, becoming at the same time Assistant Inspector of Weights and Measures, Explosive Substances, and Petroleum. March of the same year saw him senior inspector.

A large number of offences have been investigated by the ex-Inspector, and for many years past scarcely an Assize or Quarter Sessions have been held without his presence in charge of a series of cases. In one very revolting case of which he was in charge, the prisoner was sentenced to penal servitude for 15 years.

"There is no comparison," said Mr.Vickers, "between the Hanley of today, and that of my younger days, especially at the election times down to 1874. The cut down my forehead," continued the veteran, drawing his finger down a long scar, "was inflicted by a brick which was thrown at me by one of the rioters in the election of the year mentioned. The cause of the disturbance was the return of Mr.Arthur Heath's father as a Conservative for the old Parliamentary constituency. The place prior to this time had always shown itself to be Radical. They were peculiar elections in those days. The people had an idea that they enjoyed immunity from the law at election times, and drink, previous to the passing of the Corrupt Practices Act, used to be served free at certain public-houses. Consequently there was great disorder. The disturbance which I remember best of all was after the declaration of the poll in 1874.

Around the Town Hall, which is now Lloyds Bank, and in all the neighbouring thoroughfares, a vast crowd had assembled, numbering, probably, between 20,000 and 30,000 persons from all parts of the Potteries. What turned out to be a riot commenced with some rough horse-play, and the throwing by members of the crowd of herrings, and other missiles at each other. A donkey which had been paraded round the town during the day, dressed in blue ribbons had caused a good deal of excitement, and it was felt by many that the tension was so great with many of the crowd that the slightest provocation would be sufficient to create a disturbance. The announcement of the return of a Conservative was like applying a match to a oiled rag. The excitement soon became intense, and stones were thrown. The corner of the National and Provincial Bank was being rebuilt at the time, and the crowd found plenty of the 'munitions of war' For a long time the fight went on, but the police were ordered not to leave the Town Hall, despite the fact that the windows of the building were being smashed, and glass was flying about in all directions. " The late Alderman Cartlidge was the Mayor in that year, and he placed himself in a very perilous position in reading the Riot Act from one of the windows of the Town Hall opening on to the Market square. As he stood there, stone and brick ends were flying round him, fortunately he escaped any serious injury. Inside a council of war was held. Some thought it was advisable for the police to remain inside the building until the reinforcements which had been wired for arrival. Outside, however, things were rapidly becoming worse; property was being destroyed, and not a hand had been raised to protect it. At the time the Volunteers had their armoury underneath the Town Hall buildings; and it was eventually decided by the Volunteer officers that we should be armed with rifles. No time was lost in getting the weapons, and out we marched through the side door into Tontine square. The crowd saw us, and the rifles too, and not knowing that they were not loaded dispersed helter-skelter in all directions. We could not get within 20 yards of any of them except those who were thrown down in the panic that ensued and trampled under foot. The affair was not yet over though, for the rioters placed themselves at the ends of the streets and hurled bricks at us as we passed. While against Morris's shop I saw one of the roughs Trike a man with a stone. I caught him, and took him back to the police station. His pockets were filled with stones. The next morning he appeared before the Bench and was sentenced to six months imprisonment without the option of a fine. When I came back with my prisoner I found the lower story of the Town Hall was like an infirmary. Dr. Spanton and his assistants and other doctors were fully employed in attending to the injured in the fray. A little later I went out again, and was met near Morris's by a man who hurled a brick at me. It hit me on the forehead, cutting it severely, and rendering me unconscious. Soon after we were reinforced by a number of County Constabulary from Burslem, and a detachment of soldiers were brought down by a special train from Manchester. Things soon settled down after this, though one or two very respectable tradesmen, who had been sworn in as special constables during the morning, got nasty knocks from the 'foreign' police because they stopped in the streets after the order had been issued for everybody to return to their homes.

The next morning, with head bandaged. I attended an inquest on the body of a well-known cab proprietor in the town of that day - Charles Kent- who was killed on the day of the election by being thrown from his box while driving down Etruria road just below the Antelope Inn. The majority of our men were 'crippled' after the fray, and we came in for a good deal of sympathy. I have also had exciting times when I have been drafted to Nottingham elections, where one occasion the crowd, after being driven from the streets, went to the bedroom windows and threw ginger-beer bottles, brick ends, and all sorts of things at us. But to come back to home affairs. There is no comparison between my today now, and that of my younger days in the force. On Sunday morning then you would see more drunken men between nine and twelve than now you would see in a month on Saturday night now. The people are much more refined today."

Yes, they are more refined now, but there is plenty of room for improvement yet, as any daily visitor to the local police courts can testify." Inspector Vickers now rests from his labours in receipt of a well earned pension.

Policing The Potteries

The new pay scales were as follows:-

Inspectors

	Old Scale.	New Scale.
On appointment to the rank ,	38/-	44/-
After 4 years in the rank	41/-	46/-
After 7 years in the rank	44/-	48/-
After 10 years in the rank	46/-	50/-

Sergeants

	Old Scale.	New Scale.
On appointment to the rank ,	31/6d	35/-
After 4 years in the rank ,	33/-	37/-
After 7 years in the rank,	34/-	39/-
After 10 years in the rank	----	42/-

Constables

	Old Scales.	New Scales.
On appointment	23/-	25/-
After 6 months service	26/ 4d	28/-
After 12 months service	27/6d	29/-
After 3 years service	29/-	30/-

This pay scale replaced one that had been in existence since 1892.

SERGEANT DISMISSED FROM THE FORCE 1900.

Sergeant Tobin, who had only recently joined the force, as sergeant on transfer from Bootle Borough Police, appeared before a meeting of the Watch Committee to answer a charge made against him. It was that he had been borrowing money from licensed victuallers in the town. When the allegations were put to the sergeant, he tendered his resignation. This the Committee refused to accept, but dismissed Tobin from the force. His stay with the Hanley force had been less than 12 months.

QUALIFICATIONS FOR SERGEANT 1900.

In April, 1900, the Watch Committee decided that good conduct, and long service, would not in itself be the only qualification for promotion to the rank of sergeant. They requested the Chief Constable to prepare a list of questions relating to police duty, and draw up a form.

In future all applicants for promotion would be required to answer the question paper placed before them, before promotion could be considered.

GOVERNMENT INSPECTION 1900.

At the annual inspection of the force in May, 1900, Her Majesty's Inspector of Constabulary complained that not all the members of the force were wearing regulation uniform pattern boots.

The authorized strength of the force at this time was 61 officers, and men, but the actual strength was only 58, as 3 members of the force, who were Army Reservists, were away fighting in the Boar War. Of the 58 men on parade, 36 were holders of the St. John's Ambulance Certificate.

At the next months Watch Committee meeting, the Chairman reported that the Army Reservists could be away from police duty longer than was first thought, and told the Chief Constable to advertise for three more officers as replacements. To which the Chief Constable replied, that when the reservists did return to police duty, they would then find themselves with more men than they needed. The Chairman told him to advertise for 3 more men, and when the reservists returned, they would sort things out then.

Some time later one man retired, and the force strength was increased by 2 men.

With effect from March, Constable Longmore, the plain clothes officer was to be allowed £6 in lieu of uniform, plus £1 per quarter out of pocket expenses.

Members of the force were to allowed two additional days leave per year, which was to take effect from January the following year.

A Little Social Life 1900.

Members of the force at this time seemed to have a little bit of spare time to enjoy a little of the social side of life. The Town Hall Committee had installed a billiard table in the recreation room at the police station, in 1898.

Two years later members of the force formed a football club, and one of the first games played was against the Liverpool City Police. This game was played on the recreation ground in Hanley, and all money taken at the gate was donated to the Hanchurch Holiday Home for Children.

In the final month of 1900, the Hanley Borough Police Football Club was allowed to join the Half Holiday League.

The force also had a tug of war team.

Retirement of Mr. Windle Chief Constable 1901.

The year opened with Inspector Bloor acting as Chief Constable. This was due to the absence of Mr. Windle, who was indisposed by sickness. In fact Mr. Windle was not to recover sufficiently enough to allow him to take up the reins of office again, and in May, he tendered his resignation. Mr. Windle had been a member of the force since its formation in 1870, and Chief Constable since 1875. During Mr. Windle's service with the force, he had seen the population of the Borough increase from 39,000 to 61,000, and the strength of police force to rise from 31 men in 1870, to 64 in 1901.

Due to the pending retirement of Mr. Windle, the Watch Committee had to select a successor. The Watch Committee decided, after due deliberation that a Chief Constable not over 40 years of age be appointed.

Advertisements were placed in a number of newspapers, and 28 applicants applied. From this number a short list of five were chosen for interview. They were as follows:-

Inspector William A. WILKS,	Manchester City Police.
Chief Constable Roger CARTER,	New Windsor Borough Police.
Chief Constable John STIRLING,	Newcastle-under-Lyme Borough Police.
Superintendent Thomas EARNSHAW,	Wigan Borough Police.
Detective Inspector Thomas QUIGLEY,	Stockport Borough Police.

A few days before the interviews were due to take place, Mr. Stirling, of Newcastle-under-Lyme, wrote to the Watch Committee, informing them that he had been successful in securing the post of Chief Constable of Grimsby Borough Police, and therefore would not be attending the interview.

The Watch Committee decided that five persons should still be interviewed, and Captain J. Hall-Dalwood of Chatham, was added to the list. Captain J.Hall-Dalwood later became the Chief Constable of Leicester and then Sheffield.

MR. ROGER CARTER, CHIEF CONSTABLE 1901 - 1936.

The successful applicant for the post of Chief Constable was Mr. Roger Carter, who commenced his new duty on the 31st August, 1901. In addition to his office as Chief Constable, he also held the post of Inspector under the Explosives Act , Inspector of Hackney Carriages for the Borough, Inspector of Common Lodging Houses, and Superintendent of the Police Fire Brigade.

He was to be paid £300 per year on appointment, with a annual advancement of £20 rising to a maximum of £400. He would also be allowed three weeks paid holiday each year, and £10 each year in lieu of uniform.

Roger Carter, was born in 1867, in Kendal, Westmorland, where his father was a builder, and timber merchant. He was educated at Kendal Grammar School, and on leaving school joined his father's business, but due to the death of both his parents in a short space of time, led him to join the local police force at the age of twenty. He moved to Rochdale, and quickly won promotion. In 1898, when a detective inspector, he was appointed Chief Constable of Windsor. Twice in the next three years while at Windsor, his abilities were tested, when during the celebrations of Queen Victoria's eightieth birthday, and the occasion of the her funeral, he was responsible for controlling the crowds. This experience later enabled him to improve control on Saturday night crowds control in Hanley.

He was later to be made a member of the Royal Victorian Order in 1913 for his previous services to Queen Victoria, and later received the Kings Police Medal

FURTHER DIFFICULTIES WITH POLICE ACCOUNTS 1901.

In June, 1901, certain discrepancies found in monies paid into the police office for licenses, fines, etc., was reported to the Watch Committee. They ordered the Borough Accountant to investigate the matter immediately, and the Acting Chief Constable Mr. Bloor was instructed to give him the necessary help he required. In the mean time Sergeant Dodd, the clerk sergeant would be suspended from duty.

Three months later the Borough Accountant reported to the Watch Committee, that he was able to prove 12 cases where money had been handed to Sergeant Dodd, but no official receipt had been issued, or the money entered in any official book. He also reported that a total of £48 17s 4d (£48 86p) was not accounted for.

After careful consideration of all the facts the Watch Committee decided by a vote of 4 to 3 not to instigate any proceedings against Sergeant Dodd for embezzlement in the Magistrates Court. Some members of the Watch Committee seemed to think that he had been more negligent than criminal. He was however, dismissed from the force.

The new Chief Constable asked that his residence be connected to the Police office by telephone, which was agreed to. At the same time 50 new police bulls eye lanterns were purchased at a cost of 6/- each.

Photograph Elane Bryan.

Chief Constable Carter in centre of photograph mounted.

In October, 1901, the strength of the force was increased by four men. However, the boy employed in the office was dispensed with.

The Museum Committee requested that the force supervise the building at night, which was agreed providing that the Museum Committee paid all the cost. The following month the caretaker of the Free Library was sworn in as a constable, and provided with a suitable uniform. Prior to this records show that members of the force performed duty at the Free Library in their own time, for which they received remuneration.

Inspector Bloor who had been Acting Chief Constable during Mr. Windle's illness, and until the appointment of Mr. Carter, received the sum of £10 from a grateful Watch Committee, for all the extra work that had been force upon him, and he had so willingly carried.

COMMENDATION FOR *P. C. BLOXHAM 1901.*

Police constable Bloxham was awarded a gratuity of £1 by members of the Watch Committee, for the arrest of two men who he found breaking into the rear of Mayers butcher's shop, in Hope Street, late one night. Two men, Mr. William Hancock, coal cart driver, also of Hope Street, and John Knapper, a soldier on leave, both went to Bloxham's assistance, helping to secure the prisoners, and convey them to the police office. Both men also received the same award of £1 each.

At the final meeting of the Watch Committee in 1901, the Town Clerk was asked to write to the Shelton Iron and Steel Co regard the danger of the blasting that was being carried out by the company. After the Chief Constable had reported about the danger, when he said that pieces of metal had been travelling some distance from the site, some of it falling in the streets of the town. It was only luck that no one had been injured, or killed.

SERIOUS ASSAULT AND STABBING OF POLICE OFFICERS 1901

In the July, 1901, a John Collings, residing at an address in West Street, Hanley, appeared before the magistrates, charged with assaulting Police constable George Roberts of the Borough force.

P.C. Roberts told the court that he had been on duty in Bucknall Road at 11 pm on Friday, 12th July, when he heard screams, and shouts of murder. He immediately hurried to the scene, where he saw the defendant, who was obviously drunk, having difficulty in standing without assistance, and using indecent language. He told the accused to go home, but he refused. P.C. Roberts took hold of him, but was immediately knocked to the ground by Collings, who drew a knife and stabbed him in the left leg. He then blew his whistle, and P.C. Kelly then came to his assistance. The defendant then became very violent, and kicked both constables several times.

By this time a crowd had began to gather, and became very hostile towards the officers, and began to throw bricks and other missiles at them. At one point a dolly tub of water was thrown which struck Kelly on the head. It then became necessary for both officers to use their staffs to defend themselves.

Collings was later sentenced to 14 days imprisonment, for being drunk and disorderly, and 3 months for the assault. Inspector Bloor informed the court that it was Collings's 42 appearance before the court.

OFFICERS RETURN FROM BOER WAR 1901.

Before the year was out Police constables George Bowler, George Pember, and Enock Davenport, returned from service in the South African (Boer War), and resume duty.

DEATH OF MR. WINDLE, EX-CHIEF CONSTABLE *1902.*

The new year was only 26 days old when members of the force were to hear of the death of their former Chief Constable Mr. Windle, at the age of 59 years. His funeral took place at Hanley Cemetery a few days later. Besides family mourners, the Mayor, magistrates, and other civic dignitaries attended, also the present Chief Constable Mr. R.J.Carter, and all members of the Hanley Borough Police force, that could be spared from duty. The County police were represented by Chief Superintendent Longdon, Deputy Chief Constable of Staffordshire, Chief Superintendent Hill, Burslem, Superintendent Oakden, Longton, Superintendent Dodd, Tunstall, and Superintendent Gilbride, Stoke Division.

The Town Clerk was instructed to write a letter to the Management of Parkers Brewery, Burslem, telling them that they must refrain from giving, or sending presents to members of the Borough Police force, and if it should continue, the Licensing Justices would be informed.

PROBLEMS WITH HORSES *1902.*

It would appear that both the Davenport brothers were experiencing difficulties with horses during the year 1902. Constable 43 Enock Davenport, who had only just returned to duty after service in the Boer War, was thrown from his horse, when taking part in the Life Boat Parade. He was taken to the infirmary, but his injuries were not life threatening.

Only a few days later his brother Constable 39 Albert Davenport was awarded 5/- by the Watch Committee, for his brave conduct when he stopped a runaway horse in Tontine Street.

In May, 1902, the Watch Committee received a letter from the Public Health Committee request-ing the force to assist them in its endeavours to abate the nuisance arising from the emission of black smoke in the Borough during the times of epidemic, when the smoke inspector was fully employed with cases of infectious disease. Once again the police were found yet another job.

During the same month members of the force placed a petition before the Watch Committee, asking for monthly, and annual leave to be increased. Their petition pointed out that most larger industrial towns, allowed 2 days per month. Constables 7 days, sergeant 10 days, and inspectors 14 days annual leave each year. The Committee granted their request.

The Chief Constable was instructed to enforce the regulations with respect to the return of items of uniform clothing. No doubt this was as a result of a member of the force appearing before the Watch Committee, on a charge of improperly selling items of used uniform clothing.

In the December, the Watch Committee ordered a new die for the uniform buttons.

TRANSPORT AND LICENSING LEGISLATION *1903.*

Two pieces of legislation that had been passed, which were to cause the force extra administration, and work, came into being on the 1st day of January, 1903. They were the Motor Car Act, part of which made it mandatory for every mechanically propelled vehicle on the highway to display an identification mark. The County Borough of Hanley was allotted the registration letters E.H.. Records of the registration numbers, and owners had be kept, and that job at that time fell to the police.

The second act with which the force had to keep records was the Licensing Act, 1902. From this date the police forces had to keep record, and photographs of all known habitual drunkards, and distribute same to all licensed premises, and clubs within the force area.

Mr. Carter made representation to both the Watch Committee, and the Licensing Justices to have the number of licensed premises reduced in certain parts of the Borough, namely the High Street, Lamb Street, Hope Street, Bryan Street, Union Street, and Bow Street areas. He said that he thought it would be desirable for the number of licensed premises to be reduced in this immediate vicinity.

DANGER OF TRAMS IN THE BOROUGH *1903.*

Members of the public were complaining to both the police, and members of the council, regarding the speed of the tram cars in the Borough. Mr. Carter was requested to investigate these complaints, and to let the Watch Committee have a full report regarding the problems.

Mr. Carter was able to furnish the Committee with the following information:- Over the previous 12 month period four young children had been knocked down by tram cars, one of whom was a girl of 3 years of age who had been fatally injured in Etruria Road.

He had kept observation and reported that the average speed of the tram cars in the Borough was 9 m.p.h..

In November, 1903, one inspector, one sergeant, and fourteen constables, two of which were mounted were loaned to the Newcastle-under-Lyme Borough force, to assist with crowd control at the unveiling of the statue of Queen Victoria, by the Grand Duke Michael of Russia, in Nelson Place. Newcastle Council later received a bill for £4 7s 7d (£4 38p).

Inflation must have been with us in the 1900's, as the Chief Constable requested that the petty cash he was allowed to hold be increased from £10 to £20, to which the Watch Committee agreed

He also made a further suggested to which the Committee agreed, which was that both the prison van, and ambulance should be completely overhauled, and painted. Also that the ambulance should be adapted to be drawn by two horses instead of one.

The Chief Constable with the Watch Committee's blessing arranged for classes in educational subjects to be held for constables who wished to attend them. These classes were held at the Higher Grade School (Hanley High School), and were taken by the Head Master Mr. Wilson.

At the close of 1903, the total strength of the force was sixty four men, there were no vacancies. The total cost of the force for the year was £6,332 0s 10d, half of which was reimbursed by the Central Government.

COMPLAINT OF POLICE OFFICERS DRINKING ON DUTY 1904

In 1904, a letter written by a Mr. Ball appeared in a local newspaper, complaining about member of the local police drinking when on duty, and of two licensees who were supplying police officers with drink, when they knew them to be on duty. Mr. Ball, however, refused to substantiate his statement when later interviewed by the Chief Constable.

Thomas Rowley, a local man was awarded 10/6d by the Watch Committee for going to the assistance of Police constable Roberts, who was attempting to arrest a violent prisoner in the town

The force purchased the following items at the beginning of the year, four new pairs of riding boots, from Brassington Bros, of Hanley (who are today, still dealers in footwear), at a total cost of £12s 6d.

A new oak book case for the Clerks Office, at a cost of £11, and a portable tin bath was also purchased for use in the police department. It is not recorded whether this was for use by policemen, or prisoners.

SENIOR OFFICERS PROMOTED 1904.

Inspector Bloor, who had been a member of the force for 17 years, and had held that rank since 1896, was promoted to Chief Inspector. He was the first officer in the force to hold that rank. His salary was to be £2 12s 6d (£2 63p) per week, rising to £2 15s 0d (£2 75p) per week after three years service in that rank.

It also meant that the Chief Inspector would be in charge of the force, in the absence of the Chief Constable.

THE FORCE IS EMBEZZLED AGAIN 1904.

Problems of five years previous were to embarrass the force yet again, when Sergeant Simpson, the Chief Clerk, absented himself from duty. The Chief Constable later informed the Watch Committee, that Simpson had absconded with a married woman, and that £40 in cash was missing from the accounts. The sergeant was dismissed from the force in his absence, and a warrant issued for his arrest. The sergeant left behind a wife and seven children.

A search of local newspapers, and records have failed to show whether he was ever arrested, or dealt with for the offence.

No doubt due to this and previous problems that the force had suffered at the hands of previous incumbents, the Watch Committee decided that in future, the Police Clerk would be required to give a bond of up to £100. The Watch Committee would pay the annual premium.

Members of the Borough force held their first annual outing in August, 1904, when they visited Trentham Gardens, accompanied by the wives and guests. Among the invited guests, were the Mayor, the Chief Constable, the Deputy Chief Constable of Staffordshire, and the Superintendents of all the Pottery divisions of the County Constabulary, and Mr. J. H. Watson, Chief Constable of Congleton.

CHIEF CONSTABLE'S REPORT FOR 1904.

The Chief Constable reported to the Watch Committee for the year 1904, as follows:-

The strength of the force was 64 men, of whom 49 held the St. John Ambulance medallion.

242 indictable offences had been committed within the Borough, 698 non indictable offences had been committed, of which 348 were for drunkenness. 616 persons were summoned for a variety of offences, 88 Inquests were held. 162 dogs were seized, of which 17 were returned to their owners, 6 sold, and the rest destroyed. 27 fires were attended by the Police Fire Brigade, which possessed two steam fire engines, one hose cart, and one escape ladder.

The Watch Committee at the suggestion of the Chief Constable purchased a number of enamelled signs at a cost of 4s 3d (22p) each. The signs were to be fixed to the front of the house of every member of the force. It is not recorded whether the Chief Constable had one of the new signs fixed to his house.

At this time the Chief Constable moved his residence from 41 Lichfield Street, to 81 Park Road. The telephone was then connected to his new residence.

Attitudes have changed considerably over the last ninety or so years, certainly in relationship to behaviour, as the following case shows. Charles Humphrys, aged 16 years was charged in 1904, under the Lords Day Observance Act, when it was stated that he had been crying "Newspapers" in the street on a Sunday. It was said that he had been previously warned. Humphrys was discharged on promising not to offend again.

AMBULANCE DUTIES 1905.

In the June of 1905, a new ambulance of the most modern design was purchased, along with four new stretchers from John Roberts and Co., of Manchester, at a total cost of £108 2s 0d. The old ambulance was to be kept for the removal of fever cases.

Doctor J. Aldridge, the Chief Superintendent of the area St. John Ambulance Brigade, said of the new ambulance. " I would like to see every town in North Staffordshire equipped with one. It is capable of carrying two persons on stretchers at the same time. It is something that the town can be justifiably proud of. Doctor Aldridge was present with an inscribed silver cigarette case by the Chief Constable from members of the force thanking him for the instructions he had given in St. John's Ambulance duties.

Repairs were also carried out to the prison van, at a cost of £7 3s 6d (£7 17p). At this time the force had under it's control two ambulances, one prison van, and two steam fire engines, all of which were horse drawn.

BIRCHING OF YOUNG OFFENDERS 1905.

Three young boys, Samuel Thomas, aged 10 years, William Briggs, aged 12 years, John Howlett, aged 14 years, all appeared before the police court at this time charged with throwing stones off a bridge onto a passing train, on the loop line. Briggs, and Thomas, were each ordered to be birched, but Howlett, who was too old to be birched, was bound over, it being his first offence.

Reports of malicious damage, and theft in Hanley Park and Cemetery, were causing problems at this time. One night in August, the park pavilion was broken into, and money, and goods to the value £1 10s 0d (£1 50p) were stolen. To alleviate this problem the police were issued with a key to the park, in order that the night duty men were able to gain access to check it better.

In September, 1905, part of the Parish of Milton was added to the County Borough, and the force increased by one man. The force also opened a branch police station in the Birches Head area.

In the same month the Chief Constable Mr. Carter got married, and was presented with a Gladstone bag by members of the Watch Committee.

MUTUAL AID 1906.

The year 1906, opened with a General Election, and to assist with the policing of these elections, sixteen members of the County force, and ten members of the Macclesfield Borough Police, were loaned to Hanley. A few days later Hanley officers travelled to Macclesfield, and Congleton to assist their colleagues with their election duties. One days extra leave was granted to the Hanley men, for the extra work involved with the election.

BEGGING YOUNGSTERS 1906.

Complaints about juveniles begging in the streets of the town were made to a Watch Committee meeting in February, 1906. The complainant said that the situation was worse on the Market days between the railway station, and the Market Square.

A request from the Market Committee, was read, asking if it were possible for a policeman in uniform to patrol the covered market. The Market Committee were informed that there request was possible, but they would have to pay for the service.

It seemed to be quite common during that time for all other Committees of the Council to request the loan of police officers for help, and assistance, but then decline the offer when the Watch Committee insisted on payment.

C.I.D AID FROM OUTSIDE 1906.

A communication was sent out from the Home Secretary to every Chief Officer of Police in the Country, informing them that Detective officers from Scotland Yard would be available to every provincial force to assist them with all serious, and difficult cases, if so requested by the Chief Constable.

In June, 1906, a horticulture fete was held in the Hanley Park, and the force had the assistance of two Detective officers , one from Manchester, and the other borrowed from the Birmingham force. The main purpose of these two officers was to watch for pickpockets. They were both employed for the two days of the fete.

Chief Inspector Bloor Retires From Force 1906.

In the same month Chief Inspector Bloor who had been in the force 19 years, and had held the rank of Chief Inspector for two years, retired from the force. He was replaced by Inspector Higgins, who had been a member of the force since 1879, and at the time of his promotion was the Detective Inspector in charge of the Detective Department.

Commendations 1906.

Both Police constables Alfred Bailey, and Ralph Coffey received 5/- (25p) from the Watch Committee, for the capture of fowl stealers. Coffey had only been a member of the force for about eight weeks. The following month David Longdon, of 25, Elizabeth Street, and John Cope, of 11, East View, were also awarded with the customary 5/- by the Watch Committee, for going to the assistance of P.C. Smith, when he was being assaulted by a drunk he was attempting to arrest.

The Watch Committee agreed to the suggestion from one of it's members, that the Chief Constable be allowed to send the ambulance outside the Borough, and levied the following charges:- 5/- or 7/6d depending on the distance, plus charges for special duty allowance for the police officers.

These charges would come into effect on the 1st July, 1906.

Government Inspection 1906.

Captain the Hon C.G. Legge, H.M.Inspector of Constabulary, paid his annual visit to the force in March., 1906. The following officers were on parade for his inspection.:-

1 Chief Constable,	1 Chief Inspector,	
2 Inspectors,	5 Sergeants,	42 Constables.

The following were unable to attend due to being on duty, sickness, or leave:-

1 Sergeant On duty,	6 Constables On duty,
3 Constables Off sick,	2 Constables On leave.
2 Vacancies.	Total Strength of the Force 65,

Actual Strength of the Force 63.

After he had inspected the men at the Drill Hall, he then inspected the police station cells, and books, the Inspector said, "I am pleased with all I have seen, but I would suggest that it is advisable to appoint a female to attend to women, and accompany them on their travels to Stafford Gaol".

Captain Legge then informed the members of the Watch Committee, and the Chief Constable, that it would be the last time that he would inspect the force, has he would be retiring later in the year.

ALLEGATION OF ASSAULT AGAINST POLICE OFFICERS 1906.

Chief Inspector Higgins, along with Police constables Brassington, Roberts, and Bailey, appeared before the Watch Committee in November, 1906, to answer the charges made against them. As a result of the inquiry by the Watch Committee Chief Inspector Higgins was found guilty of assaulting a prisoner, who had been brought to the station by P.C. Brassington. He was charged with assaulting the same prisoner.

Constable George Roberts, and Henry Bailey, were charged with making a false report to the Chief Constable in relation to these allegations.

Chief Inspector Higgins was fined £5, and severely reprimanded by the Mayor. Each of the constables were fined £2.

RETURN OF MERIT CLASS 1907

In June, 1907, after a laps of 7 years, the Watch Committee, at the suggestion of the Chief Constable, reintroduced the class of Merit Constable, but laid the following qualification for it. Not more than 10 constables were to be in the Merit Class at any one time; men chosen must have no charge of misconduct recorded against them for at least 3 years. Men appointed to Merit Class would receive 1/- (5p) per week extra to their pay, and be allowed to wear a badge. Police constable 33 Harry Hardey Glover, and Police constable 14 George William Pember, were the first two recipients of the award.

The Watch Committee received a letter from the Rev. Jenkin Edwards, in which he was complaining about the action of the Chief Constable, who he said had refused him the services of a police constable, to assist him to get rid of some troublesome tenants he had in one of his properties. The reverend gentleman was informed by the Watch Committee to apply to the County Court.

A safe was purchased for the Clerk's Office, after £2 in cash had gone missing from the same office, and had been written off as a bad debt. Mr. Carter told the Committee that the cash was at present kept in a draw, which could not be locked.

AREA FIRST AID CHAMPIONS 1907.

Hanley Borough Police managed to win the area First Aid Competition for the third years in succession. The members of the winning team were:- Inspector Middleton, P.C. 33 Glover, P.C. 20 Perry, and P.C. 42 Bloxham.

COMMENDATIONS TO COUNTY POLICEMEN 1907

Police constables Arthur Scott, and William Harman, both members of the County Police, were awarded 10/6d (52p) each by the Hanley Borough Watch Committee, for the arrest of two local men who they apprehended breaking into a pottery situated in the Borough , and stealing ware.

CIVILIAN DRIVER HAVING DIFFICULTY WITH HORSES 1907

In October, 1907, Mr. William Keeling, a civilian employed by the force as a driver, and groom was taking the prison van to Stoke Railway Station, when the horse was in collision with a cart, which resulted in Mr. Keeling being thrown from the van, and sustaining injuries to his neck. He was off sick for a number of weeks. Exactly twelve months later Mr. Keeling assisted by two constables, was removing a body from a house in Hinde Street. As the two constables were having difficulty in lifting the body into the ambulance, Mr. Keeling got down from his driving seat to assist, and as he did so, both horses together with the ambulance bolted into Mollart Street along Windsor Street, Charles Street, where it collided with a wall, and continued on into Eastwood Road, where it collided with a dray. There was only slight injury to the horses, but considerable damage to the ambulance, which had to be repaired.

Mr. Carter informed the Watch Committee that he had applied for the post of Chief Constable, of Leicester City Police, and had been called for an interview. However, he was not successful with his application.

At the last meeting of the Watch Committee for 1907, the Chief Constable was complaining regarding the attitude of the newly promoted Inspector Collier, in his dealing with the men under his command. He said that the inspector lacked tact.

SUNDAY SHOPPING 1908.

Just as a matter of interest to readers, when so much is spoken about present day Sunday shopping . It does not appear that it was very different in those days when compared with the Chief Constables report to the Watch Committee of the number of shops open in the Borough on Sunday, 16th February, 1908, which is as follows:-   Sweet shops 157; grocers 53; greengrocers 45, newsagents 28; tobacconist 19; hairdressers 6; confectioners 3; fish and chips shops 10; dairies 4; herbalists 1; butchers 2; photographers 1; Total 329.

GOVERNMENT INSPECTION 1908.

Lieutenant Colonel Eden, the newly appointed Inspector of Constabulary inspector the Hanley Borough force, and the station, and declared all to be satisfactory.

Mr. Thomas Bickley complained in a letter to the Watch Committee in March, 1908, about the nuisance that was taking place in Morley Street. He stated that unsavoury characters were gathering in the street, and doing damage to his premises. He complained that it was not properly supervised by the police, and that it was poorly lighted.

CONSTABLE COMMENDED FOR SAVING CHILD 1908.

Police constable Preston was awarded one guinea by the Watch Committee in May, 1908, for saving a young boy from drowning in the canal at Etruria. He was also commended for his action. The Town Clerk was asked to write to the owner of the land adjoining the canal where the incident had occurred, and ask them to fence the area.

The Watch Committee were to receive a further complaint in June, 1908. This time it was regarding school children throwing stones , and creating a nuisance in the town. The Education Committee was asked to put up notices in the schools, and improve supervision of the children when they were leaving school.

The North Eastern Railway Company wrote to the Chief Constable requesting the name and addresses of the owners of all motor cars registered in the County Borough of Hanley. The Town Clerk was requested to reply to them, and inquire why they required the information.

POLICE SOCIAL WORK *1908.*

In the days before any social services as we know today existed, it was often the police who were called to assist, although they appear to receive gratuity for it. Police constable Glover received 2/6d (12 p) from a Mr. Schofield for assisting him to convey a gentleman to the Lunatic Asylum. A few months later a letter of thanks was received from the Wolstanton and Burslem Union, from their offices in Burslem, in which they thanked the Hanley Council for the use of the Police Ambulance in removing a Mr. Roberts to the workhouse.

With effect from October, 1908, the Chief Constable was to see his petty cash increased from £20 to £40.

The Watch Committee were asked to provide more police supervision in the park, and it was suggested that constables in plain clothes be used.

IMPROVED CONDITIONS OF SERVICE *1908.*

The men were to see an improvement in their conditions of service before the year was out. The Chief Constable announced that in future, each member of the force on night duty would be allowed a 30 minute break to take his meal in the police station. Prior to this a man would leave the police station at 9.45 pm, and remain on his beat until 6.am the following morning. He would be expected to eat his sandwiches standing in a shop doorway, or somewhere similar, and on a cold night, it would be virtually impossible to obtain a hot drink. So can we blame them for seeking a little warmth, and comfort on a cold night in the local hostelry.

In December, 1908, an additional constable was added to the force.

FIREARMS *1909.*

1909 opened with the Council receiving a letter from the Town Clerk of Newport, Monmouthshire, in which he was complaining about the prevalence of crime, and the ease by which revolvers could be acquired. He said it was of the opinion of his Watch Committee that further restrictions should be placed on the sale of revolvers, and he requested the Hanley Council to be a signatory to an attached document, and forward the same to the Home Office. The document was duly signed, and forwarded to the Home Office.

Constable Rescued from the Canal *1909.*

At 11.pm on Saturday, 30th January, 1909, Police constable 31 Craddock was walking his beat in the Etruria area, when he slipped, and fell into the canal lock, and had to be rescued by a Mr. Thomas Wilkinson, and George Meadowcroft, both employees of Twyfords Pottery Ltd, Cliffe Vale. The men were each given a gift of 5/- by the Watch Committee.

Mr. Challinor the Town Clerk was asked to write to the owners of the land bordering the canal, and inform them of the unsatisfactory state of it.

It was now costing the Council 8/- (40p) per week for the maintenance of each boy sent to the Werrington Home.

The Chief Constable was requested by the Watch Committee to ensure that every member of the force attended ambulance lectures.

Police constable Pember was promoted to the rank of sergeant in October, 1909, and placed in charge of the detective department, and would in future work directly under the control of the Chief Constable.

Certain members of the force complained to the Watch Committee about the selection of men for the detective department. The complainants were informed that the selection of the men for this duty, was left to the Chief Constable.

The cost of employing private constables to the Shelton Iron and Steel Co. Ltd., was now £110 per officer, per year. There were then 3 constables employed on this duty.

Officers and men who were involved in the pit boys strike in the July, 1909, were granted one extra days pay for the extra duty involved. The Chief Constable was awarded the sum of £5 5s 0d (£5.25p), for the tact he had displayed during the dispute.

A little obscure law was used at this time, when the occupiers of land in Leek Road, were served with an order under the Barbed Wire Act, which required them to remove the wire in seven days, or face court action.

Heroic Rescue By Police Constable *1909.*

On the 17th October, 1909, Police constable 53 Henry Seabridge, almost lost his own life while making a heroic rescue of Thomas Hughes from the canal in Hanley. Hughes, who in an attempt to commit suicide, threw himself into the canal lock and resisted, most violently, any attempt to be rescued. The man was finally got out of the water after a struggle. As a result of the injury he received in the rescue

P.C. Seabridge was off sick for some considerable time. He was granted a Merit Badge, and in January the following year the Town Clerk was requested to apply for the Carnegie grant for him.

Seabridge was awarded the Royal Humane Society Bronze Medal for his heroic action.

Constable Thomas Hugh Davies, who had joined the force in May, 1909, was dismissed from the force, after only seven months service. It was found that he had forged discharge papers from the Royal Marine Artillery, to obtain his employment.

ELECTION DUTIES 1909.

Forty constables from the Staffordshire County force were on duty in Hanley for the Parliamentary Elections, and a few days later twenty constable from the Hanley Borough force travelled to Sedgley to assist there County colleagues with their election duties.

Staffordshire Police.

Hanley County Borough Police. This Photograph was taken only a few months before federation in 1910. Chief Constable Carter seated centre.

THE FINAL YEAR 1910.

Members of the force submitted a petition to the Watch Committee at the beginning of the year, requesting one days leave in seven. However, the Committee said they would take no action, but the request would be placed before the new council in April.

Over a considerable number of years there had been discussions, and proposals in town halls within the Potteries to form a federation of the six towns within that area, namely Burslem, Fenton, Hanley, Longton, Tunstall, and Stoke-upon-Trent. Finally after a number of readings of the bill put before Parliament for the federation, Royal Ascent to the bill was given, and the formation of the County Borough of Stoke-on-Trent would take place as from the 1st April, 1910.

This would directly effect the policing of the area, as up to that time it was policed by two forces. The towns of Burslem, Fenton, Longton, Tunstall, Stoke-upon-Trent by Staffordshire Constabulary, and Hanley, by Hanley Borough Police. As a result of the federation Hanley Borough Police force was to merge with the County Divisions of the remaining five towns to form the County Borough of Stoke-on-Trent Police. This also came into effect on the 1st April, 1910.

Most of the Watch Committee meetings for the early part of 1910, were taken up with the setting up of the new Stoke-on-Trent County Borough Police force, and which included appointment of over forty extra men

Mr.E.B.Bateman.

Constable William Bateman sitting Centre. Bateman was one of three constables who were loaned to the Shelton Iron and Steel Company for duty at their factory. Shelton Iron and Steel Company would then be required to reimburse the Watch Committee all costs that would occur. These constables were usually know as private constables and were in addition to the normal strength of the force as set by the home office, but were, for pay, pensions, leave and discipline, treated as normal members of the force. They were appointed by the Chief Constable and Watch Committee and not the management of the factory.

who would commence duty on the 30th March, 1910, ready for the policing of the enlarged area of the new County Borough.

These men were appointed mainly from other police forces, from various parts of England, Scotland, and Ireland, as a result of advertisements placed in the Police Review, Staffordshire Sentinel, Staffordshire

Policing The Potteries

Advertiser, Penrith Herald, and newspapers in Scotland, and Ireland. In addition to these men, nearly seventy men from the Staffordshire County Police, who had been stationed in the Potteries District of that force, transferred to the County Borough force.

The majority of the Hanley Borough men continued to serve in the new Stoke-on-Trent Borough Police Force for sometime, some climbing to higher ranks. One such officer later became the first Chief Constable of Wallasey Borough Police, when it was formed in 1914.

The Chief Constable Mr. Roger Carter remained as Chief Constable of the Stoke-on-Trent County Borough force, which later became the City of Stoke-on-Trent Police, until

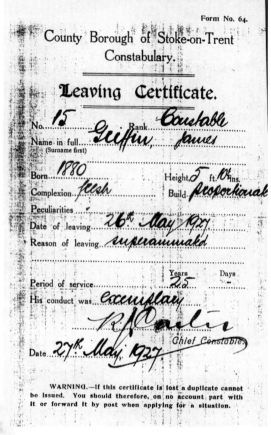

his death while still serving on the 13th April, 1936.

The 31st March, 1910, ended forty years policing of the town by the Hanley Borough Police Force.

P.C. James Griffin who served from 1902 to 1927. This photograph would have been taken shortly after Griffin joined the force. Also Griffin certificate of service.

Loaned by family.

84

THE POLICE FIRE BRIGADE.

TRAGIC FIRE. 1871.

A most serious, and destructive fire, resulting in loss of life, broke out early one morning in February, 1871, Market Terrace, Hanley. The terrace was a row of stone built three story houses, with shops on the ground floor, and living accommodation on the upper two floors. It also formed one side of a covered market. The fire was first discovered at about 6.am in the morning, in the premises of Mr. James, grocer, but had apparently been burning some considerable time. It soon spread to the premises of Mr. Tirrell, next door, and then to the home of Mr. Day, boot, and shoemaker. Within a short space of time, the entire frontage of the three shops was well ablaze.

On the alarm being raised, messengers were at once dispatched for the fire engines, and in the meantime desperate attempts were made to rescue the occupants of the premises. After great difficulty a side door was broken open leading into Swan Passage, and Mr. and Mrs. James and their children just managed to escape in their night clothes, although they were scorched by the flames.

After a lapse of about a half hour, the Hanley engine arrived with Superintendent Alexander in charge, followed by engines from Etruria, Cobridge, and Stoke. A mounted messenger was also dispatched to Burslem at 7.am to request the loan of the steam fire engine belonging to that town (at that time Burslem was the only town in North Staffordshire to possess a steam fire engine), and that arrived at 8.10am. There was ample water in the mains, and all the engines were kept busy. Thanks mainly to the Burslem engine the fire was soon under control, but it was several hours before the last smouldering embers were quenched.

Although the occupants of the premises were safely rescued from the premises, during the fire, Mr. Wyatt, a young sergeant in the Etruria Artillery Corps, who was helping some bricklayers to render what assistance that was in their power, fell through the glass panelling of the market roof, sustaining fatal injuries.

The total cost of damage caused was in excess of £1,000.

THE FORMATION OF THE POLICE FIRE BRIGADE *1871.*

After this disastrous fire the local newspaper, and towns people were complaining of the attitude of the local council, with regards to it's fire cover for the town. A local newspaper went on to say , " We have time, and time again brought to the council's attention the inefficiency of the fire brigade in this town. The plant, and equipment of the fire brigade is wholly inadequate for a town the size of Hanley, and the brigade is undisciplined, and incompetent."

The council met the following week, and decided to purchase a steam fire engine, and the best fire escape that they could purchase, regardless of cost. This was purchased from Merryweather Ltd, and was delivered about three months later, at a total cost of £500. It included 16 ft of suction hose, and 400 ft of delivery hose. The new escape ladder cost an extra £10.

At this same meeting, the town council decided to transfer the control of the fire brigade from the General Purpose Committee, to the Watch Committee, and form a Police Fire Brigade, with the Chief Constable being in charge. It was normal practice in most towns at that time, for members of the police force to also perform duties as firemen, and was no doubt cheaper, saving the councils considerable cost.

The brigade now possessed one steam fire engine, one manual engine, and one wheeled escape ladder.

The new steamer did not have long to wait, for it was to receive it's baptism on the 12th August, when it attended a rick fire in Leek Road, Hanley. Mr. Alexander was in charge of the operation, water being pumped from the River Trent nearby.

Mr. Tozer, Superintendent of the Manchester Fired Brigade, visited Hanley at the request of the Borough Council in 1873, to inspect the manual fire engine, and report on the same. He was allowed £2, plus travelling expenses, by the Hanley Council for his trouble.

GAINING EXPERIENCE.

On the 24th July, 1885, a large fire occurred at Palmer's timber yard which was situated at the junction of Bucknall Road, and Wells Street. The brigade were in attendance for nearly 12 hours, and the damage came to just over £3,000, quite a considerable amount in those days.

The Council agreed to allow both the town's fire engines to travel to Rudyard on Easter Monday, 1886, to take part in a display, providing the cost would not be incurred by the Borough. I dread to think what would have happened if a fire had occurred in the town on that day.

Members of the force seem to have been spending most of their time fire fighting in the months of November, and December, 1886. They attended two fires on the 5th November, one on the 10th , two again on the 11th . The following month seems to have been no better, with the brigade attending two fires on the 7th December, and a further five fires in the next seven days.

In 1888, the Chief Constable, along with the Borough Surveyor, were instructed to travel to Newcastle-under- Lyme to inspect the new telescopic fire escape, then in use in the town, and report on it to the next meeting of the Watch Committee. The Committee then decided to purchase one, complete with canvas shoot. The total cost was £81.

At the end of 1888, Mr. Thomas Shaw, senior, and his son Thomas Shaw, junior were appointed engineers of the fire brigade. Members of the Committee said it would be very convenient to have a father and son employed like this.

Mr. Heath, a farmer from Bucknall, wrote to the Watch Committee in 1891, complaining that a bill for £14 9s 0d sent to him for fire brigade attendance at a hay rick fire at his farm, was too excessive. The Committee reduced the bill to £7 2s 0d.

THE OLD ENGINE KEEPS GOING 1891.

In 1891, Mr. Shaw, the engineer of the fire brigade reported to the Watch Committee that the steam fire engine was 21 years old, was in a bad condition, and he did not have confidence in it. The engine required a thorough overall, or a new one purchased. The Watch Committee lost no time, and made contact with Merryweather Ltd, asking them to send one of their engineers to inspect the engine. Several days later a report was placed before the Watch Committee, in which it was stated that the repair of the engine would cost £250, or that a new one could be supplied for £410, plus the old one in exchange.

The Committee also wrote to Shand Mason, the only other manufacturer of steam fire engines in Britain at the time, asking for an estimate for a new engine. In the meantime the Council decided to have the fire engine examined by an independent engineer. He reported that the engine would be all right, and only needed a few minor repairs. These repairs to the engine were carried out locally at a cost of £8 10s 0d (£8.50p).

In August, 1892, the National Telephone Company, were instructed to connect the fire brigade engineer's house to his works for fire brigade purposes.

A new Tozer hand operated pump, together with 300 ft of hose were also purchased at this time.

At the beginning of 1893, Thomas Shaw and his son resigned from their positions, as engineers to the fire brigade. Their successor was Mr. George Quick, who was to be paid £10 per annum, plus 3/- for each drill attended, and 3/- per hour when attending fires. Mr. Quick's house, and place of work were also connected by telephone.

Representatives of all the fire brigades in the Pottery towns held a meeting at Stoke in 1893, to set a scale of charges, and which the following were decided upon:-

Chief Officer, 10/6d for the 1st hour, for every successive hour 2/6d.

Engineer, 5/- for the 1st hour, for every successive hour 2/-.

Sergeant, 2/6d for the 1st hour, for every successive hour 2/-.

Constable or Fireman, 2/- for the 1st hour, every successive hour 1/-.

It seemed to be a regular occurrence for the Chief Constable to be complaining to the Watch Committee regarding the water pressure in various parts of the town. The Committee instructed the Town Clerk to write to the Staffordshire Potteries Water Works Company. Numerous correspondence passed between the council, and the water works company, complaining about the unsatisfactory state of the water supply, in particular the pressure in the town.

The water problems were highlighted on one Sunday night in June, 1894, when the brigade were called to an outbreak of fire at the factory of Bullock and Bennett, in Pelham Street.

The management or the company latter sent a letter to the Mayor, in which they expressed their thanks for the splendid work carried out by the Superintendent, and the members of the fire brigade. However, they said that they had been handicapped by the lack of water. They complained that this was the second time that they have been forced to standby and watch part of their factory burn down, due to the lack of water in the mains.

In the following September, there was a third fire at the same factory (perhaps a visit from the fire prevention officer, had they existed at that time, may have assisted). At this time the Council purchased a new horse for fire brigade purposes.

In September, 1895, the Chief Constable was instructed to have the fire escape put in proper repair, and repainted . Twelve months later the Council decided to purchase a new 60 ft escape from Merryweathers and Co Ltd, of London, at a cost of £78.

At the September, 1897, Watch Committee meeting, it was decided that Mr. Quick the engineer to the fire brigade should be issued with a uniform.

Mr. Windle was instructed to drill every man in the force, in the use of the fire escape. This was to be carried out at the same time as the normal fire practice, which took place once every month. Two months later the Chief Constable was able to report that to the Committee that every man was now proficient with the escape.

Busy Period *1898.*

The Police Fire Brigade attended four fires during May, 1898. The first of these being to an empty house in Spice Street, which was extinguished by them with a hand pump, and the engine was not required. A few days later, the brigade was called to the works of Messrs. Doultons, in Nile Street , Burslem, but on their arrival, they discovered that it had been already extinguished by the Burslem Brigade.

The next call was to the factory of Messrs. Powell and Bishop, in Stafford Street. The hand pump was again used on this fire. The last fire of the month was at the American Oil Stores, at Cliffe Vale, but the brigade were late again, for the fire had been attended to by the North Staffordshire Railway Co Fire Brigade, on whose premises the building was situated.

The Council received a letter from the Endon and Stanley Parish Council, requesting the Borough of Hanley to enter into an agreement with them for the use of their fire brigade, and engine, in their respective district. However, the Borough Council replied that it could not see it's way to enter into such an agreement, stating that they already had agreements with adjoining towns. If however, the engine is not required, it may be sent into their district on the terms already fixed.

In October, 1899, the Council received a letter from the Town Clerk of Sunderland, requesting the Borough of Hanley to concur in a petition to the Government in favour of a bill being put before Parliament, that would provide for the payment of half the cost of maintaining a fire brigade in each city, and borough in England, and Wales. The Town Clerk was instructed to write back, and inform them that they would have the full support of this Borough.

It was to take close on 50 years for local councils to get this grant, for it was not approved until the Fire Service Act of 1947.

Acts of Bravery in a Tragic Fire *1900.*

At about 10 minutes past four in the morning of Tuesday, the 5th June, 1900, Police constable Shenton was on duty in Broad Street, Hanley, when he heard shouts of fire, and noticed smoke bellowing from the shop of Herbert Baker, clogger and boot repairer, which was situated in the same street. P.C. Shenton hastened to the scene, and now accompanied by Inspector Bloor, were met at the scene by Mr. Baker, who was handicapped, and his wife who informed them that their children were still trapped in the house. P.C. Shenton and Mr. Baker entered the burning house, and managed to locate the eldest daughter Mary Ellen, aged 10 years, but they themselves became trapped. They only managed to escape when Alfred Dalton, an Army Recruiting Sergeant living next door to Mr. Baker, came to their rescue. It was now impossible for any further rescue attempts to take place due to the thick smoke issuing from the shop.

The bodies of Harold, aged 9 years, and Ada, aged 6 years, were later recovered by Sergeant Collier, and P.C. Tildsley, after the fire had been extinguished.

The Watch Committee later held an investigation into the tragedy, and came to the conclusion that it could not have been avoided, and stated that the workings of the fire brigade were in no way to blame.

Later at the Inquest into the deaths of the two children, the jury added that the conduct of Police constable Shenton was deserving of commendation, and that he ought to receive some recognition for his courage. Both P.C. Shenton, and Mr. Alfred Dalton were to receive 5 guineas each from the Watch Committee.

REORGANIZATION OF THE FIRE BRIGADE 1901.

The new Chief Constable Mr. Carter had not been in office long, when he decided to take a close look at the organization, and equipment of the Police Fire Brigade. He submitted the following report, in October, 1901, only one month after taking office:-

"A number of alterations are required in the fire brigade. There is no system of calling out the Brigade.

The present system of the men running with the hose cart is unsatisfactory, and slow, the men are then unfit for active duty on arrival at the fire if a considerable distance has to be covered. I ask the Committee to purchase a horse drawn tender.

Secondly, in fairness to myself, I must ask your Committee to have an engineer to inspect the steam fire engine, and report fully on its condition. The engine is I am informed 30 years old, and his not satisfactory to me."

The engineers report was read to the Committee a few weeks later, this informed them that if the repairs to the old fire engine were carried out by Merryweather's own engineer, the cost would be about £250, but an independent engineer had quoted between £150 to £175 to put the engine in good repair After considering the report, and the following tenders submitted for replacing the old engine, the Watch Committee decided that a replacement be purchased. Tenders received were as follows:-

Merryweather and Son,	£354.
Messrs. Shand Mason Ltd,	£460.
William Rose and Co,	£440.

A new engine was purchased from Merryweather and Son, and the old one was then repaired and brought up to standard. This repair work was carried out by Mr. Quick the Borough Engineer himself, who later received a reward of 10 guineas from the Watch Committee, for all the extra work he had put into getting the engine in full working order, at a total cost of £25, thus saving the council over £150. The Hanley Borough Brigade then possessed two steam fire engines, both in working order. It was the only town in North Staffordshire to do so.

Mr. Carter also reported that the hose cart, and fire escape were in need of repainting, and that the engine house need lime washing. He also asked the Committee to arrange for metal plates to be fixed to walls, indicating the positions of each fire hydrant.

At this time a hanging harness was purchased for the use by the fire brigade at a cost of £9 15s. This was a form of harness which would be suspended in the air ready for quick fitting to the horse at the time of turning out.

The Committee received an application from the manager of Huntbach's shop, asking that a fire hydrant be positioned in Lamb Street opposite the main door of his shop, and that from time to time, they be allowed to attach a hose to it for the purpose of giving the shop assistants practice in fire drill. This was agreed to, providing that Huntbach's paid the water company for the water used.

The Chief Constable placed another report before the Watch Committee in September, 1902, saying that a new fire station should be built, capable of housing two steam fire engines, a hose tender, and the ambulance. There should also be a small store room, work shop, hose tower, drill yard, stabling, and a house for the inspector. The fire escape might be retained in it's present position as it was more central.

A system of fire calls, or alarms ought to be placed in various points throughout the Borough, and eight to ten men should reside very near to the station.

He said that he horsing of the Brigade was an important matter, as at present they were experiencing the greatest difficulty in obtaining horses in the day time. Occasionally the ambulance was delayed for ten to thirty five minutes, before even one horse could be found. There ought always to be two horses available.

All the men ought as at present be drilled in the use of the fire escape, but he did not like the system of the whole force forming the fire brigade. When a fire occurred, the beats were in many cases, entirely neglected. In many cases police uniform was damaged, because the men had attended fires in their best uniforms, as no fire fighting uniform with the exception of helmets was provided. He suggested that the men be allowed to retain their old uniform for this purpose. The Committee agreed.

A more efficient call out system should also be devised, as the noise of the traffic in the day time had drummed out the sound of the police whistles, except over a small area. Sometimes it took considerable time to locate sufficient numbers of men to man the hose cart.

FIREFIGHTER FATALLY INJURED *1903.*

Members of the Hanley Police Fire Brigade were called to a serious fire at the premises of W. R. Renshaw and Company, carriage works, situated in Cliffe Vale, at 4.am on Thursday, 4th June, 1903. On their arrival they found that a large three story building was well alight, and requested assistance from the Stoke Brigade, which arrived a few minutes later. The building involved was surmounted by a large iron chimney some 30 ft high, and weighing between 2 to 3 tons. This structure came crashing down, striking Police constable Brassington, and Sergeant Cooper. Doctor Folker was immediately summoned to the scene. P.C. Brassington whose injuries were only slight was able to resume duty after treatment by the doctor. Sergeant Cooper's injuries were, however, far more serious, and the doctor immediately had him removed to the North Staffordshire Infirmary at Hartshill, by the police ambulance, where on the 23rd of June, he succumbed from injuries.

The total cost of the fire was in the region of £3,000.

Several months later, in October of the same year, Sergeant Cooper's son Joseph Cooper followed in his foot steps and became Constable No. 24 in the Hanley Borough Police.

The Mayor, Chief Constable, and Mr. Quick, the Borough Engineer, attended the Fire Prevention Congress at Earls Court, London, between the 7th and 10th July, 1903.

PLANS FOR A NEW FIRE STATION *1903.*

During the same month it was suggested that a new fire station be built on land in Lichfield Street, next to the swimming baths. It was to consist of rooms for two steam fire engines, stables, the ambulance, and a shed to house the escape ladder. Mr. Carter said that he thought that this would be advantageous, as there was direct access from the police yard, which could also be used for training. There were also plenty of houses in the vicinity, for the police firemen to reside in.

The Council were informed that it would cost approximately £2,000

ANOTHER SERIOUS FIRE *1904.*

On the 27th February, 1904, the police fire brigade were called to a fire at the Imperial Pottery Company owned by Johnson Bros. The fire was so serious that the brigade had to call for assistance from the Burslem, Tunstall, Stoke and Longton brigades. The outcome of the fire was such that 300 employees lost their jobs.

The Watch Committee received a letter from the manager of the Imeprial Pottery, in which he said that the fire could have been much worse, had it not been for the efficiency of the Hanley and other brigades that attended.

At the request of the Chief Constable, the Watch Committee decided that in future, two horses would be kept in the police station stables, for the sole use of the fire brigade.

FALLING OUT AMONGST BRIGADES 1904

Members of the Watch Committee held a special meeting in May, 1904, to receive the following report placed before them by the Chief Constable :-

"At 11 p.m. on Saturday the 14th May, a fire occured at Mr. Sandland's Pottery, in Ogden Road, Hanley., One engine was sent and worked from two hydrants, one situated at the corner of Berkely Street, and the other in Ogden Road, itself. The Longton, Fenton, and Stoke Brigades arrived in that order. All were told that their services were not required.

Captain Coleman of the Stoke Brigade agreed with my decision, and returned home. The Fenton Brigade commenced pumping from the canal, and I made no effort to stop them. The Longton Brigade, however, fixed their engine at the corner of Derby Street, and tapped into the supply of water to the Hanley engine, and rendered it useless. They were requested to stop on several occasions, but refused to do so. The only alternative left to us, was to cut their hose, this was done on the suction side, as near to the joint as possible, so as to minimize the damage to their hose. Directly this was done, the Hanley engine was able to resume work, and extinguish the fire."

The Mayor of Longton, who was present at the meeting, expressed regret, at what had occurred. A conference was arranged between the captains of all the local fire brigades several months later.

In May, 1905, the Chief Constable was given permission to send one of the steam engines to Great Haywood to assist in the draining of a pool to help in the recovery the body of a woman who was trapped in her vehicle.

One of the steam fire engines was loaned to the Midland area of the National Fire Brigade Union, for use in a competition, and display which was held on the old Port Vale ground (where the Potteries shopping centre now stands), on the 25th and 26th of August, 1906.

1,000 ft of new hose was purchased at this time from Morris and Sons, of Salford, at a total cost of £35 8s 4d.

In 1908, the Chief Constable reported to the Watch Committee that himself, Councillors Ball, and Kirkham, along with Mr. Burntwood, the vet had just purchased two horses at a total cost of £125 for fire brigade purposes.

On the last day of the year a fire occurred in one of the store rooms of the second floor of the Town Hall, in the part occupied by the police, only slight damage was caused.

At the beginning of the year 1909, the brigade purchased a Phoenex fire extinguisher at a cost of £3 15s 0d (£3.75p).

Members of the Police Fire Brigade received a special service call via telephone on the 2nd February, 1909, to the effect that a building at the New Hall pottery had collapsed, and a number of persons were thought to be trapped. It was later discovered that no one was in the building at the time of the collapse, and no one was injured.

THE END OF THE POLICE FIRE BRIGADE 1910.

On the 1st April, 1910, not only did the new County Borough of Stoke-on-Trent become responsible for the policing of Hanley, and the other five towns in the federation, but also for the fire brigades. On that date the brigades of Burslem, Fenton, Hanley, Longton, Stoke, and Tunstall, came under the command of Mr. Frederick Bettany, the Borough Surveyor (formally in charge of the Burslem Brigade), who acted as the Captain on a part time basis, in addition to his duties as surveyor.

Although the new brigade came under the control of the County Borough of Stoke-on-Trent Watch Committee, it was no longer a Police Fire Brigade.

PUNISHMENTS FOR BREACH OF DISCIPLINE

It would not be possible to list all the charges recorded for breach of discipline, against members of the Hanley Borough Police force during it's existence, so a few have been selected at random.

Sergeant Cook   -   Missing from the police office at 7.30.am, later found drinking in the Baker's Vaults.   Reprimanded.

1880.

P.C. Maycock   -   Improper conduct; Gossiping with a known prostitute while on duty. Dismissed.

P.C. Keary   -   Not working his beat correctly between 1.30. am and 2.30.am, and failing to discover a burglary that had taken place on his beat. Fined 5/-

Sergeant Jones   -   For being drunk when off duty in uniform. Fined £1.

P.C. Dulson   -   For being in the company of Sgt. Jones on the same day , and not reporting the facts to the Chief Constable. Fined 10/-.

P. C. John Smith   -   Failing to report himself off duty at 9.pm, and later found asleep in the watercloset of the Blue Bell by the sergeant. Fined £1 to be

paid   at 5/- per week.

1883.

P.C. Turner   -   Reported for using obscene language in the theatre. Fined 5/-.

P.C. Rabone   -   Not changing his residence when ordered to do so. Dismissed.

P.C. Le-Doux   -   Changing his residence without permission.   Dismissed.

P.C. John Wooding   -   Insubordination, and using profane, and indecent language to the Duty Sergeant. Reduced from 1st to 2nd Class, also to lose long, good conduct pay.

and

P.C. Barratt   -   Charged with disgraceful conduct; Did associate with a Mary Kidd in the cells, who a criminal charge was pending; Also supplying excessive amount of drink to a woman prisoner, thereby accelerating her death. Dismissed.

1892.

P.C. George Davis   -   This constable was not at any of his points. Last seen by
the   sergeant at 1.15.am, found by the sergeant at home,
and in   bed at 5.30.am. Fined 5/-

P.C. Thomas Turner   -   Behaving improperly to a female prisoner while she was
                                       detained in the cells, also with assaulting the same person
                                       outside the police office. Dismissed.

P.C. George Balamay   -   Not entering time, and place of visits by the sergeant and
                                       inspector in his journal. Dismissed.

P.C. Sherwin   -   Conversing with a woman of immoral character, and giving
                                       hearsay information to her concerning her husband.
                                       Reprimanded.

P.C. Harry Oakes   -   Immoral conduct with his landlady. Dismissed.

P.Cs William Jackson,
James Jackson, Joseph Turner   -   all charged with being careless when giving evidence before
                                       the Quarter Sessions Court. All reprimanded by the Mayor.

1894.

P.C. Longmore   -   For falsely representing himself to be a single man to a
servant   girl, and attempting to induce her to walk out with
him.   Reprimanded.

P.C. Taft   -   For immoral conduct with one Martha Prince. Dismissed

P.C. Hollings   -   For immoral conduct with his brothers wife. Dismissed.

1895.

P.Cs Jackson, and Watts -   Both charged with fighting in the town centre when on
                                       duty in uniform. Both men ordered to resign.

1898.

P.C. Perkins   -   Drunk on duty, and assault on a female named Sarah Ann
                                       Lockett. Dismissed after court case.

1898.

P.C. Shenton   -   Assault on a male prisoner while taking him to the cells.
                                       Fined £1 and reprimanded by the Mayor.

P.C. Hall	-	1st May, Drinking in uniform off duty. Fined 5/- 30th May, Drunk on duty. Fined 10/- 10th June, Improperly arresting a man. Dismissed.
P.C. William Sayers	-	7th August, Drunk and using indecent language when off duty. Reprimanded. 13th August, Drunk on duty. Fined 5/-. 27th August, Drunk on duty, and associating with a known prostitute. Dismissed.
P.C. Enock Davenport	-	25th October, Neglect of duty. Reprimanded. 27th November, Improper conduct on licensed premises. 6th December, Improper conduct with a woman, and assault on a man. Dismissed, then reinstated by the Watch Committee, and fined 50/- to be paid at 5/- per week. Also severely reprimanded by the Mayor.
P.C. Henry Blackman	-	Levying blackmail on licensee. Dismissed.
Inspector Higgins	-	10th January, Using bad language to a Mr. O'Reilly, and ordering him out of the police station. 21st January - Misbehaving himself in the police office, and having to be forcibly ejected. Watch Committee decided to take no action.
P.C. Baddesley	-	Absent from his abode when on sick leave, and assaulting an unknown person. Cautioned.
Inspector Higgins	-	Drunk, and interfering with the uniform members of the force. Advised by the Watch Committee to work more amicably with Inspector Bloor the Acting Chief Constable.
Inspector Higgins	-	Drunk on duty. Reprimanded by the Mayor.
P.C. Jackson	-	Charged with selling worn items of police clothing. Reprimanded.
P.C. Isack Glover	-	1. Improper conduct, absent from his home all night when on sick leave. 2. Telling falsehoods to the Chief Constable. 3. Making false entries of sergeants visits in his journal. 4. Bringing discredit on the force by getting into debt, and being arrested for same. Dismissed.
Sergeant Sherwin	-	Gaming in licensed premises with a subordinate. Reprimanded.

P.C. Bowler   -   Attempting to defraud the Potteries Electric Traction Company Ltd., by saying that the person who was accompanying him from Hanley to Goldenhill on the tram was a police officer, when he knew that not to be true. Fined 10/- and also lose 5 days pay.

P.C. Perry   -   Charged with using obscene language in a public place . Fined 10/-

P.C. Bloxam   -   Permitting a recruit in his company to consume intoxicating liquor while on duty. Suspended without pay for 14 days.

1905

P.C. Paul Gennis   -   Made his second appearance before the Watch Committee on a charge of being drunk on duty. Reprimanded, and ordered to sign the pledge. Dismissed in June, 1907, for the same offence.

P.C. William Coats   -   Improper use of the staff, and improper charge against a prisoner. Reduced to 2nd Class.

P.C. Thomas Hodgkinson   -   Missing from his beat, and found at home in a drunken state. Reduced to 4th Class for 2 years.

P.C. George Roberts   -   Charged with insubordination to the Chief Constable. 5 days loss of pay, and 5 days deducted from service.

P.C. John Smith   -   Drunk on duty, and threatening the sergeant with violence. Dismissed.

P.C. George Roberts   -   Making a false charge against Lydia Hackney for being drunk on licensed premises out of permitted hours . 2. Making a false charge against John Neil, licensee for permitting Hackney to be on licensed premises during closed hours. Ordered to resign.

Chief Inspector Higgins   -   Reported for assault on a Mr. Davies, in Percy Street. Fined £1 and reprimanded by the Mayor.

P.C. Cooper   -   Charged with gross neglect of duty, failing to take any action when a complaint of robbery with violence against an old man was reported to him. Reduced to 2nd Class for 6 months.

P.C. Hugh Davis   -   Had to appear before the Watch Committee when it was found out that he had forged his discharge papers from the Royal Marines. Dismissed.

P.C. Kelly   -   Unfit for duty through drink. Fined £1. His duty can only continue, if he becomes a total abstainer.

Readers will see that most officers transgressed discipline regulations through strong drink. It must be remembered that policing one hundred years ago was considerably different than todays policing. The constable of that error would patrol his beat for 10 to 12 hours a day or night, in all weather conditions, with no meal break. The only place he would be able to get a little refreshment, would be from the local hostelry on his beat.

Tea, and coffee were somewhat of a luxury in those days, so beer seemed to be the normal refreshment for most working men, regardless of their occupation. The police were no better, or worse than the majority of the working class at that time, but just part of every day life as it then was.

CHIEF CONSTABLES OF
HANLEY BOROUGH POLICE

Mr Stanford ALEXANDER	1870	- 1872
Mr George WILLIAMS	1873	- 1875
Mr.Herbert WINDLE	1875	- 1901
Mr Roger CARTER	1901	- 1910

MEMBERS OF THE FORMER HANLEY BOROUGH POLICE FORCE UP TO AND INCLUDING 30TH MARCH, 1910.

Rank	Name	Approved service in Hanley Borough Police up to and including 30/3/1910.		Service In other Force.
		Year	Days	
Chief Constable				
	CARTER, Roger Jas	21	5	Rochdale Borough, then C.C. Windsor Borough
Chief Inspector				
	MIDDLETON, George Henry	12	318	
Inspector				
	COLLIER, John	19	191	
	BARRY, Percy	8	117	
	BOULTON, James	19	73	

Rank	Name	Year	Days
Sergeant			
1	MICKLIN, Charles	17	46
2	BOWLER, George	13	178
3	BATEMAN, William	21	125
4	GUNSTON, Robert John	8	152
5	PEMBER. Geo.William	12	50
6	GLOVER, Harry Hardy	18	349
Constable			
1	BROWN, Joseph	20	64
2	LOOSKAN, James	10	175
3	KELLY, Thomas	10	66
4	SHENTON, John	22	73
5	THREADGOLD, Arthur	8	121
6	TILDSLEY, Richard	23	282
7	COOPER, Percy	3	61
8	TURVEY, George Walter	9	4
9	BAILEY, Alfred	11	272
10	JOHNSON, Thos.William	1	-
11	HARRISON, Saml. Henry	3	354
12	SAUNDERS, Frederick	-	353
13	HAMMERSLEY, Thos	3	321
14	JAMES, Thos Bagnall	-	335
15	GRIFFIN, James	7	309
16	HARRIS,Robert	15	275
17	TUNNER,Joseph	17	152
18	CLOWES, Tom	24	172
19	BRASSINGTON, Charles	9	361

Rank		Name	Year	Days
	20	PERRY, Alfred William	10	227
	21	WALKER, Henry	6	317
	22	LINGARD, John	7	217
	23	BETTANY, Arthur	6	203
	24	COOPER, Joseph	6	290
	25	WALKER, Albert Horace	6	335
	26	TURNER, Thomas	18	282
	27	PRESTON, Charles	7	201
	28	TURNER, Thomas	5	301
	29	BOSTON, Arthur	7	341
	30	JAMES, Thomas	2	15
	31	CRADDOCK, Arthur Bernice	3	278
	32	PICKFORD, Fred	4	119
	33	PARR, Leonard	-	94
	34	MARSHALL, Harry Hadfield	-	178
	35	KELLY, William	10	9
	36	BEARDMORE, Arthur	20	17
	37	BLAND, John Vaulkard	1	120
	38	NORREY, Ernest	2	63
	39	DAVENPORT, Albert	9	128
	40	DAY, Thomas	20	51
	41	BLOXHAM, Charles	13	351
	42	HARVERY, Thos Samuel	2	273
	43	APPLETON, Frank	1	139
	44	CARTER, Harold W.E.	-	363
	45	CLARKE, Alfred James	6	326
	46	BROWN, Thomas	1	287

Rank		Name	Year	Days	
	47	BUNNEY, Robert	10	158	
	48	POTTS, William	8	206	
	49	LEESE, Matthew	9	289	
	50	LONGMORE, Arthur	18	322	
	51	HALL,Fred	8	182	
	52	TONKINSON, Albert	3	362	
	53	SEABRIDGE, Henry Albert	7	22	
	54	DILLON,Arthur	8	114	
	55	APPLETON, Paul	2	19	
	56	BAILEY, John	-	93	
	57	SUTCLIFFE, Benj.Butterworth	-	1	Birkenhead Borough, 4 years 86 days
	58	DAVID SON, Walter	-	I	Blackpool Borough, 2 years 136 days
	59	COOPER, William	-	1	Derby Borough, 2 years 271 days
	60	PRICE, Thos.William	-	1	Oxford City, 3 yesrs 18 days
	61	FAULDS, John	-	1	Lanark County, 4 years 108 days
	62	POVER, Samuel	-	I	Manchester City, 2 years 358 days
	63	SALT, Charles	-	1	Hull City, 4 years 86 days
	64	DUNCAN, Alexander	-	1	Kendal Borough, 1 year 94 days
	65	BINGHAM, Jas. Frederick	-	1	Hull City, 5 years 233 days
	66	KETTLETY, Harry Ernest	-	1	Gloucestershire, 2 years 119 days
	67	PLANT, Joseph	-	1	Preston Borough, 175 days
	68	BASEY, Charles	-	1	Grantham Borough, 2 years 173⁻y⁻
	69	WOODINGS, James	-	1	Derbyshire, 275 days
	70	JONES, James	-	1	Cheshire, 2 years 204 days
	71	BIRKETT, John	-	I	Burnley Borough, 2 years 55 days
	72	WILKINSON, George	-	1	Hastings Borough, 6 years 242 days
	73	LONG, Arthur George	-	I	Wiltshire, 3 years 241 days

Rank		Name	Year	Days	
	74	HUNT, Fred.	-	1	Worcestershire, 2 years ¯80 days
	75	CHADWICK, John Porter	-	1	Burnley Borough, 2 years 52 days
days	76	GLOVER, James	-	1	Warrington Borough, 2 years 12
	77	COX, Maurice Joseph	-	1	Warrington Borough, 6 years 363 days
	78	HODGKINSON, James	-	1	Manchester City, 1 year 177 days
	79	WALMSLEY, Thomas	-	1	Salford City, 3 years 55 days
	80	JONES, Chas. W.	-	1	Manchester City, 2 years 38 days
	81	BENNETT, Wm. James	-	I	Manchester City, 3 years 221 days
	82	DIGGLE, Charles John	-	1	Nil
	83	FEWTRELL, Albert Sidney	-	I	Reigate Borough, 3 years 121 days
	84	McLEOD, Alexander	-	1	Renfrew Borough, 277 days
	85	HARNDEN, Hubert Chas Noel	-	1	Nil
	86	DILLON, Dennis	-	I	
	87	MURRAY, Alexander	-	1	Nairnshire, 2 years 172 days
	88	OLDHAM, Albert	-	1	Barnsley Borough, 252 days
	89	WATKIN, Thomas	-	I	Shrewsbury Borough, 2 years 250 days
	90	HEBDIGE, Frank	-	1	Cheshire, 1 year 217 days
	91	McEVOY, Patrick	-	1	Royal Irish Constabulary, 2 years 19 days
	93	JEFFRIES, John Wordley	-	1	Nil
	94	BUTLER, John	-	1	
	95	DRAIN, Walter Daniel	-	1	
	96	WOODS, Horace Edward	-	I	Barnsley Borough, 4 years 227 days
	97	WORDEN, William	-	1	Preston Borough¯ 5 years 162 days
	99	RICHARDSON, Charles Henry	-	1	Cheshire, 5 years 23 days

CHAPTER V

THE BIRTH OF THE STOKE-ON-TRENT POLICE FORCE

At midnight on the 31 March, 1910, the six Pottery towns (for there were six, and not five as the local author Arnold Bennett would have us believe) of Burslem, Fenton, Hanley, Longton, Tunstall and Stoke-upon-Trent were all amalgamated to form on local administered area, so was born the County Borough of Stoke-on-Trent, for it did not become a city until June, 1925.

The policing of the area at the time of the Federation, was being undertaken by two separate police forces. Hanley which was the largest of the six towns at that time having a population in excess of 62,000 and was a County Borough in it's own right which maintained it's own police force which numbered 68 officers and men. The remaining five towns were policed by the Staffordshire County Constabulary. The towns of Burslem, Tunstall, and Longton were all Divisional Headquarters having a superintendent in charged. Fenton was a sub divisional station of Longton with an inspector stationed there. At the Stoke-upon-Trent Police Station which stood in Copeland Street, resided the Chief Superintendent who was not only in charge of the division, but also in charge of the whole of the Potteries District, and as such was answerable to the Chief Constable at Stafford.

The new federated County Borough had a population of just over 235,000 and covered an area of 11,147 acres.

The new police force that was established to police this area consisted mainly of men from the Hanley Borough, and Staffordshire County forces.

The setting up of the force to police the new federated County Borough did not run as smoothly as at first anticipated. Councillors representing all the six towns held a meeting in February 1910 in an attempt to sort out problems which had arisen. Members of the Hanley Borough Watch Committee who were at the meeting, seemed to think that it was a foregone conclusion that the Hanley force would merely increase in strength, and then take over the policing of the enlarged area, with Mr. Carter in charge. This, however, was not to the liking of some members. Alderman Green who represented Stoke, replied that he had made enquiries from the Local Government Board, and they had said that "Federation did not make Mr. Carter, Chief Constable automatically. I do not wish to do an injustice to Mr. Carter, but we must examine the matter further."

Some members of the meeting suggested that Capt. G. A. Anson, the Chief Constable of Staffordshire be approached and asked to act as Acting Chief Constable until they were able to sort things out. Another councillor asked if he thought Capt. Anson would be prepared to take on the extra responsibility. One member of the meeting representing the Hanley Borough Watch Committee, stated that he understood that a member of the Stoke Council was very friendly with a certain gentleman who was at present stationed in the Potteries and was being nursed by the County to be the new Chief Constable when the new force was established.

A number of councillors from the Longton area seemed to favour a consolidation agreement with the County, this they said would be cheaper than setting up their own county borough force. It was then pointed out that if they did go for a consolidation agreement, they would then have no control over the County men at all, so we might as well disband the Watch Committee.

A vote was then taken, 32 being in favour, and 37 against the agreement. One member even suggested that the Hanley men continue to police the area now under their control, and that the County police the remainder of the federated borough. It was pointed out to him that this would be impossible under the present legislation.

At the close of the meeting the members had decided that a new force for the area would be set up, but the stumbling block was the appointment of a Chief Constable to head it

A few days later the Committee sitting to deal with problems they were facing due to the impending federation received a communication from the Home Office. In this they were referred to article 5 of the act covering the Federation, and to which the Committee had agreed. This act stated that all the powers and duties of all the constables and other officers of the Borough of Hanley shall extend to the new County Borough. They also stated that as Mr.Carter was the only officer holding the premier position in that force, he should continue to do so in the new force.

The new force was to consist of all the members of the Hanley Borough force, and such members of the County force as the Home Secretary shall determine.

All police stations, fixtures, and fittings situated in the new borough will also be transferred to the new authority.

By the time the Stoke-on-Trent County Borough Police force was formed in 1910, police forces were well established, and had ill fact been with us for over 80 years. A large part of the area that was to make up the federated County Borough had seen uniformed policemen on it's streets since 1842, when the Staffordshire County Constabulary, which was established in that year stationed a detachment of men in the Potteries.

Chief Constable R. J. Carter

Authors Collection

BUILDING UP THE STRENGTH OF THE FORCE.

One of the first tasks that confronted Mr. Carter on being appointed the first Chief Constable of the new force, was to combine both the Hanley Borough men and the Staffordshire County men into one efficient police force. The combined strength of the force on the 1st April, 1910, was 137 officers and men, which was 41 short of the establishment. The Watch Committee to try and alleviate the problem instructed the Chief Constable to place adverts in a number of newspapers and police publications asking for serving police officers to transfer to the new force. In total the required number of 41 officers transferred from a number of various police forces far and wide, such as Renfrew Burgh, Kendal Borough, Nairnshire County, and even the Royal Irish Constabulary. It was not unusual before 1919, when the pay and conditions of service were set by local agreement, for men to transfer from one force to another for perhaps just a few pence a week, but to put it in prospective a terraced house at that time could be rented for about 15 pence per week. The rate of pay at that time paid by the Stoke-on-Trent force was slightly above that paid by most forces, especially the rural ones.

On the 16th October, 1910 the total strength of the force was 178 officers and men made up as follows:

Hanley   72 men

Longton   24 men

Burslem   23 men

Tunstall   21 men including Goldenhill

Stoke   24 men

Fenton   15 men

Now that the force was up to it's full establishment, it meant that the remaining 20 County police officers who had been on loan since the 1st April, were able to return to their force. The Home Office now agreed to an increase in the establishment of 12 men, bringing the total up to 190.

The tours of duty that were in operation at the beginning of the force were as follows:

1st Relief:-   6am to 9am and then 1pm to 6pm.

2nd Relief:-   9am to 1pm and then 6pm to 10pm.

Early Night Duty:- 6 pm to 2 am.

Night duty:-   10pm to 6am.

The men on early night duty, and night duty were allowed 30 minutes in which to take refreshments at the station.

FIRST INSPECTION OF THE FORCE *1911.*

On the 29th March, 1911, the first inspection of the force took place when it's members were paraded at the Drill Hall, Shelton, and were inspected by Lieut. Colonel. J.H. Eden., H. M. Inspector of Constabulary. The men were ordered to parade in their best tunics and trousers, day helmets and white gloves. They may have looked smart, but their drill must have left a lot to be desired, for the H.M. Inspector was far from pleased with what he saw. The Chief Constable remarked that it was the first time in his 24 years police service that the Government Inspector had made an unfavourable comment on the standard of drill. He said, "I have therefore instructed that a drill parade will be held at 2.30 on the last Friday of each month at the Drill Hall, Shelton. Officers in charge of the various divisions will have present as many men as possible, no time off will be allowed." These parades were later changed to Wednesdays, and Sergeant Bowler who had previously served in the army was made drill instructor on a part time basis. With effect from 1st August, 1911, men who had been transferred from the County force, were informed that they would no longer receive an allowance for lamp oil, instead the oil would be supplied by the corporation.

PROBATIONARY CONSTABLES.

It seemed to be normal practise at this time for the Chief Constable to appoint men to the force on a period of probation. Then after a period of between six to twelve months, these men would be called to appear before the Watch Committee, who would then decide on their suitability for permanent appointment.

The force was just over twelve months old when two of it's members were convicted of warehouse breaking involving the theft of pottery when on night duty. However, no other details of this case are known.

Authors Collection

Sgt No. 11 William Warden, born New Years day 1881, joined Preston Borough Police 1905, transferred to Stoke-on-Trent force 1st April 1910 as a P.C. Served in both the Boer War and the First World War

ROYAL VISIT 1911.

The force had hardly time to establish itself, when in 1911 their Majesties King George V and Queen Mary paid a visit to the Potteries. This necessitated the force being assisted by the loan of 490 extra men to assist with crowd control. Some of these men were loaned from the Metropolitan and Staffordshire police forces. Owing to the large number of persons who assembled to see the Royal couple, the police were moved from one area of the Borough to another by means of tramcars.

CHANGES IN UNIFORM

In October, 1911, the Chief Constable issued an order to the force instructing that all men in possession of helmets with white metal fittings, will continue to wear them for day duty until the supply of new helmets now on order, are delivered. Those who are not in possession of the above helmets, will wear others in their possession, using the bright metal badges from their summer helmets. The wearing of caps must be discontinued (this order was no doubt meant for the transferred County men, who at the time wore kepis not helmets. It would appear that by 1912 members of the force were in possession of three different styles of helmets. A ball top helmet complete with metal fittings including insignia and chain, which was worn for day duty in the winter, and on ceremonial occasions. In the summer months a white straw helmet with a lightweight serge uniform was worn. The night helmet was the normal Metropolitan Police type Home Office pattern with black insignia and fittings.

City Museum

P. C. 78 Joseph Jackson

It seemed that in May and October each year that the change over from winter and summer uniform took place, with overcoats being taken into use sometime in November.

When the annual inspection of the force took place, all available personnel would parade before His Majesty's Inspector of Constabulary, in their ceremonial uniform. Each man also had to take with him his second uniform, including greatcoat, cape, spare helmet, staff, lamp, and handcuffs. These parades were usually held in the Drill Hall, Victoria Square, Shelton, which must have been a tiresome journey travelling from Goldenhill or Normacot with all this equipment to the inspection. This journey was however, made easier from 1917 when special tramcars were arranged from all areas of the County Borough.

INCREASE IN PAY *1912.*

Members of the force were to see their pay increased from 30th May, 1912. Sergeants and Constables were to receive 1/- (5p) per week, Inspectors and Chief Inspectors £5. 4s.0d (£5.20p) per annum, and Superintendents received £6. 10s.0d (£6.50p) per annum. The new pay scales were as follows:-

Superintendent on appointment	£166. 10s.0d per year
After 2 years service	£181.10s 0d
4 " "	£196.10s.0d
8 " "	£231.10s.0d
10 " "	£251.10s.0d
Chief Inspectors on appointment	£2. 14s 6d per week
After 5 years service	£2. 19s 6d
Inspectors on appointment	£2. 7s 0d per week
After 4 years service	£2. 10s 0d
7 " "	£2.12s0d
10 " "	£2.14s 0d
Sergeants on appointment	£1 17s 0d per week
After 2 years service	£1.18s.0d
4 " "	£1.19s.0d
6 " "	£2. 0s.0d
8 " "	£2. 1s.0d
10 " "	£2. 4s 0d
Constables on appointment	£1. 6s. 0d per week
After 6 months service	£1. 7s. 0d "
1 years service	£1. 8s.0d "
2 years service	£1. 9s.0d
3 " "	£1.10s.0d
4 " "	£1.11s.0d
6 " "	£1.12s.0d
8 " "	£1.13s.0d
10 " "	£1.14s.0d
18 " "	£1.15s.0d

Merit Class of Sergeants and Constables will receive 1/- per week extra.

At this time quite a number of officers were called before the Watch Committee, to receive the customary award of lOs 6d for stopping runaway horses.

In February, 1912, an order was issued reading as follows: - " The Chief Constable has noticed that during the daytime a number of men are in the habit of walking about with their hands in their greatcoat pockets. This practice must be stopped."

INDICATION OF PROBLEMS AHEAD *1912.*

The Home Office in 1912, issued a circular to all police forces, a directive urging them to form a police reserve. It stated that only fit and able bodied men should be chosen, preference being given to ex-military personnel. These would be paid when called on duty.

It also asked Chief Constables to recruit suitable men for service in the Special Constabulary in the event of any emergency.

This was no doubt due to the unsettled state of affairs, then existing in the mining and industrial areas of the country.

In July, 1912, members of the force were issued with new dress belts bearing the Stoke-on-Trent County Borough crest. These were to be worn by men on day duty, and the existing belts would be worn on night duty.

P. C. 79 Leonard Wilson joined the force on the 9th March 1911. Born Walsoken, Norfolk 29th June 1889. Seen here in Winter Uniform

Authors Collection

CHANGES IN THE FORCE *1913*.

In March, 1913, Chief Inspector Percy Berry resigned from the force to take up the appointment as Chief Constable of Wallasey Borough Police, Cheshire. He had originally joined the Hanley Borough Police in 1901.

At this time single policemen resided at the various police stations throughout the County Borough, and were looked after by a cook come cleaner, who was employed to tend to their domestic needs. These men were informed in 1913, that they may now obtain outside suitable lodgings, which must be first approved by the superintendent.

In April, 1913, the Chief Constable issued the following order :- In future when a constable seeks permission to marry, he may apply direct to the Chief Constable, marking his application "Private", and giving the necessary information respecting the Lady, so that the matter may be heard confidentially. The superintendent of the Longton Division was asked to explain why his requirement for stationary was so large. It was explained to him that the number of forms issued to his station, and the number returned to Headquarters, showed a wastage of between 400 to 500. The Superintendent received a mild rebuke, and was informed, that more care must be taken in future.

The seven police clerks employed at the various police stations applied to the Watch Committee for a clothing allowance in lieu of uniform, this was agreed to, and became effective from the 1st April, 1913.

Mr. E. B. Bateman

Sgt. William Bateman photograph taken on the day of his retirement. Bateman joined the Hanley Borough Police in 1880 and transferred into the Stoke-on-Trent County Borough Police on its formation in 1910 and retired in 1913. He is seen here wearing the George the IV coronation medal.

TELEPHONE COMMUNICATIONS *1913*

Since the turn of the century a telephone system had been in existence in all of the larger divisional police stations within the Potteries area, and by 1913 some of the smaller stations, such as Birches Head, Goldenhill, and Hartshill, had been equipped with telephones. These stations had sergeants in charge of them, who were informed that the telephones were only to be used for police purposes.

At this time the Chief Constable ordered that all handcuffs on issue to sergeants and detective officers were to be returned to headquarters, and replaced by snips.

OUTBREAK OF WAR *1914.*

With effect from the 27ᵗ July, 1914, the police weekly rest day became operational in the force, which applied to all officers up to the rank of superintendent, and to enable all the beats to be covered, eighteen extra men added to the strength of the force. On the 10th August, 1914, due to the outbreak of war, a order was issued, saying that the weekly rest day would continue as far as practicable, until further notice, but no man was to leave the division without written permission of the officer in charge. Later in March, 1916, this was reduced to one day off in every fourteen days, the extra day lost would be paid. Sometime later, due to the depleted strength of the force, members were asked if they wished to forego their annual leave they, would be paid for it according to his rank or service.

At the outbreak of the war, three members of the force, all ex-regular soldiers, were seconded to Whittington Army Barracks, Lichfield to instruct and train new recruits. They were instructed to go in their police uniform. While there they received their normal police pay, plus army separation allowance. Some months later thirty members of the force together with three police ambulances, were sent to Stoke Railway Station to assist with the repatriated wounded soldiers, who were to receive treatment at local hospitals. No doubt there would be more to follow.

NEW POLICE STATION FOR FENTON *1915.*

A new police station was opened in Baker Street, Fenton, in 1915. The total cost of this building was £342 12s lOd (£342 64p). However, less than 18 months after the station had been opened structural alterations were made to the building. The reader may find it difficult to believe that for the first years of it's life, the station was lighted by oil lamps.

Only a few months after this station had been opened, the Chief Constable visited all the police stations within the County Borough to inspect the new uniforms having just been issued to the men, which was to be worn by them on the H.M.I's annual inspection several days later. This was supposedly a full dress

Author's Collection

*The first Helmet Badge worn by the County
Borough Force.
Note the officers collar number in the centre.*

rehearsal, but the Chief Constable was apparently not a happy man, and on his return to his office had the following order dispatched to all divisions.

I was not impressed by the standard of turn out this morning. Only at Fenton Station were all the men properly dressed. There was a slackness through the force. I hope to see a marked improvement at the subsequent inspection, otherwise explanations will be called for".

Inspector Davies, the officer in charge of Fenton Sub Division was promoted to Chief Inspector, and transferred to Stoke. Mr. Davies was presented with a gold watch by the local trades people in the area, as a thank you for all the good work he had carried out for charity. He was later called to appear before the members of the Watch Committee, to explain why he had not first obtained their permission. He was permitted to keep the watch.

ABSCONDER FROM THE FORCE *1916.*

Police constable 76 James Glover absconded from the force on the 5th September, 1916, and was dismissed in his absence by orders of the Watch Committee. The Chief Constable was instructed to instigate proceedings against him, if and when he was found.

Miss Kittson

B (Burslem and Tunstall) Division 1916 Senior Officers sitting centre Inspector Hall,
Superintendent Hickson, Inspector Kittson, Constable 8th from left second row wearing medal is
P.C. H. Bird, later Inspector at Tunstall. Note the peculiar way the men are carrying their capes.

DANGER LOOMING OVERHEAD 1916.

On the 5th March, 1916, people in the Potteries were alarmed and frightened when a German Zeppelin was spotted in the sky over the area. The air raid alert was sounded, but no enemy action took place. One member of the force was later fined 1/- for failing to report to the police station when the alert was sounded.

The force received a circular in 1916, sent out from the Home Office, and addressed to all Chief Constables throughout the country, requesting them to release all younger men for service with H.M. Forces. A order was issued at this time by the Chief Constable, stating that the uniform of men who have enlisted in the armed forces, must be returned to headquarters stores as soon as possible. Also that great care must be taken of all uniform on issue to members of the force, as there was much difficulty in obtaining new uniform.

It was also in 1916, that the Chief Constable ordered all members of the Detective Department to meet at headquarters each Tuesday evening at 6.30 to discuss crime within the County Borough, so as to make the department more efficient.

Miss G. Scarrett

P.C. Harry Scarratt

CHANGES IN RATES OF PAY 1918.

During 1918 the force saw several changes in their rates of pay starting with the following new pay scale which became operative as from January, 1918:-

Superintendents on appointment	£185. 0s. 0d		per year
After 2 years service	£200. 0s. 0d	"	
4 " "	£251. 0s. 0d	"	
Chief Inspectors on appointment	£165. 0s. 0d		per year
After 2 years service	£170. 0s. 0d	"	
5 " "	£175. 0s. 0d	"	
Inspectors on appointment	£2. 15s.0d		per week
After 2 years service	£2. 17s.0d	"	
4 " "	£3. 0s.0d	"	
Sergeants on appointment	£2. 4s. 0d		per week
After 2 years service	£2. 6s. 0d	"	
4 " "	£2. 8s. 0d	"	
7 " "	£2. 10s. 0d	"	
Constables on appointment	£1. 10s. 0d		per week
After 1 years service	£1. 11s. 0d	"	
2 " "	£1. 12s.0d	"	
4 " "	£1. 14s.0d	"	
6 " "	£1. 16s.0d	"	
8 " "	£1. 18s.0d	"	
10 " "	£2. 0s 0d	"	
15 " "	£2. 1s. 0d	"	
18 " "	£2. 2s. 0d	"	

As from the 1st October, 1918, there was a further increase in pay, and in addition each man up to and including the rank of superintendent received a War Bonus of 12/- per week, plus an allowance of 2/6d for each child under the age of 14 years. A boot allowance of 1/- per week was also paid.

The Chief Constable was not to be left out, because he received an increase of £50 per year. Rampant inflation must have been present then, no doubt due to the war, because the rates that had been adopted in the October, 1918, were again replaced only a month later. These pay rates which were recommended at a meeting held in Birmingham, and attended by representatives of all police authorities in the Midlands, were as follows:-

Superintendents on appointment	£280. 0s. 0d	per year
After 2 years service	£285. 0s. 0d	"
3 " "	£290. 0s. 0d	"
4 " "	£295. 0s. 0d	"
Chief Inspectors on appointment	£239. 0s. 0d	per year
After 2 years service	£245. 0s. 0d	"
3 " "	£250. 0s. 0d	"
4 " "	£255. 0s 0d	"
Inspectors on appointment	£201. 0s. 0d	"
After 2 years service	£206. 0s 0d	"
3 " "	£211. 0s. 0d	"
4 " "	£216. 0s. 0d	"
5 " "	£227. 0s. 0d with merit	
Sergeants on appointment	£2. 16s 0d	per week
After 1 years service	£2. 17s 0d	"
2 " "	£2. 18s. 0d	"
3 " "	£2. 19s. 0d	"
4 " "	£3. 0s. 0d	"
5 " "	£3. 1s. 0d	"
6 " "	£3. 2s. 0d	"
Constables on appointment	£2. 3s. 0d	per week
After 1 years service	£2. 4s. 0d	"
2 " "	£2. 5s. 0d	"
3 " "	£2. 6s. 0d	"
4 " "	£2. 7s. 0d	"
S " "	£2. 8s. 0d	"
6 " "	£2. 95. 0d	"
7 " "	£2. 10s. 0d	"
8 " "	£2. 11s. 0d	"
15 " "	£2. 12s. 0d	(Subject to recommendation
20 " "	£2. 13s. 0d	of Chief Constable)

These pay scales were again soon replaced by National Rates covering all police forces within the United Kingdom were agreed in 1919.

The Chief Constable's salary was increased from £500 per annum to £600. The Superintendent who acted as Deputy Chief Constable, also received an allowance of £25 per annum, added to his normal pay as a superintendent.

The Watch Committee, and Chief Constable acted with foresight, when they allowed the members of the force to set up a Police Representative Committee. This committee was to consist of two inspectors, four sergeants, and seven constables. There was to be one sergeant elected from each division, and two constables were be elected from Hanley, Burslem, and Longton Division, and one constable from the Stoke Division. The representatives were to be elected annually.

The Committee would be able to represent members of the force in all matters relating to pay, and general welfare, other than discipline.

Perhaps it was due to the setting up of this representative committee, that the Police Strike which occurred in the cities of Birmingham, Birkenhead, Liverpool, and London in 1919, did not effect the Stoke-on-Trent force.

Authors Collection

Group of Stoke-on-Trent policemen obviously taken just after the first world war, as most of the men are wearing their medals. Are the men at the back in civilian clothes and uniform cap new recruits to the force waiting delivery of uniform, we wonder?

RETURN FROM THE WAR *1919*.

Members of the force who had been serving with H.M.Forces, started to return to their peace time occupations from early in 1919, but it was to be April before the last members of the force actually returned. No doubt pleased to exchange the mud and blood of Flanders for the smoky streets of Stoke. Sixty seven members of the County Borough Police force had served with the armed force in the war, of whom eleven made the supreme sacrifice. This was over 25% of the forces establishment.

Men who had stayed on in the force to serve their country, in the way they knew best, after qualifying for pension, were allowed to retire. They were to be replaced with a new intake of men, mostly with military service. By 1922, almost a quarter of the total strength of the force, had joined since 1919. Two members of the North Staffordshire Branch of the National Council of Women held a meeting with members of the Watch Committee, and the Chief Constable, as to the desirability of appointing a police woman. The Committee and Mr. Carter decided to take no action.

CONTINGENCY PLANS *1919*.

On the 12th July, 1919, the Chief Constable sent out the following circulation to all stations within the force.

In the event of a serious demonstration on the part of the public at any of the following places in consequence of an arrest or other cause, or additional help being required. Divisional officers will follow, as circumstances will permit the undermentioned instructions as to the transfer of men :-

Station where help required.	First move of men from.	Second move of men from.	Third move of men from.	Fourth move of men from
Goldenhill	Tunstall	Burslem	Hanley	Stoke
Tunstall	Burslem	Hanley	Stoke	Longton
Burslem	Tunstall	Hanley	Stoke	Longton
Hanley	Burslem	Stoke	Longton	Tunstall
Stoke	Hanley	Fenton	Longton	Burslem

Fenton	Longton	Stoke	Hanley	Burslem
Longton	Fenton	Hanley	Stoke	Burslem

The men will be moved by the quickest available method. Motor conveyance if possible, or tram, to a point near to the place where the disturbance is occurring, and then marched in a body to the place where their assistance is required. If the demonstration is one of violence at a police station, the men should be set down at the following places:-

(1) Goldenhill Main road near to police station.

(2) Tunstall Top of Amicable Street, and then marched to the side entrance in John Street.

(3) Burslem Market Square.

(4) Hanley South Street for rear entrance, Bagnall Street for side entrance.

(5) Stoke King's Hall in Wolf Street, and marched along side of canal where facilities will be provided for scaling the wall into the police station yard

(6) Fenton Gimson Street and taken across allotments where facilities will be provided for scaling wall into the police station yard.

(7) Longton First Street on right off Anchor Road, across the vacant ground, over the wall and into the rear off the police station.

The position of the nearest fire hydrant should be noted, with a view of obtaining a standpipe if required. If the mounted men are required, Inspector Plumber will make arrangements, and take charge of the section.

The Chief Constable Mr. Carter was elected President of the Chief Constables Association for the Cities and Boroughs of England and Wales for the year 1919.

The first decade of the force ended with the Chief Constable being a very happy man, for he was to see his annual salary increase from £600 per annum to £900 per annum, when the Desborough pay agreement was accepted.

CHAPTER VI

FURTHER DEVELOPMENT OF THE FORCE *1920-1929.* EARLY

TRAFFIC PROBLEMS *1920.*

Traffic problems seemed to have been increasing in 1920, because the Chief Constable was contemplating using mounted officers to regulate the flow of traffic on some of the main streets, where at that time, horse drawn vehicles, motor vehicles, and electric tramcars, were all competing for space on the crowded roads.

GOVERNMENT INSPECTION OF THE FORCE *1920.*

Major General Sir Llewelyn Atcherley, C.M.G., C.V.O., His Majesty's Inspector of Constabulary, inspected the force in May, 1920. The Chief Constable issued the following instructions as regards to dress on the day of the inspection.

Inspectors; Dress coats, sling belts, and caps. Sergeants and Constables; Tunic, day helmets, belts, white gloves, and rolled capes. Staffs, handcuffs, whistles and chains and lamps must be carried. The last issue of serge uniforms, great coats, and straw helmets must be displayed at the inspection. All decorations must be worn. Ambulance badges, and Merit badges to be worn on the left arm. All accoutrements must be perfectly clean and in good order.

Sergeant Saunders, P. C.s Clarke, Davenport, Harrison, Wilson, Tennant, Wase, Flowers, and Basey will be mounted. All stations will be thoroughly cleaned.

Authors Collection

P.C. No. 6 Stoke-on-Trent Force Circa 1918

The H.M.I. had only one complaint, that was about the cramped conditions that the office staff were working in. This resulted in the force being allotted the use of two more offices in Hanley Town Hall Headquarters, that had previously been used by the Education Department.

TRAINING OF RECRUITS *1920.*

Owing to the large number of recruits having joined the force over the previous twelve months, the Chief Constable decided that some form of instruction must be provided to the new members. All new recruits would in future be sent to Headquarters in Hanley for training in police law, and first aid. The classes would last one week. They were informed by the Chief Constable that he would not certify any probationary constables as efficient, or recommend him to the Watch Committee for permanent appointment, until they had passed their ambulance examination.

The Chief Constable also decided to reintroduce the divisional drill parades, which would be held each week, and all sergeants would take their turn as instructors. (This no doubt went down like a bomb with all those recruits who had just returned after a number of years in the armed forces).

These instructions classes were to continue for the next five years, until in 1925, all new recruits appointed to the Stoke-on-Trent force were sent to the Birmingham City Police Training School.

RETIREMENT OF DEPUTY CHIEF CONSTABLE *1920.*

Superintendent William Williams, the Deputy Chief Constable, retired from the force at the end of 1920. Mr. Williams had originally joined the Staffordshire County Constabulary in 1881. He was to be replaced by Superintendent Charles H. Bowler.

In the Chief Constable's Annual Report to the Licensing Justices for the year 1920, he reported that 356 persons had been convicted for drunkenness, and that proceedings had been taken against 24 licensees. At the close of that year, the strength of the force stood at 223 men.

SHOOTING OF HEROIC CONSTABLE *1920.*

Palmerston Street, Hanley, was to be the scene of intense police activity on the night of the 28 May, 1920, when at approximately 2.am Police constables Appleton, and Madew made an attempted to execute a warrant on the occupier of number 47. Police constable Madew went to the rear of the property, and Appleton to the front, there was no light on in the house, and no reply was received to their knocking. Madew then entered the house, and was confronted by the occupier Edward Thomas Reynolds, who pointed a double barrelled shot gun at the constable, and said, "I know who you are. If you come any closer, I will blow you inside out."

A Mr. Kennedy, Reynold's next door neighbour also attempted to persuade him to come out, but Reynolds ran upstairs, and again threatened to shoot anyone who came near him. Both constables and Kennedy then left the premises. A message was then sent to Hanley Police Station, requesting assistance, and some time later Sergeants Boston and Harvey along with Constables Blackhurst, and Seabridge arrived. In the meantime Reynolds had barricaded both doors, and the downstairs windows. The police then obtained a fire hose, which they attempted to train on him. While this was taking place Constable Seabridge was able to obtain the loan of a ladder, which he placed to the bedroom window and ascended it, however, as he reached the top of the ladder, and was about to enter the house through the window, he was shot at by Reynolds, and fell to the ground. Other officers who had by now managed to gain entrance to the house, managed to overpower and arrest Reynolds.

Reynold was charged with assault with intent to murder, and later received a long custodial sentence at the Stafford Assizes.

Authors Collection

Five members of the force obviosly taken in a studio about 1922 Left to right P.C. 131 James Taylor, P.C. 165 Joseph Axhorne, P.C. 105 Thomas Willett, P.C. 20 Charles Henry Crow and P.C. David Sidney Strachan

Police Constable Seabridge was never to return to police duty, and received a special pension. He had had quite a memorable service with the police force, if only a short one.

In 1909, while a member of the Hanley Borough force, he almost lost his own life while making a heroic rescue of a man from a canal lock. As a result of the injury sustained during the rescue, he was off sick for some considerable time.

In 1917 while attempting to stop a runaway horse, he was struck by one of the shafts, and received injuries which resulted in hospitalisation for several days.

MINERS STRIKE *1921.*

1921 was to see a strike taking place in the coal mines of North Staffordshire, which meant many extra hours of duty for members of the force.

The Chief Constable informed the Watch Committee, that all rest days had been cancelled due to the prevailing situation. The number of days lost by each individual officer varied from 7 to 12 days, and that it would be necessary to pay the men, or grant them time off in lieu. The total cost in payment to the men would amount to £1390. 19s. 1d (£1,390.96p).

The Watch Committee were in favour of payment, and one member said, "It would be inadvisable to grant leave at this moment in time." The Home Office, however, refused to sanction payment. During the strike a hostile crowd of several hundred strong, stoned members of the force, who were on duty outside Hanley Colliery. Several policemen, and a number of police horses were injured. The strikers were eventually dispelled, and afterwards the Watch Committee paid tribute to the patient, and efficient way in which the police had handled the situation.

The Watch Committee decided that all the police stations situated within the County Borough were to be painted. The total cost of this operation was £305. 1s.6d.

EARLY SPEED TRAPS *1921.*

It would appear that speeding motorists have been around for a long time, as on the 11ᵗ September, 1921, the force operated a speed trap for motorists along a measured mile in London Road, Stoke. A total of 20 speeders were caught, who were all later fined £1 plus costs, when they appeared before the local magistrates.

ENLARGEMENT OF THE COUNTY BOROUGH *1922*.

On the 1st April, 1922, the whole of the Urban District of Smallthorne, along with Abbey Hulton, Bucknall, Meir, Blurton, Hanford, and part of Trentham, all became part of the enlarged County Borough of Stoke-on-Trent. The area of the County Borough increased from 11,147 acres to 20,762 acres, and the population increased from 234,553 to 267,597. To compensate for this the strength of the force was increased by 18 men.

COURAGEOUS POLICE WORK *1922*.

The Chief Constable reported to the Watch Committee in 1922, that he had received a report from the Police Surgeon, which stated that it was unlikely that P.C. Alfred James Clarke would ever return to police duty. P.C. Clarke had been off sick since April, the previous year, when he had been thrown from his horse, which resulting in him sustaining a fractured scull. He finally retired from the force on sickness grounds in 1929, never having returned to duty.

Police constables Charles Heath, of the North Staffordshire Railway Company Police, stationed at Stoke, was awarded £1. 1s.0d by the Watch Committee for his assistance in the arrest of a notorious thief

POLICE ECONOMIES *1922*.

In May, 1922, all police forces received a circular from Central Government asking for economies in police administration. They outlined the following: - a 5% reduction in the authorised establishment of the force. No new building construction to be undertaken. That the issue of new uniform to be left to the discretion of the Chief Constable. Members of the police forces throughout the country would also see a reduction of 2 % in their pay, along with a reduction in their allowances.

The tender for the supply of uniform in 1922, went out to John Hammond and Co. Ltd., Newcastle, Staffs, and consisted of the following items:-

Inspector's Overcoats, Inspector's Dress Coats, Inspector's Serge Patrol Jackets, Inspector's Dress

Trousers, Inspector's Undress Trousers, Inspector's Capes.

Sergeant's Overcoats, Sergeant's Dress Coats, Sergeant's Serge Patrol Jackets.

Constable's Overcoats, Constable's Dress Coats, Constable's Serge Patrol Jackets, Constable's Riding Breeches, Sergeant's and Constable's Trousers, Sergeant's and Constable's Capes, Sergeant's and

Constable's Winter Gloves, Sergeant's and Constable's White Summer Gloves.

Policewomen's Tunics, Skirts, and Caps.

Inspector's Brown Leather Gloves

The Inspector's brown leather gloves cost 17s 6d (85p) per pair, the black woollen gloves for the sergeants and constables cost £1. 1s 0d (£1.5p) per 12 pairs. The cost of helmets in 1922 was 13s.9d (68p) each.

At the close of 1922, the authorised strength of the force stood at 251, and was made up as follows:-

Chief Constable	1
Superintendent	1
Chief Inspectors	3
Inspectors	6
Sergeants	31
Constables	209

Staffordshire Police

P.C. 17 George Samuel Scragg seen here in his summer uniform complete with Straw Helmet. Scragg joined the force on the 20th July 1911. Photograph circa 1914

Chief Constables and Superintendents Cap Badge, embroidered. Inspectors wore embroidered Crown only

Authors Collection

County Borough Helmet Plate
The Coat-of-Arms were granted in 1912.
This badge would have been taken into
use about 1913. The oval centre was
used as a cap badge. see page 220

This badge would have been taken into
use about 1925 when the City status
was granted. It would have been worn
on the Ball Top Helmets.

FALSE ALARM 1924.

A rather amusing incident took place during the early hours of one morning in July, 1924. A Mr. and Mrs. Scott, who resided in a flat next door to Pidduck Jewellers, Market Street Hanley, were awoken by an alarm bell ringing. They notified Hanley Police, who immediately responded by dispatching six constables to the scene in one of the ambulances. On arrival the constables discovered that a number of alarm clocks had sounded in the shop, all at the same time.

CONSTABLE INJURED BY A BOLTING HORSE 1924.

On the 24th August, 1924, Police Constable John Peat was on duty at the junction of Etruria Road and Marsh Street, Hanley, when a horse owned by Boyce Adams Limited, made a dash for freedom, pulling a small bread cart behind him. P.C. Peat shouted a warning to a number of pedestrians in the near vicinity, and then made an attempt to stop the horse. Unfortunately the constable was knocked down, and bowled over several times, along with a civilian who tried to assist him. Both men were later seen by a doctor. P.C. Peat suffered from severe shock, and bruising, and was off duty for over a month. The horse was finally brought to a halt, by a young man named Arthur Meakin, who ran down Etruria Road, managed to climb onto the back of the cart, and bring the horse to a standstill by the reigns. All three men involved were later rewarded by the Watch Committee.

ACCIDENT STATISTICS AND ROAD SAFETY 1925.

Like speeding drivers, road accidents and parking problems are not something new, as the Chief Constable's Annual Report for 1925, shows that 15 persons were fatally injured on the roads of the County Borough, and that there were 352 non fatal road accident. (In comparison the number recorded for 1997, were 8 fatal, and 1100

Mr. Peter Saunders
Sgt F. Saunders D.C.M. and three constables taken outside the old Copeland Street Police Station. c. 1925

injury only road accidents) There were over three times the number of road accidents, but less fatalities in 1997, than in 1925. This is no doubt due to the advanced medical science, and improved ambulance service.

Returning to 1925, the Chief Constable had 50,000 handbills, and notices produced. The handbills were to be distributed to all the schools, and factories in the area, warning both children, and adults to take more care on the roads. And the large notices were fixed in prominent positions in the town. It would appear from the ever increasing number of deaths in the Borough from road accidents, that all Mr.Carter's efforts to improve the safety on the roads, were not being rewarded. In 1926, there were 34 fatalities, and the following year, 39 road deaths were reported.

The Chief Constable was to tell the Watch Committee, that the way things were going, it could be expected that one person in every 650 in the police district to meet with a road accident in the next year. Mr. Carter was also complaining about the traffic congestion in the Longton area. (Nothing changes).

Mr. Peter Saunders

Inspector F. Saunders D.C.M. c. 1934

ROYAL VISIT AND CITY STATUS 1925.

On the 5th June, 1925, their Majesties George V and Queen Mary visited the Borough of Stoke-on-Trent to open the extension to the North Staffordshire Infirmary. When the Royal couple left Stoke-on-Trent a few hours later, the Infirmary became the North Staffordshire Royal Infirmary, and Stoke-on-Trent was elevated to City status. And so from that date the title of the force was changed to the City of Stoke-on-Trent Police.

Six new pedal cycles were purchased for the use of the force at this time. The Chief Constable said that the cycles were required for the rural area of the City.

UP TO FULL STRENGTH *1926.*

The year 1926 opened with the established strength of the City force standing at 240 officers and men, there were no vacancies. Mr. Carter pointed out to the Watch Committee, that the City force had less men per population than any other force in Staffordshire, and gave the following examples: - The County force had 1 constable to every 862, Walsall 1 constable to every 881, Wolverhampton 1 constable to every 906, Newcastle 1 constable to every 890, whereas the City force had 1 constable to every 1066 of the population. The Watch Committee then agreed to add 11 more men to the strength of the force, bringing the established strength to 251.

At the same meeting of the Watch Committee, it was reported that P.C. J. L. Leak had been awarded a certificate to teach life saving. He was to receive the congratulations of both the Committee and the Chief Constable.

Staffordshire Police

Stoke-on-Trent policemen photographed outside the old Copland Street Police Station, Stoke. about 1925, note the wearing of straw helmets, summer issue.

THE GENERAL STRIKE 1926.

The General Strike took place between the 4th and 12th May, 1926. One or two ugly incidents took place within the City area, and although a small number of arrests were made, the situation did not get out of hand. The Regular Force backed up by over 1000 special constables, managed to maintain law and order. Members of the force did, however, confiscate a number of offensive weapons, which had been used by a few of the more militant strikers.

The Chief Constable was authorised to hire a number of motor cycles during the General Strike, the cost of which came to £38.15s.5d (£38.77p).

At this time the Chief Constable was given permission by the Watch Committee to reside outside the City boundary. Mr. Carter then purchased a large house in Basford.

Authors Collection

Men of the Tunstal Sub-Division c. 1925 Left to right: Sgt. Bettany, P. C's. Lake, Harbey, Conner - holding cup, Sgt Goulson, 6 & 7 not known, Copeland, Collier and Larter.
Inspector Joseph Reading sitting

IMPROVED WORKING CONDITIONS *1927*.

The Chief Constable informed the Watch Committee in 1927, at their November meeting, that he had received two requests from the Joint Branch Board of the Police Federation.

The first request was that the bull's eye oil lamp carried by the men on night duty be replaced by electric torches. Mr. Carter said, "I do not think that will be much of a problem, because most of the men have purchased their own anyway". This was agreed to.

The second request was that the eight hour tour of duty, be worked in one complete duty, instead of two 4 hour shifts. The Chief Constable told the Watch Committee, that at present only the night shift was worked in one complete eight hour shift. He informed them that he was completely against that, he thought that one eight hour stretch, particularly in the summer months was too long, and that if it were adopted, each man would be entitled to one half hour meal break. That meant only $7^1/_2$ hours patrolling would be carried out, and that there would be a loss of 63 hours duty throughout the force each day.

Councillor Rowley in reply, said, "The Chief Constable's interests were efficiency, but I at least think we should meet the men's representatives".

Mr. Sproston, another member of the Watch Committee, said, "I don't think there is any authority in the United Kingdom that considers its men more than we do in Stoke-on-Trent."

The men eventually got their wish, as the eight hours tour of duty was approved in May the following year. Returning to the electric torches, the Committee decided to stop paying the lamp allowance to the men, and in October, 1930, Wootton police lamps were supplied. A number of these lamps were issued to each divisional and sub-divisional stations. Each lamp was numbered, and each man signed for it on issue. The lamps were then taken to Headquarters each Monday, Wednesday, Friday, and Sunday to be re-charged, and returned to the stations during the day, so as to be ready for the night duty men. These lamps were apparently quite heavy to carry.

In his annual report for 1927, the Chief Constable was able to report that every member of the force was qualified in first aid, and that the majority were able to swim. Recruits were at this time were being sent to the Birmingham City Police Training School. The Police Recreation and Sports Ground at Finney Gardens, Bucknall had just been purchased.

Mr. Carter remarked on the amount of ordinary sickness, which he said was too high. Having regard for the rest and facilities that the men now had for sport etc. He did not think that they were looking after themselves as they should.

The crime figures for that year make interesting reading, as there were 7 cases of burglary, and 12 cases of housebreaking reported in the whole year, plus 274 cases of simple larceny. There were also 21 cases of attempted suicide, (a criminal offence in those days).

All sergeants were detailed at this time to report to Detective Inspector McEvoy at Headquarters, in order that they could be instructed in the taking of finger prints.

The Chief Constable was either not used to the North Staffordshire dialect, or was trying to provide his men elocution lessons, because he issued the following memorandum in February, 1927:-

I have noticed that among the members of the force there appear to be a general mispronunciation of the word "BUS". I have noticed that when men are giving evidence, they invariably pronounce it as "BUZZ", which is wrong.

GOVERNMENT INSPECTION *1928.*

In March, 1928, His Majesty's Inspectors of Constabulary, Mr. Charles de Courcy Parry carried out his annual inspection of the force, which was held at the Palais de Dance. Present on the parade were Superintendent Bowler, Chief Inspectors Abbotts, Smith, and Davies, Inspectors Appleton, Carter, Reader, and Rye, 28 sergeants, and 168 constables, plus Sergeant Saunders, and 10 mounted constables. The Detective Branch numbered 14 men, paraded under the command of Detective Inspector McEvoy. There were also two police women on parade.

When the Inspector was examining one of the constable's notebooks, he came across the following entry:- Premises in Longton found insecure at 2.30.am. "What action did you take", asked the H.M.I., "I aroused the occupants", replied the constable, "And were they pleased, and did they thank you", asked the H.M.I., "No, they most certainly did not," replied the officer.

FURTHER DEMANDS ON THE FORCE *1928.*

The Chief Constable was again complaining to the Watch Committee regarding the low strength of the City police, when compared with other towns, and cities of comparative size, and population. Mr. Carter said that the City Parks Committee, had requested that in view of the number of break ins that had taken place at the pavilion in Hanley Park, could a constable be detailed to patrol the park at night. The only answer he could give was that he simply did not have the men to do it. He said that he had made enquiries and had found that the total cost of goods stolen over the previous two years, only amounted to £2.4s.0d (£2.20p).

Alderman Sproston said at the meeting of the Watch Committee, "I think that we should support the Chief Constable in his request for more men. I believe we are the lowest staffed force in proportion to population in the Country. I do not think the Chief Constable is seeking to increase the force unduly, or unnecessarily, but when he does ask for them, I don't think the Finance Committee should refuse them altogether.

Councillor Dale, asked, "Apart from controlling the traffic during the day, and patrolling at night What else was there for the policeman to do?" He said that crime was decreasing in the City, and didn't think it was necessary to recruit any extra policemen in this City.

The Lord Mayor Thomas Clarke Wild, replied "I don't think that it is the Chairman's or the Chief Constable's idea, to add extra expense for the City. I think, it is their idea to increase the strength of the force now, instead of waiting for something serious to happen." The Chief Constable's request for more men, was deferred.

At the same meeting of the Watch Committee, a letter of complaint was received from business people in Hanley, was read out. The letter was referring to the cars belonging to shoppers being moved on from some of the main thoroughfares. Mr. Carter replied, "My men do allow shoppers a reasonable time. The problem is business people themselves, who leave their cars outside their premises all day. My men have a duty to facilitate the free flow of traffic. I think the time will come when we will see parking grounds at the entrances of all large towns." (obviously a man of foresight).

In his Annual Report for 1928, the Chief Constable reported that 45 persons had been convicted of driving at excessive speed on the road of the City, the fines varied between 10/- (50 p) to £10 plus costs. 33 of these cases were against the drivers of omnibuses.

Six boxes containing first aid equipment were purchased at a cost of £2. 15s.0d (£2.75p) each. One to be placed in each of the police stations.

TRAFFIC CONTROL *1929.*

For some considerable time the Chief Constable had been inundated with requests from schools all over the City, asking for constables to escort children across busy main road. Most of the requests, however, had to be refused by the Chief Constable, the reason given was that there were too many schools, and not enough policemen.

A debate over the issue of white or black mackintoshes for police officer performing point duty, took place at the February meeting of the Watch Committee. The Chief Constable favoured black coats, with white cuffs, saying, "I have made enquiries with a number of forces that use white coats, and they tell me that they are unsatisfactory, the white runs onto the uniform in wet weather.

Councillor Kemp a member of the Committee, "I am thinking of the safety of the policemen. I think we should have white ones, they show up much better, especially in the dark, and the safety of the policeman is paramount."

A vote was taken, and it was decided to purchase six white coats as an experiment.

While on the subject of point duty, the winter weather in 1929, must have been quite severe, because the

Chief Constable ordered that the men on this duty should be relieved every 15 minutes, and that they should also have two 20 minute breaks, instead of one 30 minute break, so that they could obtain hot refreshments.

It was also at this time that the force obtained it's first lethal chambers, which were made locally, for destroying dogs.

POLICE TELEPHONE BOXES 1929.

Discussions took place at the March meeting of the Watch Committee as to whether to bring the City police up to it's establishment, by the addition of 11 men, or to adopt the police telephone box communication system. The Chief Constable said that the Committee had allowed the extra cost for the 11 extra men some time previous, and then the numbers had been later reduced by the Geddes Committee. Mr. Carter said, "Manchester had quite recently adopted the police box system, and were able to dispense with men. It has been suggested that they might do the same here, but my table shows that a Stoke-on-Trent policeman has to cover 12 times as much area as a Manchester man.

Stoke-on-Trent	82	acres	per	man	1,103	population	per	man
Coventry	61	"	"	"	808	"	"	"
Newcastle-on-Tyne	22	"	"	"	771	"	"	"
Nottingham	28	"	"	"	736	"	"	"
Sheffield	43	"	"	"	700	"	"	"
Bradford	48	"	"	"	621	"	"	"
Manchester	15	"	"	"	513	"	"	"

I think that the police box system would result in increased efficiency, but it will not reduce the number of men I require. I think the members of the Committee would be very surprised to learn that the numbers of men that are available in the various districts. At Tunstall there were stationed 15 constables, 3 sergeants, 1 inspector, and 1 plain clothes man, 3 off sick, and 3 reserve men, plus men on days off; that leaves just 7 men to cover the beats for 24 hours." The matter was adjourned pending the Chief Constable's report. A few weeks later Mr. Carter stated that he had submitted his report to the Finance Committee, only to have it thrown out. The question of police boxes, was to be debated again the following year.

The opening of Finney Gardens Sports Ground in the 1930's
Pictured centre is Chief Constable Carter

CHAPTER VII

THE PRE WAR YEARS *1930-1939.*

The year 1930, opened with the debate regarding the adoption of the police box system of policing in the City, still taking place. The Chief Constable suggested that only a small number of boxes, say seven be situated at certain strategic points.

Councillor John Hughes, said, "Why stop at seven,? I suggest that we adopt a complete police box system. These boxes don't only serve the police, but are used by the general public to get in contact with the fire, and ambulance services."

Mr. Carter seemed to fear the use of boxes in the City, for two reasons. In Manchester the adoption of the boxes had meant the closure of eleven police stations, and in Newcastle-on-Tyne, Sheffield, Coventry, and Manchester, it had resulted in the reduction of the strength of those forces. Mr. Carter, no doubt did not wish to see his understaffed force depleted still further, and went on to say, It is no use having the boxes, if I have not got the men to operate the system.

It was to be 1931 before the Finance Committee allowed the £3, 000 for the erection of a small number of boxes in one division. The Watch Committee were informed that the boxes were to be of concrete construction, and would be manufactured by the City Works Department. The cost of the boxes would be about £65 each.

Councillor Kemp wanted to know why the boxes were costing so much, when they could build quite good one in wood, for between £10 and £15 each. Why have they got to be of concrete, is it to stand attack from tanks and guns?.

FURTHER ROAD SAFETY MEASURES *1930.*

In 1930, the City was to see the first automatic traffic light signals erected at the Marsh Street, Trinity Street cross roads, others soon followed at Miles Bank, Hanley, Cobridge cross roads, and Ely Place, Burslem. These measures were no doubt brought about by the first Road Traffic Act, which came out in that year, and the City Council receiving a grant of 60 % from the Ministry of Transport, towards the erection and maintenance of these lights. The Chief Constable stated that the lights would only operate from 7.am. and 11 pm., and would be switched off at night.

PROMOTIONS *1930.*

In the October, the Chief Constable asked the Watch Committee to approve his proposed promotions of Inspector Marshall to Chief Inspector, and Sergeant Clarke to Inspector.

Alderman Dale, replied that he objected to promotions being carried out this way. "I understand that the last 10 or 11 persons promoted have all come from the office staff at Hanley. If this is correct, what chance does the ordinary man on the beat stand. If we are just going to rubber stamp all promotions like this, we may just as well not be here.?"

Councillor Kemp, replied that he disagreed. "I think the Chief Constable should be able to make his own decision. He knows the men better."

Mr. Dale, replied, "He only knows the ones in the office."

A vote was taken, and it was decided that in future the Committee would be supplied with all the particulars of service of at least two men, and that they would then decide which one to promote after being interviewed by the Watch Committee under the following circumstances:-

The Chief Constable prepared a number of questions on law and procedure, and members of the Watch Committee were supplied with model answers. The questions were put to the candidates and generally those who best answered the questions were promoted.

This system of promotion was to remain with the City police until the Police Act, of 1964, placed promotions and discipline in the hands of the Chief Constable.

INCREASED CRIME IN COBRIDGE *1930.*

During the months of October, and November, 1930, a large number of cases of shop breaking, and warehouse breaking took place in the Cobridge area of the City. The Chief Constable stated that he had drafted extra men in to the Cobridge area, from other districts, and doubled the availability of the men on night duty." I have also increased the number of men on pedal cycle and motor cycle patrol in the area. It is just as big a source of annoyance to me, as to anyone else. It means a lot of extra work for the men. We are at a disadvantage because of the poor lighting in the district."

When the question regarding the situation in Cobridge, was brought up at the next meeting of the Watch Committee, Mr. Carter, said, "I just have to keep plodding along with a totally inadequate force. The majority of cities and Boroughs have one policeman to every 650 to 700 of the population. In Stoke-on-Trent we have one policeman to every 1,200. Year after year I am given the money by the Watch Committee to bring the force up to it's establishment of 251, and then it is refused by the Finance

Committee." The Chairman replied, that all the members of the Watch Committee would support the Chief Constable in his quest for more men, whatever the Council would say.

A letter appeared in the local newspaper at this time. The writer saying that the signs placed on policemen's houses, defeated their own purpose, as the 'law breakers' just moved into the next street.

NOISY NIGHT STICKS 1930.

The Chief Constable issued the following order in February, 1930:-

No Inspector, Sergeant or Acting sergeant visiting men on night duty, will be allowed to use the stick for the purpose of knocking to attract the attention of a Constable on duty; it is a direct means of letting any night prowler know exactly where there is a Superior officer, and that there must be one or more police constables in the immediate neighbourhood. Further, it reverses the proper order of things, and causes the Constable to visit the Sergeant, and not the Sergeant to visit the Constable. Similarly neither flash lamps nor other lamps must be used for intimating the whereabouts of an Officer or Constable; in fact, lamps should be used as seldom as possible.

If a Sergeant is unable to find a Constable he should already know how to act.

The stick referred to was a walking stick which for many years even as late as the 1960's were carried by Sergeants in mainly the Lancashire police forces, such as Liverpool, Manchester, it had been the practise of the Sergeant to knock or tap the pavement with his stick to attract the Constable he required to meet

GOVERNMENT INSPECTION 1931.

Lieut-Col W.D. Allan., O.B.E., His Majesty's Inspector of Constabulary, inspected the City force at Finney Gardens, (the force sports ground) in June, 1931. Present on the parade were Superintendent Bowler, Inspectors G. Rye, and P. Appleton, Hanley Division. Chief Inspector H.H. Marshall, and Inspector H. Bird, Burslem Division. Chief Inspector Reader, and Inspector H.W.E. Carter, Longton Division. Chief Inspector P. McEvoy, Stoke Division. The C.I.D. were paraded under Detective Inspector C.J. Diggle, and Inspector A.J. Clarke was in charge of the office staff, The two policewomen Miss Broadhead, and Miss Andrews were also on the parade, so were 30 constables, with their cycles under Sergeant Fowler.

In December of that year the Chief Constable sent the following memo to all Divisional Officers:-

Please find enclosed a list of outstanding ambulance accounts. The Chief Constable desires these accounts cleared up as soon as possible. Divisional officers will make every effort to collect them. In cases where the defaulter cannot be traced, or where genuine poverty exists, a report should be submitted in order that the account may be written off.

WEAK STRENGTH OF THE FORCE 1931.

In 1931, both the Watch Committee and the Chief Constable were receiving complaints from the residents of the Chell, Pittshill, and Fegg Hays areas the City, regarding the lack of police patrols. It was reported that the only time that the people saw a policeman in those areas, was when passing through on either motor cycle, or horse. This was ammunition for the Chief Constable, for when he was questioned about this complaint by members of the Watch Committee. His reply to them was to appeal for more men.

Mr. Carter stated that he had not had an increase in the strength of the force for the last 10 years. He said, "I have applied annually, and received the support of this Committee, but my request has always been turned down by the Full Council. Police boxes would not in anyway effect my conviction that the force should be increased. The present strength of 251 was fixed 10 years ago, then the Government recommended a 10% cut, and the force was reduced to 240. In 1922, the City was extended by the addition of 9,620 acres, and 27,000 population. The area that was taken into the City was originally policed by 27 members of the County Constabulary. Many miles of new roadway have been built, and added to the City. The population of the City is now 276,000, that makes each man responsible for 89.6 acres, and 1,163 of the population. The average population to each constable in each City, and large town in England, and Wales is 700, and the average acreage is 45."

Alderman Dale said, "Some town must be the lowest in police strength. Crime was diminishing, and I think we should congratulate the Chief Constable, on the efficient way he his running the force." The Chief Constable obviously did not have his own way with the Committee that year. There is no doubt that he had a justifiable complaint, when he kept referring to the under staffing of the City force, if a examples of several other forces within the country taken from Home Office Police reports for 1932, are compared.

Police Force	Population.	Force strength.
Nottingham	276,000	349
Stoke-on-Trent	276,000	251
Salford	223,000	369
Birkenhead	151,000	259

Sequel to Demonstration Against Unemployment 1932.

A sequel to a demonstration against unemployment that took place on the 17th December, 1931 ,was heard at the City Stipendiary Court, on the 4th January, 1932, when a Hanley man who had been charged with assault was sentenced to 21 days imprisonment.

Chief Inspector Patrick William McEvoy told the court that he was in charge of a number of men who were on duty in the Kingsway, Stoke, when a meeting of the unemployed was taking place. The Chief Inspector went on to say that over 200 people had gathered by the Cenotaph, when at about 3.50 pm a few of the crowd, about a dozen in number, came up to the main entrance, and tried to force their way into the hall. He then gave the order for them to be removed. The crowd then broke up into two sections, and about 1,000 of them came up to the Glebe Street entrance, and attempted to force their way into the building. The accused was leading them, and when the Chief Inspector tried to reason with him, he said, "To hell with the C.I.D., we are going in" The accused then struck P.C. Leak at the side of his head. A number of the crowd then split away from the main body, several of them going into the nearby churchyard where they then threw stones at the police, several of them being hit. Chief Inspector McEvoy then ordered his men to draw their batons, and make a charge, this had the desired effect and the crowd dispersed.

Government Cut Backs 1932.

Members of all forces throughout the whole country received some bad news in 1932, for it was at this time, due the economic situation that the Government made cuts to the pay of policemen, teachers, members of the armed forces, and all Government employees. The City Watch Committee made representation to Central Government in London, saying that they did not agree with the cuts in police pay, but this did not have the slightest effect, they still went ahead with the cuts.

This meant that a probationary constable would now start at £2.15s.0d (£2.75p) per week instead of £3 .0s.0d a reduction of 5/- (25p). Sergeants were to lose 6s.3d (32p) per week, and inspectors 7s.6d (37p) per week.

Inspector A.L. Clarke at this time was sent on an Advanced Course of Instruction for Senior Officers, at Scotland Yard, two years later when a superintendent he attended a farther course at the same place.

STANDARDISING OF UNIFORM 1934.

At the beginning of 1934, the Watch Committee received a report from the Home Office, relating the style of uniform that was to be adopted by all police forces in England and Wales. This was to be carried out, according to the Home Office to save cost.

In the following year, one of the members of the Watch Committee suggested that a lightweight uniform be issued to the men for use during the summer months. He was informed by the Chief Constable, and other members of the Watch Committee, that the force had recently adopted the style of uniform suggested by the Home Office, and there was nothing they could do.

The Chief Constable informed members of the force, that all divisional stations, and sub-divisional stations would be issued with portable first aid boxes.

Mrs. Hollings - Daughter

Above: Insp. H. Bird Uniform pre1936

Insp.H. Bird Uniform post1936

Mrs. Hollings - Daughter

MUTUAL AID TO CONGLETON 1934.

Twenty five men consisting of one inspector, two sergeants, and twenty two constables were loaned to the Congleton Borough force for two days during February, 1934, under the Mutual Aid Agreement. This was to assist their colleagues with the Hunger Marchers who were passing through the area at the time. The total strength of the Congleton force at that time was only 12 men.

Each member of the City force was instructed to take with him the necessary articles for cleaning his buttons, and shaving etc. All men would be expected to appear clean and tidy at all times.

GOVERNMENT INSPECTION AND PROPOSED NEW POLICE STATIONS 1934.

People who were about on the streets of the City early one morning in March, 1934, knew something was afoot, as they saw their policemen, dressed in their ceremonial uniforms, and complete with spiked helmets. They may have thought that a member of the Royal Family was visiting the City, they were not far wrong, because His Majesty's Inspector of Constabulary was paying his annual visit to the force. There were over 200 officers on parade, 7 cars, ambulances, and the prison van were also lined up for inspection. After the H.M.I. had inspected the men and vehicles, he then visited the stations.

It was during his visit to Burslem Police Station that he said the station should be replaced with a new one. Mr. W. H. Kemp a member of the Watch Committee said, "The Burslem Station is certainly antiquated, and should have been condemned years ago." In fact the H.M.I. had first remarked about the condition of the station in 1922.

During the debate on the building of a new police station, some members of the Council went as far as suggesting that the police station in Tunstall, should also be demolished, and one new station be built between the two towns, and suggested it be sited on Scotia Road. The Chief Constable then remarked that he could not agree to this, as the area was too large to police efficiently from one station. Both Alderman Miss F. Farmer, and Councillor Huntbach agreed with Mr. Carter when they said the area was growing all of the time.

Mr. Carter then informed the Watch Committee that he had ordered a count to be taken of the number of visitors, and enquiries that had been dealt with at all the police stations within the City over one week in April, and gave the following details:- Burslem-217, Fenton-235, Hanley-759, Longton-529, Stoke-507, and Tunstall-179. He said' "As the members of this Committee will see, all the stations are used by the general public. I don't think we will be able to close any of them, even when we have all the police boxes in use. The boxes should be used in addition to the stations, not instead of"

The new police station at Burslem was opened in April, 1937, by Lieut Col. W.D. Allen O.B.E., H.M. Inspector of Constabulary.

The total cost of the building with fixtures, and fittings was just over £12,000. It replaced a station that had been in use for just over 102 years.

Tunstall had to wait until 1959 to get their new station, which cost £10,000, and replaced one in Wesley Street, which was about 100 years old.

Lieut Col. Allen also suggested that a police station be built in the Trentham area, due to the building that had taken place there, and the increase in population in that area. This police station with living accommodation for the sergeant and his family, was also opened in 1937, the total cost of this station was £2,610.

The Watch Committee agreed to a request from the Chief Constable, when he asked for their permission to discontinue sending the City Police Ambulance into the Leek area. The Leek Urban District Council were informed that the use of the City Police Ambulance in their area, would cease at the end of the year. The City ambulance service was, in fact, operated by the police. The ambulances were based at the City Police Headquarters, Town Hall, Hanley, and an ambulance driver, a constable with specialised first aid knowledge was always on duty. His assistance, a constable, was on 'Ambulance Patrol' which consisted of leaving Hanley Police Station, patrolling down Stafford Street, left into Piccadilly, left into Albion Street and back to the station every 30 minutes. If a call was received the driver would drive from the station, ringing the ambulance bell and he would know exactly where to find his assistant. The Chief Constable was able to report that the total number of convictions for drunkenness at the end of the year 1934, was 62, which was decrease of 9 on the previous year.

POLICE BOXES *1934.*

The first three police boxes in the City finally became operational in 1934 after the erection of them had first been originally discussed in 1929. Each box was of concrete construction and cost about £75 each to build and erect, having been built by a local builder, Ball and Robinson, who are still in the building trade to this day. The first three boxes were situated at the following locations:- 1. Penkhull Square, 2. A34 Trent Vale, opposite Black Lion public house, 3. Campbell Road junction Longsdale Street, near to the old Stoke City Football Club (Victoria ground).

In addition to the normal telephone, and signalling apparatus, each box contained first aid boxes, 1 pyrene, and 1 foam fire extinguisher, plus cleaning materials. A number of other boxes were added later. Keys to these boxes were carried on the two ambulances, the Chief Constable's staffs car, the utility van, the Detective Department car, and each of the road traffic cars. This was before the cars had been equipped with wireless.

The Chief Constable issued the following order at the end of 1934:-

"There appears a growing tendency for members of the detective force to appear in public, hatless. This in my opinion, is neither dignified nor safe. In future, all members in receipt of plain clothes allowance will wear head-dress when on duty, as also will any member called up for plain clothes duty."

RETIREMENTS FROM THE FORCE 1935.

The first of March, 1935, saw the retirement of five members from the force. They included Chief Inspector J. Reader, the officer in charge of Longton Division, Inspector H.E.W. Carter, who was in charge of Fenton Sub-Division, together with three sergeants.

ROYAL REVIEW OF POLICE FORCES 1935.

King's Crown, officers cap badge, silver. Taken into use 1935

The Royal Review of all the police forces in the United Kingdom, took place in Hyde Park, London, on the 20th July, 1935. There were a total of 8,051 police officers of all ranks on the parade, but only 9 Chief Constables of the provincial police forces, of which Mr. Roger Carter was one. He was Group Commander for "A" and "B" Divisions of the contingent from the Midlands District of England, which not only included members of his own force, of which there was 1 inspector, 2 sergeants, and 21 constables, but men from the Counties of Staffordshire, Shropshire, Northamptonshire, Rutland, Warwickshire, Worcestershire, plus all of the Borough and City forces situated in those counties. The were men from everyone of the 230 forces in existence in the United Kingdom at that time.

The Parade was inspected by His Majesty King George V., and must have been a memorable day for everyone taking part including Mr. Carter.

The Chief Constable later received the George V Jubilee Medal, along with 11 other members of the City force.

GOVERNMENT INSPECTOR'S REPORT 1936.

The year 1936 opened with Colonel Allen, His Majesty's Inspector of Constabulary, producing a very adverse report concerning the strength of the City force, which he considered was totally inadequate, considering both the size and population of the City. He went on to state that this matter had gone on far too long, and must be attended to. Eleven more men must be recruited as soon as possible to bring the force up to it's establishment of 251.

The City Council, however, always mindful of the ratepayers coppers, managed to persuade the H.M.I. to agree to the extra men being recruited over a period of five years. They were to take two additional men every year for the first four years, and three men on the fifth year. However, four years later, and with the Second World War taking place, the understaffed City police force was to cause the Watch Committee problems.

SUDDEN DEATH OF CHIEF CONSTABLE MR. CARTER 1936.

Members of the Force were saddened to hear of the sudden death of their Chief Constable, which took place on 13th April, 1936. Mr. Carter was 70 years of age, and had been the Chief Constable since the force was established in 1910.

The funeral of Mr. Carter took place three days later, and must have been a memorable occasion, for in addition to family mourners, in attendance were the Lord Mayor, and Town Clerk, followed by members of the City Council, the High Sheriff of Staffordshire, plus eight Chief Constables. A detachment of the City Police, together with members of the City Fire Brigade marched behind Mr. Carter's coffin which was draped with the Union Jack, and with the Chief Constable's helmet, and sword placed on top. Chief Superintendent A.J. Richards, M.B.E.., Officer in Charge of the Newcastle Division of the County Constabulary, was also present with a contingent of the County force.

APPOINTMENT OF A NEW CHIEF CONSTABLE MR. F. L. BUNN 1936.

Several days after the funeral of Mr. Carter, a special meeting of the Watch Committee took place, with the main object being to select a successor to Mr. Carter. After a short debate, the Committee were informed that none of the Senior Officers at present serving in the force, would be eligible for the position due to the age restrictions placed upon them by the Home Office.

Adverts were then placed in a number of police publications. The post of Chief Constable for the City of Stoke-on-Trent was advertised with a starting salary of £900 per annum, with increments of £50 per year up to a maximum of £1,150 after five years service. A rent allowance of £100 per year was allowed in lieu of a house, and an official motor car was supplied. Some time later the Watch Committee decided to purchase a house in Longton Road, Trentham, at a cost of £900, plus an extra £150 for a brick built garage to be added. This house was to be used as the Chief Constable's official residence.

The Watch Committee received a total of 57 applications for the post of Chief Constable, from this number they selected seven persons for interview, they were: -

Chief Constable	F.L. BUNN	of Grimsby Borough Police
Chief Constable	C. G. LOOMES	of Blackburn Borough Police
Chief Constable	F.T. TARRY	of Exeter City Police
Chief Constable	H. J. VANN	of Lancaster City Police
Chief Constable	Tom WELLS	of Chesterfield Borough Police
Superintendent	ABERREIN	of Manchester City Police
Chief Inspector	BUCKBY	of Birmingham City Police

The successful applicant was Mr. Frank Leonard Bunn, aged 46 years of Grimsby Borough Police, who took up his appointment on the 1st day of September, 1936.

The Chief Constable later submitted a claim for £13. 13s. 0d the cost of removal of his furniture from Grimsby to Stoke-on-Trent.

RETIREMENT OF LONG SERVING OFFICER 1936.

Superintendent C. H. Bowler, who had been Acting Chief Constable since the death of Mr. Carter, was finally able to retire from the force at the end of September, 1936. He had originally planned to retire from the force at the end of April, but this had not been possible due to the unforeseen death of the Chief Constable. Superintendent Bowler had joined the Staffordshire Constabulary in 1898. Inspector A.L. Clarke was promoted to the rank of Superintendent to fill the vacant post.

Police constable Ullyart was awarded the usual £2 .2s .0d by the Watch Committee for his brave action in stopping a runaway horse in Etruria Road.

In October, 1936, the new Chief Constable presented his first report to the Watch Committee, which was quite a lengthy one. Mr. Bunn said, "I plan to increase the efficiency of the City police. I would like to see the force's cars equipped with short wave radio, and police boxes erected on all the main roads on the approaches to the City, and at all major cross roads. I will try to reduce the number of deaths, and injuries from road traffic accidents in the City, which I consider to be too high."

Mr. Bunn then mentioned that two probationary constables had resigned after only 9 days service. He informed the Committee that both men were at the Birmingham City Police Training School. He had come to the conclusion that they were not of the temperament required, and that they did not like discipline.

At the close of the meeting the Chief Constable reported that the total cost of pay for the force in 1936, was £59,835, and the cost of pensions to retired officers, and widows came to £21,500.

Later in the year the Chief Constable had the pleasure of informing members of the Watch Committee, and the citizens of Stoke-on-Trent, that their City was the most sober of the 19 largest towns in England and Wales during the year 1936.

DISCIPLINARY ACTIONS *1936.*

Chief Inspector Rye appeared before the Watch Committee at this time on a discipline charge, he was charged with conduct likely to bring discredit on the police service, but the exact nature of the offence is not recorded. They approved the Chief Constable's recommendation that Rye should be reduced to the rank of sergeant, and transferred to another division. Sergeant Rye retired from the force several months later, after completing 25 years service. Similar charges against six constables was adjourned for six months.

During the same period disciplinary action was taken against two members of the force for not paying their bus fare.

At the close of the year, the Chief Constable held the following appointments:- Chief Inspector under the Cinematograph Act, Disease of Animals Act, Explosives Act, Petroleum Act, Pharmacy and Poisons Act, and Shops and Theatres Act. He was also responsible for the inspection and licensing of Hackney Carriages. It makes one wonder how he found time to manage the force.

INCREASE IN TECHNOLOGY AND EFFICIENCY *1937.*

The new Chief Constable had been in charge of the force less than six months, when he started to make changes in the workings and equipment of the force. A new photographic laboratory was opened, and new equipment purchased for the C.I.D.

Mr. Bunn then decided that he would set up his own training school. He said that there are peculiar difficulties in policing Stoke-on-Trent, that make it desirable to train the men locally. Previous to this, recruits to the Stoke-on-Trent force had since 1925 received their training at the Birmingham City Police Training School.

The first training school in Stoke-on-Trent began on 16th November, 1936 and consisted of the following recruits Police Constables Steele (later Assistant Chief Constable), Sargent (later Chief Superintendent), Froggatt (later Chief Superintendent), Owen, Ashworth, Wilde, Andow, Hill, Manders, and Murfitt. Hill, Manders and Murfitt resigned but the remaining seven completed their service.

First intake of men trained locally after Mr. Bunn was appointed Chief Constable in 1936. Front row left to right: Thomas Hill, George H. Wilde, Trevor Geo. Froggett, Charles F. Manders and Tom Ashworth. Back row left to right: Irwin Sargent, Raymond J. Andow, Harry Steele, William G. Murfitt, Richard W. Owin.
Harry Steel retired from the force as A.C.C.
and both Trevor Froggett and Irwin Sargent retired as Chief Superintendents

Photos Mr. H. Steele

The same intake of recruits doing physical training

In charge of the training school was Inspector Gerald Goodman who later became the Chief Constable of Newark, then Scarborough, and Police constable (1) Herbert Cross who became an Inspector.

The Chief Constable was, like his predecessor, complaining to the Watch Committee regarding the size of the force. He informed them that he considered the establishment of 251, which was set in 1921, to be inadequate for The population of the City. He went onto say, "Since this establishment was set 16 years ago, the work of the men on the beat has increased, and so have the traffic problems. This Committee will sooner or later have to consider a substantial increase in the strength of the force."

The Watch Committee, and the Chief Constable then held a discussion on the subject of the use of police pillars in the force area.

FURTHER ROAD SAFETY MEASURES *1937.*

Road safety mattrs were very much in the mind of the Chief Constable at this time. Two members of the force, who were attached to the Motor Patrol Branch, P. Cs Blanchard, and Holland, were instructed to visit every school in the City, and lecture to the children on road safety. To assist in their task, the officers constructed two large scale models, of cross roads, roundabouts, with a set of working traffic light. Each model was about 4 ft square, and the total cost was about £15, that was for the purchase of two dynamos to work the traffic lights.

Road safety lectures must have been of some benefit, because the Chief Constable was able to report that 28 persons had been killed on the roads of the City in 1938. That was a decrease of 7 on the previous year.

At the beginning of 1937, the Chief Constable, with the Councils blessing introduced a number of One Way Streets in Hanley, they were Piccadilly, Brunswick Street, and Cheapside. This was done to ease congestion in Piccadilly. Six months later, Mr. Bunn was able to report that the system was working very successfully.

The Chief Constable also had a number of notices printed, and issued to each constable. These notices were to be placed on all cars that were causing an obstruction. They read as follows:- "Parking is not authorised here, as it is liable to cause obstruction. One of the responsibilities of the police is to keep the roads clear. We would rather have your help, than prosecute you" Signed. F.L.Bunn, Chief Constable. This idea appeared in the National newspapers, and the Stoke-on-Trent Police were known as the Polite Police.

The Police Federation, at the request of the Inspectors, placed the following request before the Watch Committee. The Inspectors were seeking to be put on the same pay scale, as Inspectors in the Metropolitan, and City of London Police forces. They were informed that the Committee would not support their application. At this time all police pay rates were standard, and set by the Home Office. The Inspector's rates at the time were as follows: - London £325 per annum rising to £375 after 5 years, Provincial forces (Stoke) £320 per annum rising to £360 after 4 years. Therefore the Inspectors in Stoke did not have a valid complaint.

One member of the City Council at a meeting at this time remarked that, I felt very sorry for the policemen who were employed on traffic points in this appalling weather. Only last night, I noticed a policeman standing in a pile of wet snow. Would it not be possible for the men to have a small platform to stand on, if only to keep their feet dry. I have noticed these things in Liverpool, and I think they could be constructed here without too much extra cost.

FURTHER RETIREMENTS FROM THE FORCE 1937.

Chief Inspector McEvoy retired from the force after 27 years service in the City. Mr.McEvoy had originally joined the Royal Irish Constabulary in 1908, and transferred to Stoke-on-Trent on the 30th March, 1910. He was replaced at Stoke by Inspector Goodman, who was soon promoted to Chief Inspector.

Inspector Saunders also retired from the force in 1937, due to ill health. He had completed 28 years service. Mr. Saunders had joined the Hanley Borough Police in 1909.

PREPARATION FOR THE OUTBREAK OF WAR 1938

In 1938, preparations for the defence of the Country in the event of war, were gradually taking place. Information from the Home Office, and other Government Departments were arriving on the Chief Constable's desk on a daily basis.

The Council decided to appoint the Chief Constable, Air Raid Precautions Officer for the City, for which he would receive an additional £200 per year, for as long as he was employed as such. The Home Office, however, informed the City Council, that the rate for this appointment should be £100, and the allowance was amended accordingly. The first action Mr. Bunn took, was to place the following advert in the evening newspaper:- (Wanted 2,000 part time Air Raid Wardens to serve the City. Men under 30 years of age need not apply. Members of the Territorial Army, Auxiliary Air Force, and Army Reserve, men who have undertaken to serve with the Auxiliary Fire Service, or as Special Constables should not apply). At the end of April, the Chief Constable was able to report that he had recruited over 1,000 wardens. Now that the Chief Constable had recruited and started to train some of his wardens, he now started to think about distributing them throughout the City. 560 warden posts, and 45 first aid posts were opened the length and breadth of the City.

In his annual report for 1938, Mr. Bunn referred to the alarming increase in the amount of juvenile crime that was taking place in the City, which he said he thought was due to the lack of playing fields, and parental control. He also thought that the City Magistrates were too lenient at times.

One member of the Watch Committee, after reading the report, stated that, "We have always prided ourself with being a law abiding City, perhaps we should invest in a few more policemen." No doubt the Chief Constable would have agreed with him.

Chief Inspector H.H. Marshall who had been in charge of the Longton Division for the previous two years, retired from the force. He was replaced by Inspector H. Edge, who was promoted to Chief Inspector.

The Chief Constable announced that with effect from the 1st April, 1938, the City police divisions would in future be known by letters, and not the name of the towns. They would be as follows:-

A Division   Hanley.

B Division   Burslem and Tunstall.

C Division   Longton and Fenton

D Division   Stoke.

A slight alteration to the A and D Divisions took place in the early 1950s, but otherwise these divisions were to remain until the demise of the City force 30 years later.

New first aid appliances were issued to most of the City stations. They were portable apparatus for asphyxiation, to assist with breathing, and a tannic acid spray for use on burns.

Three members of the force
c. 1938

Authors Collection

POLICE DOGS 1938.

The Watch Committee agreed to a request from the Chief Constable, to purchase two Labrador dogs for police work. Mr. Bunn said, "These dogs would be used to accompany constables on lonely beats, on the outskirts of the City. These dogs are trained to stay outside, or inside premises while the police officer investigate the other. They are trained at the Home Office Dog Training School in Berkshire, and will cost about £12 each."

Two dogs were later obtained, however, within a few weeks of being taken into service, one of the dogs was killed by a lorry on the A34 at Trentham. The other dog survived until 1948, when it was destroyed due to age. The City then had to wait until the mid 1950s before it was to acquire any more dogs. A most interesting letter appeared in the local newspaper at this time, which reads as follows:-

"Burglars Beware. I see that our local police are to acquire two police dogs. We are informed that they will guard houses, seek out articles hidden by criminals, ascend ladder, search rooms, while officers wait outside, take messages from the man on the beat, back to the police station. In fact they will do anything, except take the oath, and give evidence. What marvels they are."

I do not think the write of the letter, had as much confidence in the dogs as the Chief Constable appeared to have.

INSPECTION OF THE FORCE 1938.

In 1938 the City force was inspected for the last time by Lieu Col. W.D. Allen, who was due to retire some weeks later. The parade of men and vehicles, including four police ambulances were inspected by the H.M.I. who then remarked on the smart appearance of the men on parade.

CRIME DETECTION 1938.

A crime of a serious nature took place in the City in 1938, involving a smash and grab raid on the premises of Pidducks Jewellers, in Hanley, when a tray of rings to the value of £2,000 was stolen. The registration number of the thieve's car was noted as it sped away. An express message was flashed from the City to all major police station throughout Staffordshire, Shropshire, and Cheshire. City cars, two of which were fitted with short wave wireless, as a trial, set out in pursuit. Five days later on the 11th July, a man was arrested in London, by Detective Inspector Till, Detective Sergeant Davenport of the City force, accompanied by members of the Metropolitan Police.

Mr. W. Bates

His Majesty's Inspector of Constabulary inspecting members of the City Police in 1938. Left to right: Inspector G. F. Goodman, Supt. A. L. Clarke, Chief Constable F.L. Bunn, The Chairman of the Watch Committee and Lieut-Col. D. D. Allan H.M. Inspector of Constabulary.

The Prosecution Barrister in the case was Mr.R.N. MacGregor-Clarkson, who only twelve months later was appointed the City Stipendiary Magistrate.

GOVERNMENT INSPECTION 1939.

A gentleman with the grand sounding name of Colonel Jacynth d'Ewes Fitz-Gerald Coke., C.M.G., C.V.O., C.B.E., visited the City for the first time in 1939, and was to cause many problems for the Council, and the Watch Committee, for this gentleman was His Majesty's Inspector of Constabulary. The Colonel inspected the force on the 9th February, and over 200 men, the patrol cars, and ambulances were lined up for the inspection which took place at the Finney Gardens Sports Ground, Hanley. The senior officers on the parade were Superintendent A.L. Clarke, Hanley, Chief Inspector Tennant, Burslem, Chief Inspector

Goodman, Stoke, Chief Inspector Edge, Longton, Inspector Guthrie, Fenton, Inspector Willis, Hanley, Inspector Downing, Tunstall, and Detective Chief Inspector Till, the Officer in Charge of the C.I.D.

The H.M.I. later visited the Headquarters, and inspected the Detective Department. He reported that he was very pleased with what he considered to be some of the latest equipment in use by that department for the detection of crime. He was not, however, very pleased with the present establishment of the force, which he said should be increased by about one third.

Some weeks later, the Watch Committee received a communication from the Home Office, reporting the Government Inspector's findings, and informing the Council that they must increase the establishment of the force by the addition of 63 extra men. One can imagine the gasps of amazement from the members of the ever cost conscious City Council. The Lord Mayor, accompanied by members of the Watch Committee, and one of the City's M.P.s, set off for London, and requested an interview with Sir John Anderson, the Home Secretary.

Sir John was ready with his answers. He told the delegation that the force had been understaffed for years. This had been pointed out to them as far back as 1925, and only the previous year the H.M.I. Colonel Allan informed the Committee that the force was seriously under strength. The existing establishment was substantially below the minimum numbers required by the regulations, and that the force must be increased by a considerable number. Members of the delegation then informed the Home Secretary that they were willing to increase the establishment by the addition of 25 men. They were, however, informed by Sir John, that the strength of the force was decided by the Home Secretary, and was not open to negotiations.

Matters came to ahead later in the year, when the Certificate of Efficiency was refused, and the Government Grant, which amounted to £50,000 was withheld. Events of a much more serious nature were to overtake the squabble between the Home Office, and the Watch Committee, when on that fatefull Sunday morning in September, the Country found itself at war.

Due to the outbreak of war, the Home Office reinstated the grant, but stipulated that the force be increased to 276 officers without delay. And that at the end of hostilities, the authorised establishment of the force would be looked at again.

At the end of the year the establishment of the force stood at 476 officers, this number was made up of 276 regular officers, 154 members of the Police War Reserve, and 46 members of the Police Reserve (these were retired police officers who had been called back for the duration of the war). In addition to these there were 12 boy messengers, 2 policewomen, and just over 300 members of the Special Constabulary, serving the people of the City during these dark years.

Five members of the force, who were reservists were called back to the Colours, on the Declaration of War, four of these went to the Army, and one into the Navy. They were followed by many more.

Chief Inspector G.F. Goodman resigned from the City force in May, 1939, to take up the appointment of Chief Constable Newark Borough Police, Nottinghamshire.

PROBLEMS FOR MR. BUNN 1939.

The Chief Constable's estimates for the financial year were placed before the Watch Committee. The Committee noticed that they were £8,000 up on the previous year. When questioned, Mr. Bunn said that the increase in the expenditure was necessary. It was for the erection of the police pillars, extensions to the force garage, uniform and equipment for the Special Constabulary. The Watch Committee up to it's old tricks again, reduced the estimates by more than half. The police pillar system was never adopted in the City, and the garage extension was not completed until after the war.

In April, 1939, a writ was issued by a firm of London solicitors acting on behalf of the Chief Constable, against Mr. W.R. Kemp J.P., a member of the City Council and Watch Committee, alleging slander. Mr. Kemp was later forced to make a public apology to the Chief Constable.

It appears that Mr. Kemp had alleged that the Chief Constable had been receiving an allowance for acting as Air Raid Precautions Officer, but had delegated the job to someone else. However, this was found not to be the case.

In his Annual Report at the close of the year, the Chief Constable was able to say that the City enjoyed a favourable position with regards to drunkenness, in relation to other towns and cities of comparative size and population. He was, however, concerned at the number of convictions for the offence of being drunk in charge of a motor car.

Road traffic accidents were still causing the Chief Constable problems. He reported that 45 persons had been killed on the road of the City, in 1939, of this number 26 of the fatalities had occurred in the last four months of the year. This increase was no doubt due to the "black out". All we can do, is urge the public to be more attentive when crossing the road, said Mr. Bunn.

Staffordshire police

The bicycling bobbies parade for His Majesty's Inspector of Constabulary in 1938

Tunstall Sub-Division 1938. Inspector H. Bird sitting centre.

C.I.D. Officers parade for the H.M.Inspection 1939. Left to right front row: Det/Supt. E. Till, D/Sgt. John Davenport, Det/Sgt. Harold Rimmer, D/C's. Thomas Jones, Fred Holdcroft, Fred Tomalin, Harry Steele, Harrold Massey, Lewis Knapper. Back row left to right: Sgt. L. Woodhouse, P.C. William Singleton, D/C's. Charles Wainwright, Fred Dilley, William Tarpy, George Curran, Percy Cooke. Note Police Ambulances in the background.

Ken Hawkins

Tunstall Sub Division 1941
P.C. Walter Hill, P.C. Dennis Langton
P.W.R. Manifold, P.C. Ken Hawkins, Insp. Cross, Sgt Dilley, P.C. A.E. Taylor

CHAPTER VIII

THE WAR AND UNSETTLED YEARS 1940 - 1949.

His Majesty's Inspector of Constabulary, Colonel J.d'E.F. Coke inspected the force in February, 1940, but due to the war, the force was inspected under working conditions, with no parade being held.

FURTHER IMPROVEMENT IN COMMUNICATIONS 1940.

The Chief Constable suggested to the Watch Committee, that a system of wireless communication be adopted. He said it would mean that receiving sets would be installed in six of the force patrol cars, and a number of fixed stations. It would also be possible for the fire brigade to make use of the system, and should cost about £1,700. He thought it would be most desirable, considering the war.

The Watch Committee gave their backing to the idea, and instructed the Chief Constable to deal with the situation as soon as possible. Some six months later, in July, 1941, the wireless system not only covering the City, but the neighbouring force of Newcastle-under-Lyme, came into operation. The transmitting station was situated in a hut built on high ground at Birches Head, and was to remain there for the next 15 years. It was however, to be 1943, before the radio system became two way, which meant cars were able to transmit, as well as receive messages.

The Police Ambulances were later fitted with radios. This most up to date system, must have proved invaluable in the war years, and contributed to the force's efficiency in it's fight against crime. Later in his annual report in 1945, the Chief Constable stated that wireless communications, especially in the ambulances had been of tremendous use.

The City police had experimented with wireless as early as 1937, when short wave sets were placed in two of the force's cars as a trial.

BREACH OF WARTIME REGULATIONS *1940.*

A rather amusing case was heard at the City's Magistrates Court, in October, 1940, when a gentleman was fined £2 for showing an unobscured light, contrary to the Blackout Regulations. Mr. Nixon, a bus conductor, told the Court that during a air raid alert, the defendant struck 4 matches. He repeatedly told the defendant that he must not do that, but he took no notice, and just continued. Defendant apologised to the Court and said' "It must have been the drink".

The Chief Constable reported that 35 persons had been killed on the roads of the City during the year 1940. This was 10 less than the previous year. I am quite pleased. It is probably due to less traffic on the road, he said.

A new police station complete with living accommodation for the sergeant, was opened at Hartshill at this time. The total cost of the building was £3,580. (Some of the older readers may well remember Sergeant Dean, the resident sergeant who was stationed there during the 1940s and early 1950s. This building is now in use as the Coroner's Court.

1941.

The Chief Constable reported to the Watch Committee at the beginning of 1941, that 11 members of the force, who were Army Reservists, and had been called back to their regiments at the outbreak of the war, had now been released, and had returned to the force.

Mr.Bunn also informed the Watch Committee that Police Constable George Hannah, had transferred to the Derby Borough Police force. He stated that P. C. Hannah was a former member of the Port Vale Football Club. Alderman J.H. Dale, asked amid laughter, "Was a transfer fee being paid.?"

Members of the Watch Committee informed the Chief Constable, that they had received a letter, complaining that the police had removed a car that had been parked at night on the roadway, to a nearby police station, and asked whether the police had powers to do that. Mr. Bunn stated that the driver had failed to immobilise the vehicle, and the police had powers under the war emergency power regulations, to remove the car to a place of safety, and this they had done.

Mr. Bunn informed the Watch Committee that he had been on a short list of five, for the post of Chief Constable of Sheffield City Police, but had not been successful.

SHOOTING OF POLICE CONSTABLE JAMES ALLMAN *1941.*

Members of the force must have been alarmed to hear that one of their comrades had been shot and seriously wounded in the Longton area of the City. On 4th September, 1941, Police Constable James Allman, had been sent together with Police Constable Fineran to a house within the Longton Division, to apprehend an army deserter, who was believed to be at the address, and return him to the military authorities. Constable Alman entered the address and commenced to climb the stairs. As he was entering one of the bedrooms, a shot rang out, and P.C. Allman fell back, having been struck in the face by a bullet. P. C. Fineran who was standing at the base of the stairs, immediately went to his colleague's assistance, helped him down the stairs, and out of the house. P.C. Allman was then taken to the Longton Cottage Hospital by a passing motorist.

P.C. Fineran meanwhile kept the house under observations, and sent a message to Longton Police Station for assistance. A short time later he was joined at the scene by Chief Inspector Edge, Sergeant Pegg, and two constables.

It appears that the accused who was serving with the Pioneer Corps, had been absent from his army unit for some days. When the police officers had entered the house, the accused had attempted to cause injury to himself, so that he would not be able to continue serving with the army. As P.C. Allman entered the bedroom, the soldier who was lying on the bed fired the bullet which passed through his own foot, and then struck the police officer in the eye.

Constable Allman who had only been married five days previously, was 31 years of age, and had been a member of the force for just over two years. P. C. Allman was to lose the sight of one eye, although thankfully the officer recovered sufficiently to be able to return to duty. He spent the remainder of his service as a member of the C.I.D., and retired on pension.

In his annual report at the close of the year, the Chief Constable was able to report a detection rate of 80 % for indictable offences. The rise in juvenile offences was causing alarm. 136 male, and 15 female offenders had been charged with drunkenness.

VIOLENT ATTACK ON TUNSTALL POLICE STATION *1942.*

A violent attack took place on Tunstall Police Station, on one Sunday morning in April, 1942. The attack was not perpetrated by a mob of drunken rioters, or even Hitler's Luftwaffe, but - in fact by members of the Home Guard (better known as Dad's Army), who were taking part in a military exercise. Inspector Downing the officer in charge at Tunstall , reported to the Chief Constable, the following facts relating to the attack, and the amount of damage caused to the building.

Mr. Downing stated the windows, and window frames at both the front and rear of the station were broken, along with both doors. There was also some damage to the interior of the building. The inspector then went on to say, that as far as the men were concerned, one member of the Police War Reserve suffered a fractured collar bone, the Duty Sergeant received a gash to his forehead, and two members of the Special Constabulary also received injuries. One of the special constables received an eye injury from a blank cartridge, and another officer nearly lost the end of one of his fingers, when a bayonet was thrust through the door. This man had to receive medical treatment, and lost two days employment. He would be making a claim for £1.1 5s.0d, which would include 15/6d (67p) doctor's fee.

The men on duty at Tunstall at the time of the exercise said, "We are not complaining about the general fracas, it was good fun while it lasted. There was a little too much zeal shown by the Home Guard. The Home Guard later held an inquiry into the whole affair, apologised to the police for the injuries caused, and paid for the damage which amounted to £6. 10s.0 (£6.50p)

Superintendent A.E. Godden tendered his resignation to the Watch Committee at this time, to take up the appointment of Chief Constable of Wakefield City Police.

The Chief Constable Mr. Bunn resigned his post as Director of the Air Raid Precautions Department for the City. It was common knowledge that the A.R.P. Committee, and the Chief Constable were not always on the best of terms.

In 1942, the Recorder of the City complemented the Chief Constable on the exceptionally high rate of crime detection 81.5 %, a figure which has never been surpassed.

ON THE RUN 1943.

In May, 1943, two prisoners who had both been sentenced to terms of imprisonment at the Stoke-on-Trent Quarter Sessions, managed to escape from a prison van which was transporting them to Walton Gaol, Liverpool. One of the prisoners later told the police that they had both decided to escape, and when the van entered the open country, just outside Newcastle, they put their plan into operation They both threw themselves at the door, it burst open, and they both fell onto the road. When he got up, he noticed that the other prisoner was still lying in the road, in a pool of blood, and he was unable to rouse him. He then went to a nearby house, and informed the occupant that he had found an injured soldier lying in the road, and asked the lady if she could get help for him, and then left the area.

The driver of the prison van reported that they had passed through the village of Betley, when he noticed in his mirror, that the rear doors of the van were open. After stopping, examining the van, and finding the prisoners missing, he then turned round and headed towards Newcastle. After only travelling a short distance, he came across the prisoner Baker lying in the road. He could see that he was seriously injured, so he place him in the rear of the van and conveyed him to the London Road Hospital (now the City General). The other prisoner was recaptured in the City nine days later.

Both the driver and escort of the prison van were disciplined.

The Chief Constable was able to report to the Watch Committee, that the force had been able to reduce it's petrol consumption by 20 % Mr. Bunn said that the Home Office had stipulated 10 %, (so I don't think that we are doing badly.) At that time the force possessed 17 motor vehicles.

Ken Hawkins

P.C. Ken Hakins served with the City Police from 1939 until 1969 when he retired as a Sergeant

LONGTON POLICE STATION 1943.

The conditions of Longton Police Station were causing concern at this time. The station like many buildings in the City were suffering the effects of mining subsidence. Member of the Watch Committee, along with the Chief Constable, visited the station to carry out an inspection. The Chairman of the Watch Committee, said, "The men are working in deplorable conditions. We will have to try and do something, but what. The Government will not allow use to build a new station until the war is over." The City Surveyor, and Engineer were consulted, and asked to try and remedy the situation. They must have done a good job, because the building remained in use until the early 1990s when anew police station was built on the same site. Although the this new police station was built in the 1990s, the architecture was such that it would not have looked out of place in the Victorian period.

Sergeant J.W. Ash stationed at Goldenhill Police Station, descended into an old pit shaft, that had not been used for over 60 years, to rescue a small dog that had fallen down the shaft, and was unable to get out. For this brave act Sergeant Ash was awarded the R.S.P.C.A. Silver Medal. He was also presented with an inscribed wrist watch from members of the Watch Committee.

CITY OF STOKE-ON-TRENT 'D. DIVISION' (Hartshill Section) Regular, War Reserve and Special Constabulary

Back Row: S.C. R.J. Johnson, S.C. J. B. Birch, S.C. W. J. Stubbs, S.C. R. O. Poole, S.C. A. G. Dyche-Teague, S.C. H. Hand, S.C. A. Tomlinson, S. C. J. Wilbtahams.
Middle Row: S.C. E. J. Antwiss, P.W.R. J. C. Proctor, P.C. W. Barratt, P. Sgt. A. W. Dean, P.C. S. Kersey, P.C. R. Hibbert, P.W.R. E. Rogers, P.W.R. L. Oliver, S.C. G. A. Wright, S.C. W. R. Sherwin.
Froint Row: S.C. J. Goulding, S.C. F. W. Witty, S.C. W. Vyse, S. Sgt. F. Barnes, S.Sgt. G. S. Nicholls, P.Sgt. J. L. Leak, S.Sgt. W. G. Davies, S.C. J. Frost, S.C. R. E. Walton, S.C. E. O. Rose

HONOUR FOR THE CHIEF CONSTABLE 1943.

In the King's Birthday Honours for 1943, the Chief Constable Mr. Bunn, was awarded the Order of the British Empire.

Senior officers in the force, through their representatives, requested the Watch Committee, to issue them with the white shirts they wore with their uniform, instead of having to pay for them themselves . The Committee, however, refused to either issue shirts, or to grant allowance, when the Chief Constable stated that he did not think the Home Office would allow it.

1944.

The year 1944 opened with more police officers being released to serve in the armed forces. At the end of the year the strength of the Regular Force stood at 252, but to this number must be added members of the

Police War Reserve, the Police Reserve, and the Women's Auxiliary Police Corps.

When the Chief Constable asked the Watch Committee to approve his recommendation to promote one chief inspector to the rank of acting superintendent, and one sergeant to the rank of acting inspector, one member of the Committee asked the Chief Constable, why they were acting ranks. Mr. Bunn replied that the reason for this, was to give the men who were currently serving in the armed forces, a fair chance of promotion once they return. He informed them ~ he would be asking them, from then on to make all promotions as acting ranks.

WIRELESS COMMUNICATIONS *1944.*

In 1944, the Chief Constable had to issue the following order:-

'Wireless Discipline'. Valuable information may be disclosed by operators' chit-chat; This is strictly prohibited, and transmissions must be confined to official messages only. This must be strictly adhered to.

It was at this time that force was allotted the radio call sign of M2YW. The fixed stations were then allotted an individual letter, Hanley became M2YW-A, Burslem M2YW-D, and so on, until all the stations within the City and Newcastle had their own individual call signs, and all cars were each allotted an individual number. These call signs were to be used, and no reference was to be made to the name of the police station or town. With the end of the war, the need for secrecy was not so paramount, and stations would then be referred to by name again.

The Auxiliary Police Association was formed. This was to represent members of the Police War Reserve, Full time Special Constables, and members of the Women's Auxiliary Police Corps, in their dealings with the Chief Constable, and Home Office.

The Chief Constable was pleased to report to the Watch Committee, that during that year the number of road traffic accident in the City was the lowest since 1929. Also that the detection rate for burglary, shop breaking, and house breaking by the C.I.D. was 76.6 %.

SERIOUS IRREGULARITIES *1945.*

The City managed to hit the National Newspapers in 1945, regarding irregularities that had taken place in a court case within the City, where a 48 year old Roman Catholic priest had been charged with indecent assault on a 13 year old boy.

The Chief Constable ordered that this case was to be heard by the Stipendiary Magistrate, who was sitting at Tunstall Magistrates Court. However, when the accused' 5 name was called out in court, the Stipendiary Magistrate was informed that the case had already been dealt with at Longton Magistrates Court earlier that day.

Superintendent Edge the officer in charge of Longton Division, told the Stipendiary Magistrate, that he understood that the accused had been bailed to appear at the Longton Court at 10.am that day, but the case had been heard at 9.30. am. This was strictly against the Chief Constable's orders.

Mr. Bunn who was sitting in the court at the time, said' "I don't know what is going on, but I intend to find out," The Stipendiary Magistrate, replied, "I will leave it to the Chief Constable. I know he will be absolutely scrupulous, fair, and honest".

Both Mr. Bunn, and the Stipendiary Magistrate reported the matter to the Home Office, and Director of Public Prosecutions. Some weeks later the Attorney General ordered an investigation. This investigation was carried out by Lord Goddard, Lord of Appeal (later Lord Chief Justice), and Mr. W.C. Johnson, Chief Constable of Birmingham, (later Sir William C. Johnson, H.M. Inspector of Constabulary)

The investigating officers were ordered to find out why-

1.   The Chief Constable's ordered had been disobeyed.

2.   Why an indictable offence had been heard in the absence of any prosecution, police witnesses.

3.   Why the time of the court sitting had been held at 9.30.am., instead of 10.am the normal time.

The enquiry found that, Mr. Hawley, the Clerk to the Longton and Fenton Justices, both magistrates who tried the case, and Superintendent Edge, were all members of the Roman Catholic faith.

It would appear from the reports that the Rev. William Walsh, was informed by Father Whelan, that he had been charged with indecent assault. The Rev. Walsh then went to Mr. Hawley, who was not only Clerk to the Magistrates, but Father Walsh's solicitor, and personal friend. Father Walsh explained to Mr. Hawley what had happened to Father Whelan, that it would bring disgrace on the church, and asked if there was anyway it could be avoided. Mr. Hawley, then sent for Superintendent Edge, and demanded to see the police report about the case.

Heads were then put together, magistrates arranged, and a Special Court was held. Father Whelan was found guilty, bound over for twelve months, two people standing surety for him in the sum of £10. The out come of the enquiry was far reaching. Mr. Hawley, who had been the Justices' Clerk at Longton for 55 years, was forced to retire. The two magistrates who heard the case, were forced to resign, and Superintendent Edge was fortunate to be only severely reprimanded by the Watch Committee. The City then appointed one full time Magistrates' Clerk, at £1,250 salary per year, to deal with all the Lay Magistrates. The Lay Magistrates' Courts at Fenton and Tunstall were closed.

STOKE-ON-TRENT SPECIAL CONSTABULARY POLICE BAND *1945*.

The Chief Constable held discussions with the Committee in 1945, regarding the formation of a police band. Mr., Bunn informed them that there was a band in existence at that moment, which was known as the Hanley Home Guard Band. With the demise of the Home Guard, he had been approached by certain members, and asked to take over the band. He proposed to take over this band, that all the members of the band be placed on the reserve of the Special Constabulary, but would not be used for street patrol, etc.

Alderman Dale, said, "If we are going to have a police band, let us have a proper one. They have excellent police bands at Liverpool, and Birmingham".

Mr. Bunn replied that if the band was made up of Regular Officers, it would mean that the men would have to keep changing shifts.

Mr. Bunn won the argument, and the Stoke-on-Trent Special Constabulary Band came into being.

Constables and sergeants were granted an increase in pay which became effective from the 1st April, 1945. Constable's pay would start at £4. 10s.0d per week rising to £5. 17s.0 per week after 5 years.

GOVERNMENT INSPECTION *1945*.

His Majesty's Inspector of Constabulary visited and inspected the force in May, 1945. It was the first parade, and march passed that had been held since 1939, and consisted of 200 Regular Officers, 25 members of Auxiliary Divisions, which included 11 members of the Women's Auxiliary Police Corps.

CALL TO THE BAR *1945*.

The Chief Constable Mr. F.L. Bunn passed his Bar Examination, and became a barrister. He was presented with a wig, and gown by members of the Regular Force, Auxiliary Divisions, and Special Constabulary.

The Home Office, at the end of 1945, announced that all privately held arms, and ammunition, were to be handed in to the nearest police station before the 31 March, the following year. After that date, persons found in possession of such items would face prosecution.

The force received a total of 44 firearms, 764 rounds of ammunition, and 6 hand grenades.

Staffordshire Sentinel

Colonel Coke H.M.Inspector of Constabulary, inspecting men of the City Police in 1945

At the end of the year, the Police Auxiliary Messenger Service was disbanded. Three of these young men stayed on to become Boy Clerks, later joining the regular force.

RECOVERING FROM THE WAR YEARS *1946.*

1946 opened with the Country, and the City, along with it's police force, trying to recover after six years of war and austerity.

On the 21st March, 1946, the Lord Mayor Mr. Percy Williams, inaugurated the 999 Emergency Telephone System. This service covered the whole of the City, and Newcastle Borough. A few months later the Police Wireless System was updated, when it was changed over from MF (medium frequency), to VHF (very high frequency).

Residents of the Meir area of the City, were complaining at this time regarding the inadequate police cover they were receiving, and also about the police station being closed from 10.pm until 9.am the following morning.

Mr. Bunn replied that Meir had a population of about 12,000 people, which was equal to that of Congleton. It had been the intention of the Watch Committee to build a police station in the Meir area for some time, but this had been delayed due to the war. No purpose built police station was erected in the Meir, and the force operated from a converted council house in Weston Road until the mid 1960s.

FIRST RECRUITS FROM RYTON-ON-DUNSMORE *1946*.

In 1946 the Chief Constable Mr.F.L. Buun O.B.E., and the Chairman of the Watch Committee Alderman J.H. Dale, attended the first passing out parade of recruits from the No.4 District Police Training Centre at Ryton-on-Dunsmore, Warwickshire. Sergeant T. G. Froggatt, and Sergeant F. Shepheard of the City force were at the depot as instructors.

In 1948 No. 4 District Training Centre moved to Mill Meece, in Staffordshire and remained there unil the early sixties when it returned to Ryton.

Now that the war was over, and equipment seemed a little easier to obtain, the Watch Committee seemed to be spending more. Two typewriters were purchased, one costing £35. lOs.Od, and the other £29. lOs.Od, and the following year a Gestetner copier at the cost of £72 was added to the office equipment. The canteen at Hanley was also opened at this time, the cost of which to set up was £141.

CRIMES OF MURDER *1946*.

The post war crime wave seemed to arrive in the City almost as soon as the war in Europe was over, for two murders, and one attempted murder took place within the City in 1946.

The first of these took place in the Birches Head area of the City in July, when the lodger murdered the soldier son of the woman he was lodging with. The perpetrator of this crime was later executed. The second murder took place in the Burslem area, when a young wife was charged with the murder of her 71 year old husband.

The third crime took place in the Meir area, when a young son was charged with the attempted murder of his mother.

BRAVE CONSTABLE ARRESTS ARMED OFFENDER *1946.*

At 11.30.pm one night in September, 1946, Police Constable Frank Robins was patrolling his beat in the Hanford area of the City, when he noticed a light on in a cafe', which was closed. On closer examination of the property the officer noticed that one of the doors had been force, and on looking into the window he saw a soldier inside, who appeared to be carrying a rifle under his arm. The officer immediately telephoned for assistance from a local telephone box. He then asked a Mr. Frank Whitfield, who was waiting at a nearby bus stop to assist him. The constable gave Mr. Whitfield his truncheon, and instructed him to remain at the front of the premises, while he himself went to the rear of the cafe", where he entered the building via an open window.

The soldier on being discovered, struggled with the officer, and made as if to get the gun, but then attempted to run away, the officer then brought the prisoner to the ground in a rugby tackle. A further struggle then took place between the constable, and his prisoner. Mr. Whitfield on hearing the commotion ran to the rear of the premises, and then had to climb over a iron spiked gate to reach the officer, and assist him. Both men managed to subdue the prisoner, and handcuff him. The gun was late found to be loaded. The soldier, who came from Shoreham, Sussex, was 18 years of age, and was on the staff of the Officer Cadet Training Unit, stationed at Trentham. He was charged with shop breaking, theft of the shotgun, and 10 cartridges together with other property, also with using a gun to resist arrest.

He appeared before the Recorder Mr.E. Sachs, K.C., at the Stoke-on-Trent Quarter Sessions, where he was sent to Borstal for three years.

Both P.C. Robins, and Mr. Whitfield were commended by the Recorder.

CHIEF CONSTABLE'S ANNUAL REPORT *1946.*

In his report for the year 1946, the Chief Constable stated that the authorised strength of the regular force was 276, and that it was seriously depleted. This was not peculiar to this force, every force in the Country was suffering the same problems. He went on to say that the Men are resigning to take up better paid jobs in industry, and teaching. The starting pay of a constable was then £5.5s.0d (£5.25p) per week.

In the Chief Constable's report to the Inspector of Constabulary for 1946, it showed the following distribution of the authorised strength

Div	Station.	C.C.	Supt.	Ch Insp.	Insp.	Sgts.	Cons.	Total.
A	Hanley	1	2	1	4	10	64	82
	BirchesHead	-	-	-	-	I	10	11
B	Burslem	-	-	1	-	5	24	30
	Smallthorne	-	-	-	-	1	5	6
	Tunstall	-	-	-	1	3	18	22
	Goldenhill	-	-	-	-	1	5	6
C	Longton	-	-	1	-	5	32	38
	Fenton	-	-	-	1	3	17	21
D	Stoke	-	-	1	-	3	19	23
	Trentham	-	-	-		1	5	6
	Hartshill	-	-	-	-	1	5	6
	Traffic Department	-	-		-	1	24	25
	Total Strength	1	2	4	6	35	228	276

The total authorised strength for the 'B' Division in 1946, consisted of 1 Chief Inspector, 1 Inspector, 10 Sergeants, and 52 Constables Total 64. By comparison the strength 10 years later in 1956, was 1 Superintendent, 2 Inspectors, 13 Sergeants, and 73 Constables Total 89.

Mr. F. T. Tarry C.B.E., H.M.I. Inspecting City Police Women in 1947

GOVERNMENT INSPECTION 1947.

Mr. Tarry, C.B.E., H.M. Inspector of Constabulary inspected the force in 1947, and one of the things he asked the Watch Committee, was what provisions they were making for the housing of the policemen returning from H.M. Forces, and the new recruits to the service.

Members of the Watch Committee were able to tell the Inspector that they had plans to construct 47 houses on land throughout the City.

Twelve months later the H.M.I. was complaining about the slow progress the Watch Committee were making as regards to the provision of houses for police purposes.

The Watch Committee reported that they had asked the Housing Committee for 41 houses, but the Housing Committee would only allocate them 9 houses. We suppose the housing problem as it was just after the war, was such that the Housing Committee must have had a very difficult problem on their hands, and so it would be a little unfair to blame them.

Sgt. Kelly served from 1919 to 1959

SCHOOL CROSSING PATROLS 1947.

Mr. Harold Davies. M.P. for one of the City's constituencies wrote a letter to the Watch Committee, asking them to arrange for the supervision of school children crossing the High Street, Tunstall. When the Committee brought this request to the Chief Constable's attention, Mr. Bunn, replied, "We are doing everything possible, but I don't have the manpower to man every school crossing in the City. We are understaffed as it is".

The Watch Committee then said that Mr. Davies would be informed of the Chief Constable's statement.

Owing to the shortage of regular policemen at this time, the Home Office decided to retain members of the Police War Reserve, until the 31st December, 1948.

Inflation must have been with us at the end of the war, because the Watch Committee allowed extra money to the Chief Constable for cleaning materials, and the cost allowed for prisoner's meals increased from 1/- (5p) to 1/3d (7p) per day.

The Chief Constable's annual report for the year 1947, makes interesting reading. Mr. Burn stated that the Wireless Scheme, which also embraced the Newcastle-under-Lyme Borough Police, had proved most helpful, in the detection of crime, and in the connection with motoring offences and road accidents. The service was operational throughout the 24 hours.

At that time the police were also responsible for the Ambulance Service in the City, and during the year the ambulances had attended to 2,181 calls, of this number 339 were to road and street accidents. The remainder of the calls were to remove people from home to hospital. This is quite remarkable, when it is considered that the force only possessed two ambulances.

The authorised strength of the force on the 29th September, 1947, was made up as follows:-

P. C. Joseph S. Mayther
with cycle served from
1929 to 1959

P. C. A255 H. Stokes using one
of the City's Police Boxes

Staffordshire Police

Chief Constable   1

Superintendents   2

Chief Inspectors   4

Inspectors   6

Sergeants   35

Constables   228

* Police War Reserve   1 Constable

+ First Police Reserve   7

Regular Policewomen 8

Auxiliary Policewomen 3

The force had vacancies for 1 Superintendent, 1 Sergeant, and 31 Constables. 1 Sergeant, and 3 Constables were serving with the Control Commission in Germany at that time.

*   Men who were called up to serve in the police force during the war.

+   Retired policemen who were called back to the force during the war.

Women who were conscripted into the force during the war.

According to the Chief Constable's report for the year 1947, the force owned 35 pedal cycles, which were allocated to various stations.

This year was also to see the new garage accommodation, which the force had been waiting for since before the war, completed. The cost of the garage and equipment came to £1, 421.11s. 8d.

INCREASED ESTABLISHMENT *1948.*

The year 1948 opened with the Watch Committee being informed that the Home Office had decided that the authorised establishment of the force was to be increased by 62 men, bringing the total strength up to 330 men, plus 8 women. This was the final outcome of the debate that had taken place between the Home Office, and the Watch Committee in 1939, and had been put on hold due to the war. It was however, to be several more years before this number was finally achieved, due to the reluctance of men to join the police service after the war.

The authorised establishment stood at 338 and was made up as follows:-

Chief Constable	1
Superintendents	5
Chief Inspectors	2
Inspectors	12
Sergeants	41
Constables	269
Woman Sergeants	1
Women Constables	7

CITY AMBULANCE SERVICE 1948.

With effect from the 5th May, 1948, the City police ceased to be responsible for the emergency ambulance service in the City, and the two ambulances were handed over to the newly formed City Ambulance Service, which became operational on that day.

Sergeant Bennett became the first City police officer to attend the Police College, and attended the first course to be held there.

The Joint Branch Board of the Police Federation at this time requested that the men be issued with clothing lockers. 200 new lockers were purchased at a total cost of £600.

Mrs. Joyce Twiss

Sgt. Richard (Dick) Twiss served 1930 to 1962. He was the Police European Heavyweight Boxing Champion in the 1930's

CHANGE IN UNIFORM *1949.*

1949 was to see a slight change in the constables and sergeants uniform, when for the first time they were issued with open neck tunics, blue shirts, and black ties. These open neck tunics were only worn during the daytime, in summer months. The old closed neck tunics being retained for winter and night duty. It also meant that the senior officers in the force would in future be issued with white shirts, which up to that time, they had had to purchase themselves.

Constables and sergeants were also issued with raincoats, in addition to their capes. The total cost of issuing the raincoats to the force was £1,420.7s.4d.

The debate between the Watch Committee, and the Housing Committee, relating to the supply of houses to the force was still taking place. The Inspector of Constabulary wanted the problem solved as speedily as possible. The Housing Committee replied that they were only prepared to continue the present policy of allowing houses on council estates to be allocated to policemen.

1949, saw the opening of a dogs home for stray dogs in part of the old stable block at Longton Police Station. This home was manned by the R.S.P.C.A. and dealt with all the stray dogs, not only in the City, but the surrounding County police area as well.

On the transport side, two new horses were purchased at a total cost of £240.0s.0d, also twelve new pedal cycles at £12.6s.0d each.

The Chief Constables submitted a report from the Police Federation, to the Watch Committee, regarding the distribution of City Council notices by members of the force, which was referred to the General Purpose Committee.

The debate over the delivery of these notices went on for some considerable time. The General Purpose Committee wished the practice to continue, and placed on record the appreciation of the force in delivering these notices over a long period of years, and requested that the force should deliver them by car. The Watch Committee informed them that they must make alternative arrangements. This system of the police delivering council memos, although on a much reduced scale, was to continue until the amalgamation in 1968.

The police radio system was extended to embrace the City Fire Brigade by the end of 1949.

A new internal telephone system had been installed at the Headquarters by the G.P.O. at an annual rent of £63.3 s.0d.

The Chief Constable's Annual Report for 1949 shows that 130 pedal cycles were stolen within the city.

CHAPTER IX

BETTER TIMES *1950-1959*

RETIREMENT OF SUPERINTENDENT A.L. CLARKE, DEPUTY CHIEF CONSTABLE 1950.

Superintendent A.L. Clarke, the Deputy Chief Constable, retired from the force on the 4th January, 1950, after completing 30 years service. The vacancy for Deputy Chief Constable was filled by Superintendent L. Woodhouse, who took over the post on the 1st April, 1950. Mr. Woodhouse, had only been promoted to the rank of superintendent two months previous.

Mr. Harry Steele

His Majesty's Inspector of Constabulary inspecting C.I.D. Officers in 1950 L. to R. Chairman of the Watch Committee Mr. J. Hulme, Chief Constable Bunn O.B.E., His Majesty's Inspector and Det. Supt. P. F. Cooke. Parade L. to R. Harry Steel, Ray Ward, Bill Bunn, Jack Read, Ted Turner, Bill Cooper, Ivan Deeth, Dennis Billington, Frank Godfrey, Jim Allman, Tome Eaton, Fred Garrett, Jock Grant, Bill Tarpy.

FOOTBALL DUTIES *1951*.

At this time residents living in the streets adjoining the Stoke City Football Club, Victoria Ground, sent a petition to the City Council complaining of the nuisance caused on match days, by cars parked in the narrow streets surrounding the ground. This problem was never completely solved until after the Club moved to the new Britannia Ground in 1997.

Ken Hawkins

Taken on the 24th August 1950 the opening of Vale Park Football Ground. Left to right Det. Constable W. Tarpe, P.C. Jeff White, not known, Sgt Bert Poole.

The City force by this time had gained a considerable amount of experience in dealing with large numbers of football supporters, and the traffic problems, by having two Football Association team grounds within it's area. Stoke City Football Club, at the Victoria Ground, Stoke, and Port Vale Football Club, at the Vale Park Ground, Hamil Road, Burslem. It had previously had its ground at Hanley until 1950, where the Potteries Shopping Centre now stands.

The behaviour of some supporters must have changed considerably over recent years, because I am informed that in the early 1950s when Stoke played Arsenal with a crowd of over 30,000, they managed to police it with only 9 men, with very few problems. A big difference to the 1970-80s when it became necessary to parade 100 plus officers from all divisions of Staffordshire (after the amalgamation), to police match with even smaller crowds.

LONG SERVICE AND GOOD CONDUCT MEDALS *1951*.

At a meeting of the Watch Committee in July, 1951, the Town Clerk informed them that he had received notification from the Home Office, that the King had approved the issue of the Police Long Service and Good Conduct Medal. This was to be awarded to all members of the police force, who had completed 22 years service, and were recommended by the Chief Constable or Watch Committee.

The Chief Constable Mr. F.L. Bunn was one of the first recipients of this medal, along with the Deputy Chief Constable, three superintendents, two chief Inspectors, two inspectors, five sergeants, one woman sergeant, and nine constables.

Just prior to the issue of the Police Long Service and Good Conduct Medal, the Chief Constable was awarded the King's Police and Fire Brigade Medal, for distinguished service.

Twelve new pedal cycles were purchased in 1951 at a cost of £12. 14s. 0d each. Twelve months later a further nine pedal cycles were purchased, this time they cost £15. 11s. 9d each. Three new typewriters, and a Kodak specialist printer were acquired, the cost of the latter was £53. 5s. 0d, and was for use in the C.I.D. Office.

A petrol pump was installed at Headquarters Garage around this time. This necessitated the Chief Constable issuing to himself a petroleum licence, for the Chief Constable was also Inspector under the Petroleum Act. This appointment was later transferred to the Chief Fire Officer.

It was also at this time that the Force received a memorandum from the Board of Trade saying that there was a shortage of utility cloth to manufacture police uniforms. The war had been over for five years, but the country was still suffering from shortages.

Unlined serge jackets were to be issued to the policemen, as they would be cooler to wear in the summer months (shirt sleeve order had not yet arrived).

REORGANISATION OF THE FORCE 1952.

In 1952, alterations were made in the distribution and organisation of the Force. The D Division based at Copeland Street, Stoke, was downgraded to a sub division, and became a part of A Division. The new structure of the Force was as follows:

Headquarters Department (Hanley) which included the Detective Department numbered 18 men.

"A" Division (Hanley)   121 men which included 11 men at Birches Head Station.

"A" Sub Division (Stoke)   45 men, this number included 1 sergeant and 7 men at
                             Hartshill and a similar number at Trentham.

"B" Division (Burslem)   43 men including 6 men at Smallthorne.

"B" Sub Division (Tunstall) 33 men including 6 men at Goldenhill,

"C" Division (Longton)   46 men including 8 men at the Meir Station.

"C" Sub Division (Fenton)   24 men.

Superintendents were in charge of divisional stations at Hanley, Burslem, and Longton, with a Chief Inspector in charge at Stoke, and Inspectors in charge at Fenton and Tunstall.

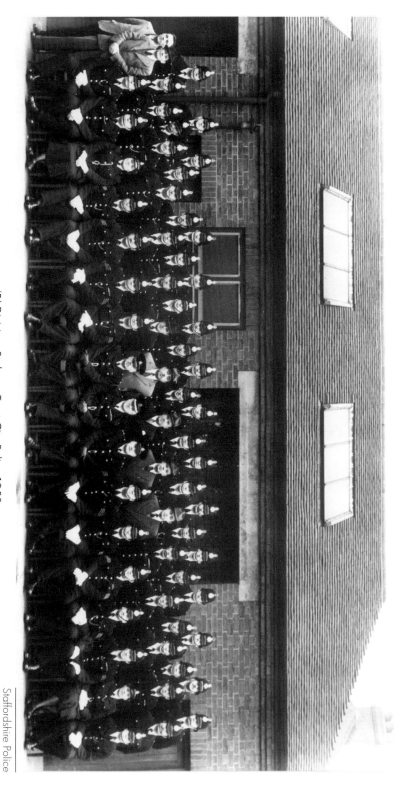

'B' Division Stoke-on-Trent City Police 1953

Staffordshire Police

Front Row: P.C. J. Hill, P.C. Hall, W.P.C. Blood, Sgt's Matthews, Wild, Reg Bird, E. Daws, Insp. H. Williams, Supt. W. Hobson, Insp. S. Baker, Sgt's H. Lewis, ????, Andow, W. Mack, Mallibone, W.P.C. M. Nixon, P.C. R. Jones.

Second Row: W. Hall, C. Johnson plainclothes, P.C.'s G. Bennett, ????, W. Lodge, A. Bateman, ????, Langton, Ken Hawkins, Geo. Curran, D.Sgt's W. Tarpie, Jock Grant, Howard Bird, P.C.'s J. Leese, W. Nixon, D. Jones, R. Swan, L. Beech.

Third Row: ????, D. Johnson, G. White, A. Cope, S. Bentley, B. Francis, M. Baddley, Ken Powell, T. Bailey, H. Ralphs, Jim Deaville, T. Taylor, ????.

Back Row: D. Kelsall, S. Brotherton, ????, D. Cheney, ????, Ted Teal, M. Mitchell, ????, A. Beaumont, ????, ????, E. Wainwright, ????, ????, J. Bould.

184

His Majesty's Inspector of Constabulary Sir Charles Martin inspecting officers of the City force in 1953. The parade was held at Finney Gardens Sports ground, Bucknall.

1953.

The beginning of the year saw a few more changes in the running of the force. Four additional civilian clerks were employed, along with seven civilian cleaners, who were employed at the larger police stations in the City. Prior to this, the policemen themselves had been responsible for keeping the stations clean and tidy. This task was usually carried out by the most junior members of the force.

The Deputy Chief Constable Superintendent L. Woodhouse, saw his allowance increased from £75 to £90 per annum. This was additional to his normal pay as Superintendent.

On the last day of March, 1953, Superintendent W. Hobson retired from the Force, he had served for over 33 years. He was replaced as Head of the B Division by Superintendent W.E. Blanchard.

CORONATION OF QUEEN ELIZABETH 11 1953.

In June, 1953, a contingent of 4 sergeants, 13 constables, 1 woman constable, and 1 special inspector, under the command of Inspector I. Sergeant, were sent to assist the Metropolitan Police, on the occasion of the Coronation of Her Majesty Queen Elizabeth II.

The Watch Committee decided that all the costs for the loan of these officers would be waived, in view of the special circumstances.

Approximately twelve months later, every police force in the United Kingdom was represented at the Royal Review held in London, before Her Majesty the Queen. The Stoke-on-Trent contingent under the command of Det. Superintendent C. Cartwright, consisted of 2 sergeants, 27 constables, 1 woman constable, and 1 special constable.

Police Constable Edmondson with his horse Silver won the First Prize at the Cheshire County Show, for the best turned out horse and rider. The prize was £15, which the officer was allowed to keep. Some months later the force was to spend £70 on new saddlery for the Mounted Section.

At the close of the year 1953, the Chief Constable was able to report that the Force had a detection rate of 65%, which was above the national average. He also reported the following numbers of fatalities due to road traffic accidents in the City over the previous four years:-

1950	28
1951	30
1952	28
1953	19

Staffordshire Police

P.C. Edmondson B.E.M., with his horse Silver

CHANGE OF POLICE DUTIES 1954.

In 1954, the Watch Committee received a communication from the Home Office, asking them to look into the extraneous duties that were performed by members of the force, and suggesting that some of these duties be carried out by other corporation departments.

After studying the document, it was decided that the following duties would no longer be performed by members of the police force.

The Chief Constable would cease to be responsible for the issue of licenses under the Petroleum Act. This would in future become the responsibility of the Chief Fire Officer. The police would no longer be responsible for enforcing the Shops Act, or serving Rates Summonses. The issue of licenses under the Diseases of Animals Act, was to be dealt with by the Town Hall staff. The inspection of registers, and the issuing of licenses under the Pharmacy and Poisons Act, and the Licensing Act, were to remain to be administered by the Force, along with the inspection and licensing of Hackney Carriages. The changing of the unilateral No Waiting signs, then situated in the town centres, and main roads of the City, were to

Staffordshire Police

Stoke-on-Trent Police Mounted Officers 1954 - 55 with The Chief Constable Mr. F. L. Bunn O.B.E., K.P.M., L.L.B. Lord Mayor Mrs. Annie Barker.
L. to R: P.C. Edmondson on Silver, P.C. Graham Wilkes on Jumbo, P.C. Dennis Sheldon on Nigger.

Staffordshire Police

Photograph of B Division taken between 1st April 1953 and 31st May 1955. All the men, with one exception, are wearing their winter uniform, of closed neck tunics and black gloves. Left to right sitting: Supt. W. Blanchard, Chief Constable F. L. Bunn, Inspector Geo. Curran, W.P.C. M. Nixon

remain the responsibility of the police, until the Highways Department took over the duty, a short time later.

The Home Office announced that with effect from December, 1954, that the officer holding the appointment of Deputy Chief Constable, should hold the substantive rank of Chief Superintendent. Mr. Woodhouse was promoted accordingly. He also received an increase in his allowance bringing it up to £105 per annum, in addition to his normal pay as a Chief Superintendent.

The Chief Constable informed the Watch Committee, that he thought it desirable to increase the strength of the force by 75 men. The Watch Committee agreed to this number, but unfortunately the Home Office did not, and would only agree to the addition of 38 men. This was a complete reversal of the situation that existed in 1939.

Junior boy clerks were still being appointed at the end of 1954. Most of these boys stayed on to join the regular force, when they came of age.

RETIREMENT OF CHIEF CONSTABLE MR. F.L. BUNN., O.B.E., K.P.M. 1955.

1955, was to see a change in leadership of the force, when Mr. F. L. Bunn., O.B.E., K.P.M., intimated his intention to retire on the 31st May, 1955. He was 65 years of age, and had held the office of Chief Constable of the City for the last 19 years. In total he had completed 42 years service in various police forces throughout the country. The Watch Committee paid tribute to the excellent service he had rendered to the City during the last 19 years.

A successor to Mr. Bunn had to be found, and the following five applicants were selected for interview:-

Superintendent	S.W.O. FERGUSON	of Leeds City Police.
Chief inspector	O. QUINTON	of Birmingham City Police.
Chief Constable	R.A.M. NOBLE. G.M.	of Burnley Borough Police.
Chief Constable	W. REES	of Stockport Borough Police.
Assistant Chief Constable	W.E. WATSON	Newcastle-upon-Tyne Police.

The man chosen to head the force was Mr. W. E. Watson and although it was not known at the time, history was to make Mr. Watson the last holder of this office.

The Chief Constable was to be paid a salary of £1,750 per annum, rising to £1,900 after three years service. He would also be supplied with a house, and a car for official use, plus £30 per annum uniform allowance.

Mr. Watson took up his duties on the 1st June, 1955.

POLICE CADETS 1955.

Within a few months of taking up office, the new Chief Constable issued his report on the state of the force to the Watch Committee. One of his requests was that more motor vehicles should be obtained. Another change he wished to bring to the force was the employment of Police Cadets. He suggested that six cadets be employed, and that this number would include the two Junior Boy Clerks, then employed at Hanley. There was to be one cadet at Stoke, Longton, and Burslem stations, and three at Hanley.

On the 1st November, 1955, Ian Alfred Grant, Brian Reginald Jones, Charles Philip Rushton, and Peter Sims, became the first Police Cadets to serve in the City.

Policing The Potteries

At the Chief Constables suggestion, the Watch Committee refused to make any application for deferment of National Service on behalf of any cadets. Two years later the Home Office informed all Chief Constables, that in future all Police Cadets would be exempt from National Service.

Within twelve months the establishment of the cadets was raised to 10.

During 1955, the Home Office Wireless Engineer visited the City, and carried out some tests, these tests were successful, and this was to be the deciding factor in the closing down of the wireless station at Birches Head. This meant that the new traffic and communications centre would be built at Headquarters, so for the first time all the communications would be under one roof It had been Mr. Bunn who had first instigated this idea, and ordered the wireless tests, but it was is successor who was to finalise the system.

Chief Constable Watson

The new Communications Department was built by Frank Hancock Construction (Stoke) Ltd., and the total cost came to £12, 674.

It was at this time that police officers were to see a reduction in their working hours from 48 to 44 hours per week.

HONOUR FOR DEPUTY CHIEF CONSTABLE L. WOODHOUSE 1955.

Chief Superintendent L. Woodhouse the Deputy Chief Constable was awarded the M.B.E. (Member of the British Empire) in the Queens Birthday Honours.

The Chief Constable informed members of the Watch Committee that he would require assistance from adjoining forces for the Royal Visit by the Queen in November, 1955. He was told to make what ever arrangements he thought necessary. A number of men were loaned from the Coventry City force. Twelve months later, a number of City officers travelled to Worcester, to assist in that City when the Queen visited there.

1956.

The year 1956 opened with the Watch Committee receiving a letter from the Rev. V. G. Ashton, Vicar of Penkhull, asking the Committee to remove the concrete police box, that then stood in the Square, and re-site it by the Grove Nursery School. The Committee refused this request, due to the cost involved.

The Chief Constable at this time attended a weeks course at the Civil Defence College, at Sunningdale, Surrey.

Mr. Watson asked the Council to erect new and larger warning signs, on all the approach roads to the low railway bridge in Glebe Street, Stoke. This was carried out, and at a later date, flashing red lights, and a klaxon were fitted, but this was to no avail, because high vehicles, and double decker buses continued to collide with it. This bridge was to remain a problem until the new road was built.

Five new pedal cycles were purchased about this time. They were fitted with a double crossbar, and three speed gears, and cost £18.6s.0d each. A number of new typewriters were also purchased.

A garage was constructed at Longton Police Station, to house the newly acquired station van, the cost was £120. 0s 0d.

One of the Police Cadets was commended for good work he carried out in a recent case.

The Joint Branch Board of the Police Federation, asked the Watch Committee to invoke Section 52, of the Police Regulations, 1955. This regulation stated that all officers must retire on the completion of 30 years service. The Chief Constable's reply was that, "While I sympathise with the men's request. I do not think this is the opportune time".

The Watch Committee suggested that the Federation submit the request in three years time.

POLICE DOGS 1956.

The force was offered the gift of a German Shepherd dog, which they accepted. This dog along with one purchased from the Metropolitan Police, were to be the first two dogs used by the City force for a number of years. The first two handlers, along with their dogs were trained at the Metropolitan Police Dog School.

Staffordshire Police

P.C. Broadhurst with his dog Prince

P.C. Ray Jones with Glen

Staffordshire Police

RETIREMENTS OF SENIOR OFFICERS 1957.

A number of senior officers retired from the force in July, 1957, they were:-

Superintendent	W. E. BLANCHARD	30	years service
Superintendent	C. CARTWRIGHT	33	years service
Inspector	C. H. HOLLAND	31	years service

The following officers were promoted:-

Chief Inspector	H. RIMMER	to Superintendent
Inspector	F. SHEPHERD	to Superintendent
Inspector	A. E. FAWCETT	to Chief Inspector
Sergeant (24)	E. E. DAW	to Inspector
Sergeant (7)	F. T. H. LAPPER	to Inspector
Sergeant (10)	G. H. STEELE	to Inspector

FURTHER CHANGES IN THE FORCE 1958.

1958 saw slight changes in the uniform worn by the sergeants and constables. They were issued with a new light weight barathea uniform, the jacket being belted. They were also issued with bush type shirts, containing two breast pockets, and epaulets, which were to be worn in the summer, when jackets were discarded.

One member of the Watch Committee asked the Chief Constable, "Do you think the belt will help the more corpulent members of the force". The Chief Constable replied, "Yes".

The Chairman of the Watch Committee, Alderman J. E. Hulme, suggested that the practice of bringing constables before the Committee, to confirm their appointments after they had completed their two years probation, should be abolished. He went on to say that he thought it utterly useless, and nothing but a waste of time. He thought the Chief Constable was best suited to inform probationers if their appointment was confirmed or not.

This system of men appearing before members of the Watch Committee, to hear if their appointment to the force was to be approved or not, went back to the Hanley Borough days, before the start of the force in 1910. Older serving officer have said that it could be quite an ordeal.

RETIREMENTS OF LONG SERVING OFFICERS 1958.

On the 6th October, 1958, Police constable Patrick Kelly retired from the force for the second time. P.C. Kelly was 67 years of age, and had served for a total of 45 years. He came from County Roscommon, Ireland, and joined the Stoke-on-Trent force in 1912, and retired in 1938, after completing 26 years service. He was called back to the force again in 1939 as a War Reserve, and went on to serve a further 19 years service.

A further retirement from the force took place, this time when Superintendent P. F. Cooke retired. He had completed 33 years service. Mr. Cooke was replaced by Chief Inspector A. E. Fawcett, who was promoted to Superintendent a few days later.

The Chief Constable at this time received a letter of thanks, from a Mr. A. J. Wakefield, of Aldbourne, Wiltshire, in which he thanked the City Police, and praised their efficiency, after they had found his stolen car in the City.

It was agreed, that in future members of the Cadet Force, would be sent to the Birmingham City Police Cadet Training Camp, which was situated in the Elan Valley.

HONOUR TO THE CHIEF CONSTABLE MR. W.E. WATSON 1958.

The Chief Constable Mr. W.E. Watson was awarded the Queen's Police Medal in the Queen's Birthday Honours for 1958. The medal was presented to him by Colonel H. Wallace-Copeland, J.P., Lord Lieutenant of Staffordshire.

In his annual report for 1958, the Chief Constable referred to the alarming increase in indictable offences which had increased by 26% in the last twelve months. Mr. Watson said, "We are just following the national trend. Our figures compare with that of other Industrial Midland Cities. The detection rate is 56.6%.

There had been 21 fatal road accidents reported, which was an increase of 8 on the previous year.

191 persons had been arrested for drunkenness, 187 men and 4 women.

The total amount spent on uniform for the entire force in 1958 came to £7,776. 13s.0d, this included the purchase of 203 caps and helmets complete with badges.

The authorised strength of the force at the end of the year 1958 was 394, which was made up as follows:-

Chief Constable   1

Chief Superintendent 1 also acts as Deputy Chief Constable

Superintendents   4

Chief Inspectors   2

Inspectors   13

Sergeants   48

Constables   299

Woman Sergeants   1

Woman Constables   15

Cadets   10

In addition to this number, there were 210 male members of the Special Constabulary, and 15 Woman Special Constables.

There were 22 vacancies for Regular Officers, this included 8 Women Constables.

1959.

At the beginning of 1959, the Chief Constable made a request to the Watch Committee that 10 pedal cycles be replaced with new ones. Councillor Evans, asked Mr. Watson if he really wanted cycles, and said, "I think nothing looks more ridiculous than a policeman wearing his cape and helmet, and riding a cycle. I think a policeman on a cycle went out with the horse and cart. If we are short of transport, we should purchase more cars." The Chief Constable replied, "I can see a considerable diminution in their use, but I would not like to see them go altogether, they afford a silent approach, and are most useful in policing some of the more residential areas of the City." The cycles were purchased.

Shirt Sleeve Order 1959.

In the summer of 1959, the public were to see for the first time. policemen and policewomen, walking the streets of the City, in their shirt sleeves, without their tunics on. They had been allowed to remove them due to the heat wave. Members of the Force had been allowed to remove their serge tunics as early as 1955, due to the exceptional hot summer that year, providing that a white cotton coat, then used for traffic duty, was worn. This coat would have been necessary to hide the officers braces, that had to be worn at that time to support his trousers.

The Chief Constable made reference to the number of resignations he was receiving due to the low pay. Some from officers with over 10 years service. It did, however, not take one member of the force, quite that long to decide that a policeman's life was not for him, for he resigned after only 19 days service. One member of the Force submitted a request to the Watch Committee, seeking their permission to be allowed to take up part time outside employment. The Committee said that this request could not be approved.

The Home Office sent out a circular at this time to all the police forces in the Country, suggesting that members of the Force should be paid by cheque each month. The Local Branch of the Police Federation, rejected this idea. They wished to keep the weekly pay, and be paid cash. They did, however, suggest that they be paid on Thursday, instead of Friday, and that they receive their annual two weekly holiday pay in advance. The Committee agreed to their request.

A number of additional civilian staffs were taken on at this time, they were as follows:-

4 Shorthand typists, 1 Male janitor, 1 Garage mechanic, 1 Garage handyman, 5 Part time cleaners

The Chief Constable ordered that with effect from 1st October, 1959, all conference points between divisions, in addition to those with the Staffordshire County Police, would cease. These conference points had been with the Force since the very early days.

On the 19th November, 1959, the new police station in Tunstall was opened by the Lord Mayor Harold Clowes. The station houses 33 men under the command of Inspector George Curran.

CHAPTER X.

THE FINAL YEARS 1960-1968.

INCREASE IN STRENGTH 1960.

1960 was to see the strength of the Force, increased by the addition of 20 men, and the adjustment of certain ranks. For the first time in the history of the Force, it was to have an officer with the rank of Assistant Chief Constable. The Watch Committee decided not to advertise the vacancy, but to appoint Chief Superintendent L. Woodhouse, the officer in charge of Hanley Division, who also held the post of Deputy Chief Constable, to fill the vacancy.

The authorised strength of the Force now stood at 414, made up as follows:-

Chief Constable	1
Assistant Chief Constable	1
Superintendents	5
Chief Inspectors	2
Inspectors	13
Sergeants	51
Constables	315
Woman Inspector	1
Women Sergeants	2
Women Constables	13
Cadets	10

There were 32 vacancies for 1 woman sergeant, one woman constable, 27 constables, and 3 cadets.

GOVERNMENT INSPECTION *1960.*

Her Majesty's Inspector of Constabulary, Sir. Charles Martin, inspected the Force, on the 25th March, 1960, at Finney Gardens Sports Ground. He was accompanied by the Lord Mayor Alderman Capewell, Councillor Gordon Dale Chairman of the Watch Committee, the Chief Constable, and Assistant Chief Constable.

There were on the parade 330 members of the Force, plus the Special Constabulary Band.

One of the police horse, Silver had to be destroyed due to becoming lame, at this time. This resulted in the Watch Committee debating as to whether it was necessary to keep the Mounted Section. The Chief Constable suggested that it was still desirable to keep a small number of horses. The Committee then decided that a replacement for Silver should be obtained.

Detective Superintendent Rimmer, who was in charge of the C.I.D. retired from the Force after 31 years service. He was replaced by Detective Inspector H. Steele, who was promoted to superintendent.

The Force acquired another dog at this time, when P. C. Gallacher returned from the Metropolitan Police Dog Training School, with Police Dog Rene.

A man who was to become well known in later years, for his expertise on the snooker table, joined the Force at this time. He was Ray Reardon, officially known to the Force as P.C. A 184 Reardon. He later left the Force and became a professional snooker player.

On the 1st April, 1960, the G.P.O. installed Telex-equipment in the Forces Information Room. This meant that the Force was now in direct dialling contact with the majority of police forces in the country.

P.C. Ray Reardon,
later to become a professional snooker
player and T.V. commentator

Ray Reardon

FURTHER CHANGES TO THE FORCE *1961.*

The Chief Constable at the beginning of the years 1961 asked the Watch Committee to purchase a number of musical instruments for the Special Constabulary Band. They were later to receive £100 from the Council for this purpose.

The Force spent a total of £14,550 on improvements to the police stations at Longton, Fenton, and Stoke, during this year.

By 1961, senior officers in the Force were being issued with fixed collars on their white shirts, while at the same time sergeants and constables still had to make do with the detachable, on their blue uniform shirts, the policewomen were also issued with detachable collars on their white shirts.

A number of new items of equipment were purchased for the C.I.D. ,at this time. The force spent more than £100 on the purchase of it's first photocopier, for use in the Detective Office, £70 was also spent of a new fingerprint camera, and a further £46.1 ls.7d on the purchase of a dictation machine for use in the C.I.D Office.

REMEMBRANCE PARADE *1961.*

Seven members of the Force, were sent to represent the City at the Remembrance Day Parade at the Cenotaph in London. They consisted of 1 Sergeant, 2 Constables, 1 Woman Constable, and 2 members of the Special Constabulary. They were under the command of Inspector T. Froggatt, who had himself served with the Royal Air Force during the war.

The Chief Constable reported that there was more crime committed in the City in the month of December, 1961, than there had been in the whole of 1936. On a lighter note, Mr. Watson was able to say, that Stoke-on-Trent was far below the National average, when it came to drunkenness, with only 0.69% of the population transgressing, while the National average for all large towns and cities was 1.93% of the population.

By the end of the year the strength of the Force was to be increased by the addition of 1 Inspector, 5 Sergeants, and 16 Constables. Twelve months later the Force was to be increased again by I Chief Inspector, 1 Inspector, 5 Sergeants, and 15 Constables.

NEW POLICE HEADQUARTERS *1962.*

At the beginning of 1962, the Home Office finally gave approval for the building of the new Police Headquarters on land in Bethesda Street, Hanley. The building operation commenced on the 2nd July, the same year, the main contractors being Messrs G.Percy Trentham Limited.

Due to the amount of mining subsidence in the area, the Police Headquarters featured some rather unique building techniques. The whole building contains a number of built in jacking facilities, which were used to overcome the result of movement taking place in the ground due to mining subsidence, this means that the building can then be lifted back into it's correct position.

A small increase in the number of civilian staff took place at this time, and the following advert appeared in the local newspapers:- "Stoke-on-Trent City Police, has vacancies for the following:- 1 Female Clerk typist, 2 Male Clerks, and 1 Male Semi-Skilled Garage Attendant" Obviously before the days of the Sex Discrimination Act.

Staffordshire Police

The main entrance to the old Police Headquarters and A. Division, the C.I.D. were housed in the building on the left of the photograph.

Fighting Organised Crime 1962.

Mr. Watson informed the Watch Committee that he had consulted with the Chief Constable of Staffordshire, and that the two of them had decided to propose a scheme for the establishment of a Crime Squad, to cover the City and County area of North Staffordshire. Six months later the Home Office gave it's approval.

The Crime Squad began operating on New Years Day the following year. Based at the C.I.D. Office in Tunstall Police Station. In addition to covering the City police area, they also operated in the three surrounding County Divisions, namely Newcastle, Leek, and Stone. They were supplied with a Morris Isis car, provided by the County.

The Chief Constable issued an order on the 17th December, 1962, cancelling all weekly rest days on Fridays, until further notice.

Staffordshire Police

'B' Division Stoke-on-Trent City Police 1963
L/ to R. Front Row: W.P.C. W. Salt, Sgt's Wainwright, F. Seabridge, E Mallibone, W. Holdcroft, Insp. Geo Curran, Supt. I. Sargeant. Insp. R. Ward, Sgt's H. Lewis, Ken Hawkins, J. Bowen, Jim Deville, W.P.C. Jill Weaver.
Second Row: P.C's R. Grocott, Ted Hall, Sam Clowes, D.C. D. Jones, H. Bird, D.Sgt. Tarpie, Pat Molloy, Ted Teal, A. Cope, P.C's R. Brayford, Bloor, A. Bateman.
Third Row: W. Carr, ????, Fred Hughes, Carl Thwaite, Ron Large, Alan Howell, P.C. Sinker, P.C.Ashby, Jim Chadwick, D. Leese, Ken Powell, W. Edwards.
Back Row: J. Gibson, G. White, H. Ralphs, A. Beaumont, ????, D. Bird, D. Kelsall, P. Baker, L. Pointon, A. Brereton, B. Hampton, H. Mitchell, C. Barsted.

SAD YEAR *1963*.

It was to be a sad year for the City police, when two of it's members, were found to have committed criminal offences. One officer who had broken into a number of properties when on night duty, was sentenced to a term of imprisonment.

The second office who had stolen from the found property store, and was awaiting trail at the Staffordshire Assizes, committed suicide.

The Local Branch of the Police Federation, suggested that all the members of the Force be given influenza:a injections. This was agreed to by the Watch Committee, who decided to pay all costs involved.

With effect from July, 1963, all members of the Force were to be paid monthly by cheque.

It was at this time that the Watch Committee decided to build a new house for the Chief Constable. The house was to be built outside the City boundary at Hanchurch, and replaced the house that had been purchased for the previous Chief Constable in 1936. The cost of the construction of the house was £8,271 .9s.7d., plus £200 to layout the garden.

At the close of the year, 1963, the Force had three police dogs, and two horses on it's strength.

OPENING OF THE NEW HEADQUARTERS, HANLEY, 1964.

1964, was to see the long awaited opening of the New Police Headquarters, which was officially opened on the 3rd July, 1964, by the Lord Mayor Alderman Joseph Edward Hulme. J.P., Chairman of the Watch Committee.

This must have been quite a momentous occasion, for the Lord Mayor, who had himself served with the City Police as a War Reserve Constable, during the Second World War.

Staffordshire Police

Opening of the new City Police Headquaters 3rd July 1964
L. to R. Mr. J. T. Manuel, H.M. Inspector of Constabulary,
Alderman Gordon Dale, J.P. Vice Chairman of the Watch Committee, Mr. W.E.Watson,
Chief Constable, Sir. Edward Dodd, Chief Inspector of Constabulary,
Alderman Joseph Hulme, J.P. Lord Mayor.

Policing The Potteries

The personnel employed in the station, must have seen a vast improvement in their working conditions at the new station. This station replaced one that had been is use for 79 years, and was originally built as part of the Town Hall, and was meant to house the former Hanley Borough force. From time to time additions were made to the building, but this station had never been quite adequate for the job.

The total cost of the building, plus fixtures and fittings, and new office, and garage equipment was close on £332,000.

One member of the staff who found it difficult to settle into his new abode, was Tito the station cat, who kept returning to the old station (perhaps there were not enough mice in the new station). Most mornings, a cadet was send round to the old station to retrieve Tito, and return him to his new abode.

With effect from the 1st July, 1964, members of the Force saw a reduction of two hours in their working week. Their hours were reduced from 44 hours to 42 hours per week. To compensate for this 3 sergeants, and 5 constables were added to the strength.

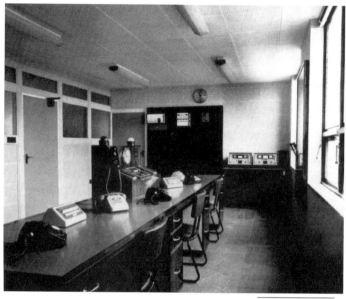

Stafforshire Police

The information room in the new Headquarters opened in 1964. By modern day standards this would look archaic

The Information room in the old City Police Headquarters situated in the Town Hall.

Stafforshire Police

Staffordshire Police

The new City Police Headquaters 3rd July 1964

Three of the Cities concrete police boxes, which had stood for just over 30 years, were demolished, when the City Surveyor reported that they were in a dangerous condition. The three boxes concerned were situated at 1. Stoke Road, near to it's junction with Station Road, 2. St. Thomas Place, Penkhull, 3. Etruria Road, near it's junction with Victoria Street.

The following three senior officers retired from the Force at this time, they were:-

Superintendent	A. RUDDICK	35 years service
Inspector	A.J. GUEST	34 years service
Inspector	Geo. CURRAN	33 years service

POLICE ROAD ACCIDENTS.

In 1964, one of the Police Motorcyclists attached to the City C Division, was involved in a road traffic accident in the Trentham Road, Longton, sustaining slight injuries. In the following year, the divisional personnel carrier of C Division was involved in a road accident, and a number of officers travelling in the vehicle at the time, sustained serious injuries, and the vehicle itself had to be replaced.

Mr. Tony Lea

Photograph taken in 1964
l. to R. Cadet Tony Lea, W.P.C. Janet Brindley, P.C. Eric Hargreaves, Sgt. Sid Ludwig. Tony Lea
ritired from the force with the rank of Inspector.

1965.

The lst April, 1965, saw the demise of the North Staffordshire Crime Squad after only two years service, which was replaced by the Regional Crime Squad. This Crime Squad would cover the whole of the No.4 Police District.

On the same day that the Regional Crime Squad was established, the City was enlarged by the addition of Badderley Green. This area had hitherto been police by the Leek Division of the Staffordshire County Police, but would in future be supervised by members of the Cities A and B Division. There would in future be no resident beat policemen stationed at Badderley Green, and the police station there would be closed. It was decided, however, to install a telephone outside the station, which was a direct line to police headquarters.

The Force purchased two additional light weight Velocette motorcycles, to assist with the policing of the new area.

The established strength of the Force was increased by the addition of 36 officers, this was made up of 4 Inspectors, 2 Sergeants, and 30 Constables, added to this was an increase in the number of Cadets by 10.

The Chief Constable was complaining at this time of the inadequate telephone system at the Longton Police Station. The Watch Committee then decided that new equipment must be installed.

It was at the same meeting of the Watch Committee, that they were informed by the Town Clerk, that they had over spent by £11,183 - 7s, - 1d., on the building and new equipment of the new headquarters. The Force also purchased five new Raleigh police pedal cycles at a total cost of £139. 17s.6d.

In his Annual Report for 1965, the Chief Constable had the satisfaction of reporting to the citizens of Stoke-on-Trent, that he was able to report a decrease in crime, this was the first time in 10 years, that he had been able to do this.

RETIREMENT OF ASSISTANT CHIEF CONSTABLE MR.L. WOODHOUSE 1965.

The 31st December, 1965, not only saw the end of a year, but the retirement of the Forces long serving officer, Mr. L. Woodhouse, M.B.E., the Assistant Chief Constable. He had completed 43 years service.

Mr. Woodhouse, was asked to appear before members of the Watch Committee, who expressed their appreciation of the loyal and efficient service he had rendered to the Force, during his long association with it.

Mr. Woodhouse had given the statutory three months notice of his intention to retire, thus enabling the Watch Committee to advertise for a replacement.

There were 23 applicants for the post, and out of this a short list of 7 were selected for interview, but only 6 attended. They were:-

Superintendent	F. SHEPHERD	Stoke-on-Trent City Police
Detective Superintendent	H. STEELE	Stoke-on-Trent City Police
Chief Superintendent	R. HAZELL	Staffordshire County Police
Chief Superintendent	AGNEW	Birmingham City Police

| Chief Superintendent | W.F. CALVELEY | Liverpool City Police |
| Chief Superintendent | R.M. McCROREY, M.B.E. | Dep Chief Constable of Bolton Borough |

The successful applicant was 49 year old Detective Superintendent H. Steele of the City Force, who had originally joined the Force in 1936.

FURTHER PROMOTIONS AND CHANGES WITHIN THE FORCE 1966.

To coincide with the retirement of the Assistant Chief Constable, and the subsequent promotion of Detective Superintendent H. Steele to fill the vacancy, a number of other promotions were to take place. Chief Inspector G.T. Froggett was promoted to Superintendent, and placed in charge of the C.I.D.; Inspector R.G. Marriott was promoted to Chief Inspector, and Sergeant T. Parton was promoted to Inspector. All these promotions were to take affect from the 1st January, 1966.

The Chief Constable held a review into the working and strength of the Force, and came up with the following. An increase in strength of the Force, and the employment of more civilian staff, including the appointment of Traffic Wardens. The first 13 Traffic Wardens were appointed in October, 1966, to be followed by 7 more in the December of the same year, bringing the total to 20.

The Force also appointed a Prosecution Solicitor.

Five new Raleigh cycles were purchased by the Force, at a total cost of £125, they were to be the last pedal cycles purchased by the Force. Cycles had been used by the Force since it's establishment, and at one time it had possessed as many as 35. These cycles had served their riders well, and had proved a most efficient way of policing the large housing estates, and suburban areas of the City.

The house at 133 Weston Road, Meir, which had been used as a police station was vacated, and returned to the City Council Housing Department. At the same time a piece of land at the junction of Dividy Road, and Arbourfield Road, Bentilee was purchased by the Council, on which it was proposed to build a new police station for that area. This, however, never materialised.

A new automatic telephone switch board was installed at Burslem Police Station at this time, which the Chief Constable said was a further stage in making the system fully automatic.

Two of the Forces senior officers retired at the end of 1966. Superintendent A.E. Fawcett, who had served for 37 years, and Detective Inspector Godfrey, who had completed 31 years service.

THE FINAL YEAR 1967.

The final year of the Force opened with the appointment of more civilian staff, when three additional short hand typists, and two clerk typists were appointed.

Information was received by the Chief Constable, at this time from the Home Office, requesting that he review his arrangement for the provision of firearms to his officers. Mr. Watson informed the Watch Committee of this, and that due to the pending amalgamation with the County force, there was a need for uniformity with them. The Chief Constable was instructed to make arrangements accordingly.

One of the last officers to be appointed to the City police was Police Constable 90 Jeffrey Virgo, who was appointed on the 15th September, 1967. Jeffrey Virgo retired from the force in 1999 as a detective superintendent, stationed at Police Headquarters, Stafford.

P.C. 301 John Dean

The last officers to be appointed to the Force prior to the amalgamation were all appointed on the 1st December, 1967, they were :- Keith John Boulton, of Hanford, Stoke-on-Trent; Thomas Paul Hammersley-Fenton, of Weston Coyney, Staffs; Geoffrey Lightfoot, of Tean, Staffs; David Wall, of Cotes Heath, Staffs; and Carol Ann Mountford, of Chell Heath, the last female officer to be appointed. The final inspection of the City force was carried out on the 25th October, 1967, by Mr. R.G. Fenwick, H.M. Inspector of Constabulary, for the Midland Area.

At the last meeting of the Watch Committee, which was held in October, 1967, an order for the purchase of 26 B.M.C. 100 motor cars, at a cost of £650 each, plus a number of personal radio sets, was placed. The vehicles were needed to provide adequate cover for the Unit Beat Police System, that was to come into operation with the forthcoming amalgamation.

P.C. 301 John Dean

The Chief Constable requested, and was granted permission to be allowed to purchase his house at Hanchurch, which was only three years old, from the Watch Committee.

In the final year the authorised establishment of the City force stood at 527. The establishment and distribution of the Force was as follows:-

Chief Constable	1
Assistant Chief Constable	1
Superintendents	5
Chief Inspectors	4
Inspectors	20
Sergeants	70
Constables	384
Woman Inspector	1
Woman Sergeants	2
Woman Constables	19
Cadets	20

Added to this were 20 Traffic Wardens, 4 male, and 24 female clerical staff, 4 male technical staff and 34 domestic staffs, both full time and part time.

At midnight on 31st December, 1967, the Stoke-on-Trent City Police, ceased to exist as a separate entity, when it amalgamated with the Staffordshire County Police. However, it's name was carried on for a number of years, in the name of the combined force, Staffordshire County and Stoke-on-Trent Constabulary, until this was changed in 1974 to Staffordshire Police.

For the past 57 years the members of the Force had served the City to the best of their ability.

Mr. Harry Steele

This photograph was taken of senior officers of the City Force at a farewell dinner
held in the later months of 1967.
L. to R. Standing: Ch. Insp. W. Holdcroft, Insp. F Seabridge, Insp. J. Reader, Insp. D. Billington,
Insp. D. Clarke, Ch. Insp. D. Johnson, Special Constabulary Commandant, Insp. T. Parton,
Ch. Insp. Fred Lapper, Insp. B. Mallibon, Insp. K. Kingsbury, Ch. Insp. Earn Daws,
Insp. Owen Gilder, Supt. J. W. Moss, W/Insp. Gladis Stokes, Insp. J. Clarke, Insp. Johnson,
Det. Supt. T. Froggett, Supt. F. Walley, Supt. I. Sargeant, Ch. Insp. R. Marriott, Insp. W. King,
Insp. R. Ward.
L to R. Sitting: Mr. H. Steele A.C.C., Mr. Edwin Holloway Lord Mayor,
Mr. W. E. Watson Chief Constable, Mr. W. Hulme Chairman of the Watch Committee.

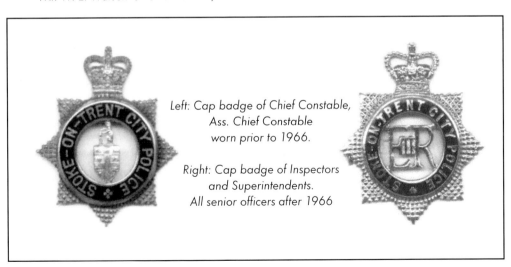

Left: Cap badge of Chief Constable,
Ass. Chief Constable
worn prior to 1966.

Right: Cap badge of Inspectors
and Superintendents.
All senior officers after 1966

Left: Kings Crown helmet badge taken into use in 1936 When the Coxcomb patten helmet was adopted

Right: Queens Crown helmet badge in use from 1953 - 1964

Bothe these badges also exist in black for night duty

APPENDIX 1

PUNISHMENTS FOR BREACHES OF DISCIPLINE

1913   P.C. 15 John Quinn   Disobeying an order of a Superior Officer, and using improper language to same. Fined 1Os on each charge, and to remove stations at own cost.

1913   P.C. 25 Herbert Bird   Improperly working his beat. Fined Is

1914   P.C. 153 Daniel Donovan   Failing to call P.C. Kelly for 5.45 am parade. Cautioned.

1914   P.C. Ralph Madew   Assault on P.C. McGuire. Fined 2/6d

1915   P.C. 171 Jabez Vodrey   Failing to deal with a telegram from the military in an official manor.   Fined   2/6d

1917   P.C. 21 Charles Bloxham   Drunk on duty. To remove from Hanley to Fenton at own expense.

1917   P.C. 16 Percy Cooper   Found on licensed premises (Dolphin Inn), Crown Bank out of hours, and obstructing Sergeant Jones. Appeared before Stipendiary Magistrates, case dismissed. Removed to Longton.

1918   P.C. Fred Hall   Conduct prejudicial to the discipline of the police force, found on licensed premises (Dolphin Inn) Crown Bank, Hanley, at 1.22.am prohibited hours. To remove to Burslem at own expense.

1921   PC 182 Ernest Barlow   Contravening the Chief Constable's orders, leaving the division when off duty during the Coal Strike without first obtaining the Chief Constable's permission. Fined 2/6-.

1922   P.C. 54 Patrick Maguire   Entering while under the influence of drink a ladies lavatory. Dismissed after conviction for drunkenness.

1922   P.C. 142 Arthur Hill   Wilfully damaging a book issued to him by the Police Authority. Fined   5/-

1922   P.C. 40 Horace Wilson   Borrowing money from a publican. Ordered to resign

1922   P.C. 24 Thomas Hammersley Neglect of duty in not taking sufficient action on receipt of a telephone call. Fine £5.

1922   P.C. 20 Alec Alcock   Found with a married woman under suspicious circumstances. Dismissed.

1923   P.C. 166 Fred Blockson   Associating with a married woman, and assaulting her husband. Ordered to resign forthwith.

1924   P.C. 125 Thomas Thorndyke Failing to report finding a stray dog. Fined 10/-

1924   P.C. 149 David Bettany   Neglect of duty allowing a prisoner to escape. To pay £3.2s.4d cost of bringing prisoner back from Durham.

1924   PC 32 Isaac Matthews   Being insubordinate in words and actions to a sergeant in refusing an order to change shifts. Fined £2.

1925   P.C. 23 Frank Weaver Absent from drill parade. Fined 2/6-.

1926   P.C. 178 Frank Morrey   Absent without leave. Fined £1.10s.0d, and to revert to uniform duty. He resigned from the force 1 month later.

1928   P.C. 133 John Liddorn   Being in receipt of rent allowance and failing to pay same to agent. Dismissed.

1929   Inspector Patrick William McEvoy   Consuming intoxicating liqueur out of hours. Convicted by Newcastle County Justices Fined 18/-. Reprimanded by Watch Committee.

The following members of the Force appeared before the Chief Constable for failing to parade for duty when the Air Raid Alarm was given on 5th March, 1916, P.C. 23 Bettany, P.C. 8 Hughes, P.C. 5 Harrison, P.C. 9 Pincham. All were fined 1/-.

THE WATCH COMMITTEE

Relations between the Chief Constable, and members of the Watch Committee, were not always as cordial as they might have been. How much of this was due to the Town Clerk, the late Mr. E. B. Sharpley, is left to conjecture.

It is said of Mr. Sharpley, that he ruled over Stoke-on-Trent like some feudal Baron, treating all officers of the City Council including the Chief Constable, as subordinate to him. This seems to have been the situation since Mr. Sharpley was appointed Town Clerk in 1910. Mr. Bunn, however, was not going to be dictated to like his predecessor.

Matters finally came to a head in 1942, when a vehicle belonging to the City Council, and on loan to the A.R.P. Department, was involved in a minor road traffic accident. The Chief Constable arranged for a summons to be taken out against the driver. This had been unheard of in the City before, council employees having always thought themselves immune from prosecution for offences committed while on duty as council employees. The Lord Mayor, and members of both the Civil Defence, and Watch Committee, all asked the Chief Constable to withdraw the summons, but he was adamant, saying, "I have made the decision, and will stand by it."

The case was heard several days later before the magistrates court, two of whom were City Councillors, who without hearing the evidence for the prosecution dismissed the case. The Chief Constable then lodged an appeal, which was successful. This appeal was to cost the City Council £1,200.

A few days later a Special Meeting of the Watch Committee took place, at which the Chief Constable was then told, that he must not in future take any case to the Appeal Court without first obtaining their permission. Mr. Bunn replied, "I will not be dictated to by this Committee. If I am in the right, I will appeal, even if it costs this Council £12,000" Alderman Dale then replied, "I hope this Committee will be able to take the necessary action to stop the Chief Constable appealing like this, and wasting ratepayer's money".

Some months later Mr. Bunn was in conflict with the Watch Committee, and Town Clerk again, when it was stated that he, Mr. Bunn, had engaged a private solicitor Mr. H. Grindley to prosecute in a case of attempted murder. The Town Clerk said that the Chief Constable should use the City Council's Solicitors Department. This was a resolution which had been passed in 1910. Mr. Sharpley then said that the Chief Constable had acted in direct contradiction of the Watch Committee's instructions, which state that all court cases, both Local, and Assizes should be dealt with by the City Council's own solicitors. Alderman Dale, then asked, "Why does the Chief Constable not have any confidence in the Town Clerk?, and that this feud between the two of you, is not in any ones interest" Mr. Bunn replied, "There are plenty of reasons why I do not see eye to eye with the Town Clerk, but I do not intend to go into them there." All he would say was that he had served in seven police forces, and had been Chief Constable of three, and he had never met with any obstructions, or interference in carrying out his duties, until he came to Stoke-on-Trent.

The Watch Committee then passed a resolution, stating that in all proceedings, other than those in which the Corporation was concerned, the Chief Constable would use the Town Clerk's Department's solicitors.

Mr. Bunn replied, "I don't think you can give me orders like that, and I intend to get it clarified by the Home Office".

Some weeks later the Watch Committee were informed by a communication from the Home Office, that they were not able to instruct the Chief Constable on how to do his duty. He was not employed by the Council, and their jurisdiction over him was very limited.

No doubt Mr. Bunn laughed heartily to himself, when he read the evening newspaper one night in 1943, to see the headlines, that the Town Clerk of Stoke-on-Trent, Mr. Edward Burges Sharpley, appeared before the City Stipendiary Magistrate, to answer 38 summonses for contravening the motor fuel regulations.Giving evidence for the prosecution was Mr. Joseph Reader, an inspector for the Ministry of Fuel and Power. There is no doubt that this Mr. Reader, was the same Joseph Reader, who retired from the police force in 1935, with the rank of Chief Inspector.

Mr. Sharpley was found guilty, and fined £300, plus £52. 10s.0d costs. His days as Town Clerk, were not to last much longer.

After Mr. Sharpley's forced retirement, and the appointment of a new Town Clerk, the Chief Constable's relationship with his Watch Committee, would appear to have been much improved.

Staffordshire Police

Members of the City Police accompany the Lord Mayor John Arthur Dale on his annual church parade, in November 1936. The Mersy combined helmet worn by Sgt. Willis on the right had only just been taken into use. The man on the Lord Mayor's left in wig and gown is the Town Clerk Mr. E. B. Sharpley. The mace bearer is Mr. Edwards.

Under the Police Act, of 1964, the constitution, and powers of the Watch Committee were changed. Prior to this date, and since the formation of the Watch Committees, under the Municipal Corporations Act, of 1835, these committees had consisted solely of elected members of the council, and this committee had been responsible for overseeing the administration of the local City or Borough police force. This was now to change, under the 1964 Act a third of the members of these Watch Committees, were to be local magistrates. The Watch Committee, would also lose the power to appoint, promote, and discipline the members of the force, which was transferred to the Chief Constable. This new act gave to the City and Borough Chief Constables, the same authority over their force, that County Chief Constables had enjoyed since 1856.

Members of the Stoke-on-Trent Watch Committee, along with representatives of Watch Committees from all parts of England and Wales, objected to these new proposals. They informed the Home Office, that there main bone of contention was the appointment of magistrates to sit on the Committee, and that they felt that as elected representatives of the ratepayers, it was their job to administer the police force, and the duty of magistrates to administer justice.

The last few meeting of the ¯Watch Committee, were taken up with discussions dealing with the pending amalgamation.

The three Members of Parliament representing the City, along with a number of other M.Ps, most of them representing the Lancashire Boroughs, had a meeting with the Home Secretary. They informed him of the objections, that most of these Cities and Boroughs had to these amalgamations. They did not like being placed under County control, and said that local policing should remain locally controlled. The Home Secretary, however, was adamant, these amalgamations would go ahead, either voluntary or compulsory.

A short time after this meeting, the Watch Committee received a communication from the Home Office, asking them, if the City Watch Committee was willing to enter into a voluntary amalgamation with the Staffordshire County force. The Watch Committee replied, that they were not satisfied with the proposals, but due to the pressure from the Home Office, they had no alternative but to reluctantly agree to this amalgamation.

The last meeting of the Stoke-on-Trent Watch Committee took place on the 24th October, 1967.

THE SPECIAL CONSTABULARY.

The first reference to Special Constables in Stoke-on-Trent was in March, 1912, when the Chief Constable issued a general order requesting Divisional Officers, to obtain names of suitable persons, who would be prepared to be sworn in, and serve as Special Constables, should the need arise.

It would appear though from records, that the first use of Special Constables in the Potteries, after the Federation, was during the First World War, and by 1916 the were 375 men servicing as Special Constables.

Each Special Constable was issued with an armlet, truncheon, whistle and chain. The reason for the armlet, was a means of identifying them as Special Constables, as they did not wear a uniform, only their own civilian clothing. However, in October, 1916, the Watch Committee agreed to issue each Special Constable with a bowler hat, to which was to be attached a helmet badge. They also ordered 42 dozen Special Constable's lapel badges, at 9s6d per dozen.

The Potteries Electrical Traction Co. Ltd., agreed to allow all Special Constables on duty, or proceeding to or from duty, to travel on all the companies tramcars free of charge.

City Museum

Men of the Stoke-on-Trent Special Constabulary. Photograph taken during the second world war. Note all the men are carrying their gas masks.

Authors Collection

This photograph of the Longton or C Division of the Special Constabulary was taken in 1917, note the helmet badge fixed to their bower hats.

In May, 1917, members of the Special Constabulary, asked the Watch Committee to issue them with boots, and overcoats. The Watch Committee refused to issue them with either, but did agree to pay a boot allowance of £1 per year, payable every six months. That, however, was not to end the matter, for members of the Special Constabulary insisted on their overcoats. All the senior officers of the Special Constabulary, were invited to a meeting of the Watch Committee, and then asked to reconsider their application, with a view to withdrawing same, due the heavy cost involved. They were informed that to issue each man with an overcoat, it would cost over £1,000, but they stood firm, and each man got his overcoat. In addition each man was issued with a uniform cap to replace the bowler hats (that were then in use.)

During the war years, on the last Sunday in May, members of the Special Constabulary paraded at the Cricket Ground in Stoke, where they were inspected by the Chief Constable. Special tramcars were arranged, and departed from various parts of the County Borough to convey men to the inspection. At this time the Special Constables were performing one hours drill per week, and one four hour night duty per week.

Special Constable Charlesworth was commended by the Chief Constable at this time, for the report he submitted, and the way which he dealt with a street accident in Burslem.

With the Armistice in 1918, the Special Constabulary, was allowed to stand down. At the final parade held in Hanley, the Chief Constable thanked all the members for their help, and saying that the Special Constabulary had acted most successfully. The Mayor then addressed the men, and thanked them for their services to their Country, and County Borough.

It was decided that the demobilised Special Constables, should be allowed to retain their uniform overcoats, caps, and Police staffs. The whistles and chains would be returned to stores.

The Chief Constable then suggested that all the members of the Special Constabulary who were serving, allow their names to remain on the Register. He would assure them that they would only be called upon in case of emergency.

In January, 1926, the Chief Constable reported that he had received from the

Mrs. Ackerley

Two members of the City's Special Constabulary.
Photograph taken about 1955

Mr. H. Steele

Stoke-on-Trent Special Constabulary Band. Photograph taken just prior to amalgamation in 1968.
Mr. H. Steel Assistant Chief Constable sitting third from left,
Mr. W. E. Watson Chief Constable sitting centre.

Home Office, regulations which referred to the enrolment, and service of Special Constables, and which the Home Office suggested should be adopted by all Police Authorities.

During the General Strike of 1926, 1,302 men served in the Special Constabulary.

From the end of the First World War, the City seemed to keep a nucleus of Special Constabulary, who would attend lectures during the winter months, but did not appear to do much else. By 1938, most of the members appeared to have resigned, no doubt due to boredom.

In 1937, one member of the Special Constabulary was commended by the Chief Constable, and the City Justices for the arrest of a thief

With the gathering of the clouds of the Second World War, the Chief Constable had inserted in the local evening newspaper, in 1938, a notice requesting men over military age, and with no other commitments, in the event of war, to enrol in the Special Constabulary.

Lectures were then started for the Specials in the latter part of 1938, and a short time later, the Chief Constable prepared an instruction book, to be issued to each member of the Special Constabulary. Shortly after the outbreak of the war, Mr. Bunn reported to the Watch Committee, that there were 350 Special Constables who would require uniform. The Committee were informed that it would cost in the region of £1,400, but they would get half of the cost back from the Central Government.

Each Special would be issued with a jacket, trousers, cap, and greatcoat. They would also receive Is (5 p) per week boot allowance.

One member of the Watch Committee said, "I am glad to see that the men are to be issued with uniform. I served as a Special during the last war, and all I got was a hat."

Alderman Dale then said to the Chief Constable, "For pity sake, relieve these Specials of their metal helmets." Mr. Bunn, replied that he intended to do so, as soon as he could obtain caps.

A Mobile Section of Special Constabulary was also formed at the beginning of the war, when the more affluent members of the Special Constabulary, who possessed motor cars, agreed to use them in case of am emergency. They would be allowed petrol for doing so.

In 1940, Mr. J.W. Moxon, a local solicitor, who at the time held the rank of inspector in the Special Constabulary, gave a talk, about the work of the Special Constabulary, to members of the Hanley Rotary Club. Mr. Moxon said, that the help and training we get from the Regular force, is second to none, but then went on to criticise the Council, by going on to say they had not been issued with uniform until six to eight months after the war had been declared. He also went onto say, that when the City Council houses it's Mobile Police in disused stables, what chance did the Specials stand. (Mr. Moxon was no doubt referring to the fact that the Chief Constable had been trying to get the City Council to build new garage accommodation since 1932.

In 1942, Special Constables were each issued with waterproof coats, and leggings, but at the same time were informed by the Chief Constable, that there would be no general issue of uniform. Items would only be replaced as and when required.

By 1944 there were over 800 men serving as Special Constables in the City. Due to the large number serving, and the easing of the war situation, the hours of duty each man was expected to perform was reduced from 24 to 16 hours per month. This meant that each man would perform one 4 hour tour of duty per week, instead of one 6 hours tour of duty each week. The Chief Constable report that most members of the Special Constabulary, did more hours duty than was expected of them.

Most of the senior officers serving with the Special Constabulary, seemed to be men of influence, or industrialists in the City. The Commandant was Mr. G.W. Huntbach, the City Coroner, while two of the Special Superintendents were Mr. J.W. Moxon, a local solicitor, and Mr. Warwick Savage, an industrialist, while other industrialists served as inspectors.

In November, 1945, the Home Office released all Special Constables from their obligations. The Chief Constable reported that resignations were pouring in by the day. Mr. Bunn said he wished to place on record, the deep appreciation in the way the Specials had carried out their duty during these troubled time.

The maximum strength of the Special Constabulary was about 800 men in 1943 - 44, in 1946 the strength stood at 501, and 12 months later only 303 men were serving.

Policing The Potteries

During the war, members of the Cities "D" Division, both Regulars and Specials collected over £400 for War Charities.

In 1950 the Force spent £2,297.8s.0d on new uniform for the Special Constabulary.

Mr. Moxon the Commandant of the Cities " A " Division of the Special Constabulary, was complaining of the inadequate accommodation, and facilities at Headquarters for the Special Constabulary, in a report sent to the Watch Committee. Mr. Moxon later had an interview with members of the Committee to discuss the report. This discussion resulted in the new accommodation being built over the existing garage and workshops. The Specials finally moved into their new accommodation in 1953. It had cost £5,000, with an additional £122.4s.0d spent on office equipment, and furniture.

The Chief Constable, Mr. W.F. Watson was to reorganize the Special Constabulary in 1958, it was placed under one Commandant, instead of three. This was to make their administration, training, and operations easier to organize.

There were at that time 210 men, and 16 women servicing, and this number seems to have been reduced still fitriher by the time the amalgamation took place.

Special Superintendent R. Hammersley retired from Force in 1960, due to ill health. He had served for just over 20 years. The following year the Commandant Mr. R.W. Moxon retired, after serving in the Specials for 35 years. He had originally offered his services during the General Strike of 1926. The Watch Committee recorded their appreciation of the excellent service rendered by Mr. Moxon during his long association with the Special Constabulary. He was replaced by Special Superintendent E. Strafford.

The Chief Constable in his Annual Report for 1958, stated that the Special Constabulary had carried out regular patrol duties in each division throughout the year. They had also provided considerable assistance at Municipal elections, Royal visits, and at both football grounds in the City. They had also been tremendous help on the six Saturday afternoon before Christmas, when they manned all the important traffic intersections, and pedestrian crossings in the City. This greatly facilitated the movement of traffic, and prevented congestion.

The uniform worn by members of the City's Special Constabulary, since they were first issued with it in 1940, consisted of an open neck tunic with white shirt, and black tie. However, the white shirts were never supplied, the men had to purchase their own. It was as late as 1966, before blue uniform shirts were worn, and issued to members of the Special Constabulary.

Special Constables off duty lapel badge.
Left; First World War issue.
Right: Second World War issue.

MOTOR TRANSPORT

When the Force was first formed in 1910, mechanically propelled motor vehicles were a rarity, and the Force did not possess any. What vehicles they did possess were all horse drawn, and consisted of one prison van and one ambulance, which had previously belonged to the former Hanley Borough force. At the time of the Federation the County police kept three horses at Longton Police Station, and a similar number at Burslem. These horses were later moved to Hanley, and the total number kept by the Force was reduced. Due to the large area of the new County Borough, the Chief Constable was supplied with a horse and trap to enable him to supervise the area more efficiently. This remained the Chief Constable's means of transport until 1920, when the horse and trap were sold for 24 guineas (£24.20p), and a Wolseley car purchased. This car remained in use until 1928, when it was taken in part exchange for an Austin Burnham saloon car.

The first motor vehicle owned by the Force would appear to have been a prison van, which was taken into use on the 20th April, 1914. A general order issued by the Chief Constable on that date stated:- Police Constable 70 Jones will drive, and be responsible for the up keep of the van. On the return journey from Stafford, he will give to P.C. 98 Wilson, who will act as escort, whatever instructions he can as regards to driving the van.

By 1915, the Force also possessed two motor ambulances, one of which had been presented to the people of Longton by the Potter's Union. In 1919, Mrs. Billington, of Porthill, presented a new ambulance to the people of Stoke-on-Trent. Less than twelve months later this ambulance was involved in a road traffic accident, which was to cost the council £750 to repair. The driver later appeared before the Watch Committee, and was told, that in future he must exercise caution, even in a life or death situation. In 1922 a new ambulance was purchased for the Longton and Fenton area to replace the older one. It was in 1928, that the Watch Committee decided that a car would be purchased for the use of the C.I.D. One member of the Watch Committee complained about the extravagant cost of such a vehicle. Alderman Sproston replied, "Don't worry, it won't be a Rolls Royce" to which the Town Clerk replied, "I hope it won't be an Austin Seven either, one can imagine what two of our big policemen would look like in that". This car remained in use until 1933, when it was replaced by a more modern one. By 1930, the Force possessed the following motor vehicles: 1 Chief Constable's Staff car, 1 C.I.D. car, 4 motor cycle combination, which were distributed 1 each to the following stations Hanley, Stoke, Burslem, and Longton, plus one prison van, and 2 ambulances.

1931 saw the start of the Road Patrol Department (later renamed the Road Traffic Department) when the City was allowed to purchase five new motor cycle combinations for this work, and for which they would receive a grant from Central Government to cover all costs. Police Constable Downing was promoted to sergeant, and placed in charge of this new department. These motor cycle combinations were stationed at the following stations: Hanley, Burslem, Stoke, Longton, and Trentham. There was also a solo motor cycle stationed at Hanley, but this was not used for road patrol work.

The City was divided into three sections, East, West, and Trentham. The dividing line was the main road running from the City boundary at Meir, to the City boundary at Goldenhill. The Trentham section was from the City boundary at Strongford Bridge, on the A34, to the boundary with Newcasfle, and up to Longton Park.

One man will be sufficient for the day time patrol, but two men will be utilised for duty after dark.

Each man will be supplied with breeches, leggings, and white mackintosh sleeves..

In 1933, four of the motor cycle combinations were replaced by four Jowett cars for road patrol duty.

1936 saw the Road Patrol Department equipped with some new vehicles. The Jowett Patrol cars were replaced by three 10 h.p. Hillman cars, and two 10 h.p. Ford cars. The Chief Constable's staff car was overhauled at a cost of £60, and £695. 14s.0d was spent on the purchase of a new ambulance, and the last motor cycle combination, which had been stationed at Trentham was disposed of

The Watch Committee agreed to the suggestion by the Chief Constable, that the cars used for traffic patrol, would in future, be replaced every year, and an agreement was signed with the Newcastle Motor Co. Ltd, to this effect.

Five cameras were also purchased at £1 each. These cameras were to be carried on each of the Traffic cars.

Mr. Neil Bradley

Photograph of what was probably the forces first mechanically propelled vehicle, the prison van, which was purchased in 1914

During the war years, the force possessed 17 motor vehicles, but this number included 8 solo motor cycles which were loaned to the force under the War Emergency Regulations. Owing to the War situation, it became virtually impossible to obtain new vehicles, and it became a case of make do and mend. Then all police forces in the country were asked to reduce their petrol consumption, if at all possible.

At the end of hostilities in Europe in 1945, the force found itself in possession of a number of motor vehicles that were in need of replacement. Although the war was over, it was to take the Chief Constable two years before he was able to replace all his worn out vehicles.

The eight motor cycles which had been on loan to the force, for the duration of the war had all been disposed of by the end of 1946. A new ambulance was purchased at this time. At the same time the force spent £71.1 5s.0d on repairs to the force's prison van. The Chief Constable requested permission to purchase a new Humber car for his personal use, to replace his Vauxhall. The Watch Committee agreed to his request, but told him to retain the old car for general police use. The cost of the Humber was £964.9s.5d.

In June, 1947, the force was in possession of the following vehicles:- 5 Traffic Patrol cars, 2 C.I.D. cars, 1 Chief Constable's Staff car, 1 Police Prison van, and 2 Ambulances. By the end of the year, 6 Austin 10 h.p. cars, which had been in use since the beginning of the war were finally replaced by 6 Wolseley cars, at a total cost of £1,567. 18s.7d., plus the old cars in part exchange.

Staffordshire Police

Left to right: Sgt R. Webster and P.C's T. Hewitt, F. Garrett and K. Lodey seen here with six of the first Velocette motor cycles taken into use by the city force in 1956

The force had not stopped spending, because in 1949, it spent £728. 1Os.Od on a new Prison van. In 1951 the Chief Constable contacted the Home Office, with a view to increasing the number of Traffic cars that were allowed to the City force, and which the force was allowed to claim for under the Road Fund Grant. Mr. Bunn wanted to increase the Traffic cars from five to seven, but his request was unsuccessfull. In the following year two of the Wolseley cars were replaced by two Austin A70's. The last order placed by Mr. Bunn when he was Chief Constable, was for the purchase of six Ford Zephyr cars, and a new Bedford Prison van. These were to replace existing vehicles. With the arrival of Mr. Watson, as the new Chief Constable, the number of vehicles owned by the force, was to be increased. The Chief Constable requested the purchase of three utility vehicles, one to be stationed at each of the following stations: Burslem, Longton, and Stoke. In 1956, a new Humber Super Snipe car was purchased for the Chief Constable's personal use. This year was also to see the arrival of the first two Triumph TR2 cars for Road Traffic Patrol, this number was later increased to four. These cars became a familiar sight on the Cities roads, and were to remain in use by the City force up to the time of the amalgamation 12 years later, when they had been updated to Triumph TR4As.

In 1957, the C.I.D. were the proud owners of a 2.4 Jaguar, which was issued to replace their Ford Zephyr, which had been in use for the previous two years.

Staffordshire Police

The yard and garage accommodation at the old City Police headquarters in the early 1960's. One of the forces Triumph TR2 traffic cars is visible, a number of police special roadmaster cycles with double crossbars can also be seen.

One of the forces Triumph TR2 traffic cars fitted with public address systems being used to appeal for information relating to the murder of a fifteen year old school girl which took place in the city in September 1962. The car is seen parked outside the old Stoke City Football ground.

The Chief Constable now decided that all drivers in the City force, would in future attend a five week specialised driving course at the Staffordshire County Police Driving School. This was to cost £37.10s.Od per man, per course.

In 1957 the force also took into use six Velocette motor cycles, after the Chief Constable said that he proposed to introduce motor cycle patrols into the City. This number was later added to, and in the following year four motor scooters were obtained for the use of the Policewomen's Department, 1 each being issued to the following stations: Burslem, Hanley, Stoke, and Longton.

The three divisional utility vehicles were replaced in 1959, by three Thames vans, each van was capable of carrying 12 passengers. A further van was added in the following year.

On the 7th December, 1960, a Portable Electronic Traffic Analyser (or Radar) as it was known to the general public was first used on the road of the City. From that date until the 31st December, of that year, 110 speeding offences were detected. The total for the previous year was 327 speeding offences detected without the use of radar. The total number of offences detected in 1961, the first full year that radar was in use, was 1,317. The use of radar in the City was well publicized. On all the main roads entering the City,

Mr. G. Hubert

A smart looking P.C. Gerry Herbert photographed with two local children and one of the city's Triumph traffic patrol cars in the Penkhull area of the city on a winters morning in 1965.

Triumph TR3 Sports Cars, pictured in Hanley in 1956, were the pride and joy of the old Stoke-on-Trent City Police Traffic Department.

were placed large signs, which read "City of Stoke-on-Trent, Police Radar Speed Checks operate in this City".

A circular was received from the Home Office in 1965, suggesting that two-tone horns be adopted as audible warning systems by all police forces. The City force was to purchase 15 sets, at a total cost of £157. 10s.0d. These two tone horns were to be fixed to the forces Traffic and Patrol cars, blue flashing lights were also fitted to the cars and divisional vans.

1965 was to see the purchase of three additional saloon cars, these cars were to be used as Crime Cars, and one was to be issued to each division. Four small Standard vans were also taken into use at the same time, these vans were for the use of the C.I.D., and were to be issued to the following stations: Hanley, Stoke, Burslern, and Longton.

In 1967, the year of the amalgamation, the C.I.D. alone had the use of seven motor vehicles, that was the exact number of vehicles that the force possessed 20 years earlier.

At the time of the amalgamation on the 31st December, 1967, the force was in possession of a total of 44 motor vehicles.

THE POLICE WOMEN

People of the Potteries were to see uniformed Policewomen on their streets, for the first time in 1921. For in that year Miss Lily Broadhead, and Miss Gertrude Nellie Cowley were appointed to the City force.

The advert for policewomen, which was placed in the National newspapers, read as follows:- The applicant must be over 25 years of age, and under 28 years of age, 5ft 7 ins or more in height, of good education, and physically fit.

The records show that Miss Broadhead was 5 ft 8 ins in height, and 30 years of age, and had previously served with the Women Police Patrol, London for 2 years. She was to serve until 1952, when she retired from the force with the rank of sergeant. Miss Cowley was 31 years of age on appointment, and 5ft 7 ins in height, she had also served with the London police since 1918, then with the Walsall Borough Police force. She resigned from the force on the 24th December, 1924 in order to marry Police Constable Alfred Henry Rye.

Exactly one month later Miss.Cowley's replacement was appointed to the force, she was Miss Majorie Della Andrews. Records show that Miss Andrews was 26 years of age on appointment, and 5ft 8ins in height. Unlike the other two women, she had no previous police experience. Woman Police Constable Andrews resigned from the force on the 31st January, 1937. She was to be replaced by Miss Gwendoline Harvey. Miss Harvey was to transfer to the Leicester City Police in 1944, with the rank of sergeant. Only two years after their introduction, the Home Office was writing to all police forces in the country, asking for economies in police administration. They suggested that all forces that employ women police patrols, should dispense with them to save money. The Watch Committee, however, stated that the women police patrol appointed by this Committee would be retained.

Staffordshire Police

W.P.C. Lily Broadhead appointed to the force in 1921 retired in 1952 with the rank of sergeant

City Policewomen both regular and auxiliary parade outside Stoke Railway Station during the 1935-45 war. L. to R. not known, Miss Harvey, Jenny Bird, Sgt. Lil Broadhead, not known, Rose Longmore, Margaret Nixon, not known. Rose Longmore was the daughter of Chief Constable Bunn.

In his annual report for 1927, the Chief Constable made reference to the Policewomen's Department, in that the two policewomen were used to patrol the parks and town centres. They had escorted 10 women to prison, and taken 25 girls to a place of detention that year. He thought that two policewomen was enough for his requirements, and had no plans to employ more.

In 1930 the Chief Constable reported that Woman Police Constable Broadhead had made 20 arrests in that year, mostly for shoplifting.

The number of policewomen employed in the City was to remain at two, until 1941, when the Home Office requested that all Chief Constables, relieve manpower with women power, as far as possible. Mr. Bunn, said, "Whatever could be done, would be done." The force was however, having difficulty recruiting enough W.A.P.C.s. The Chief Constable had the following notice published in the local evening newspaper. City of Stoke-on-Trent Police, Women's Auxiliary Police Corps. Applications are invited for appointment as members of the above corps. Applicants must be between 18 and 40 years of age, not less than 5ft 4 ins in height, and physically fit. Motor driving, Shorthand writing, and Office experience, will be considered an advantage. Pay £2.7s.0d (£2. 35p) per week, uniform provided. Applications to be made in writing to the Chief Constable. F.L. Bunn, Chief Constable.

The Chief Constable let it be known that he would consider the widows of police officers. Two of the first volunteers to join the Women's Auxiliary Police Corps, were Mrs. Rose Longinore, the daughter of the Chief Constable, and Mrs. Jenny Bird, the wife of Constable R. Bird, both of their husbands were serving with H.M. Forces. In a short space of time six members of the W.A.P.C. had been recruited, and Woman Constable Broadhead who had been a member of the force for about 20 years was promoted to sergeant, and placed in charge of the now enlarged women's section.

With the disbandment of the Women's Auxiliary Police Corps at the end of the war, the Chief Constable requested permission of the Home Office, that he be allowed to increase the strength of the Regular Policewomen's Department from two to eight. This would mean seven women constables, and one woman sergeant. The Chief Constable's request was adhered to.

Recruiting for the enlarged Women's Section of the force started in 1946, and by the end of that years the establishment stood at six women constables, and one woman sergeant. By the end of 1948, two of the policewomen had been sent to the Detective Training School, at Wakefield.

Woman Sergeant Broadhead retired from the force on the last day of June, 1952, she had served the people of the City for over 30 years. The Watch Committee had placed on record the excellent service Miss Broadhead had rendered to the City, during her service with the police forces.

Staffordshire Police

A presentation being made to W/Sgt Eileen Lea by W/Ins. G. Stokes. circa 1966
Back row Norma Johnson, Janet Dodds, Carol Spruce, Linda Lea, Jaqueline Ainsworth Kay
Wilkinson, Carol Day, Dorothy Pikin, Margaret Rodway, Pat Webster, Kathleen Jackson (in civvies),
Jesephine Brotherton, Cecilia Moss (in civvies), Margaret Nixon, Sgt. Eileen Lea, Insp. Gladys Stokes

The vacancy left by Miss Broadhead, was filled by Woman Police Constable Stokes, who was promoted to sergeant on the 3rd September, 1952. W.P.C. Stokes was one of the first women to join the force after the war in 1946.

It was in 1958 that the Chief Constable decided to double the establishment of policewomen in the force from 8 to 16. Four would be taken immediately, and the remainder the following financial year. Woman Sergeant Stokes was promoted to the rank of inspector in 1962, and placed in charge of the enlarged Women's Section, and Woman Police Constable Lea was promoted to sergeant.

At the time of the amalgamation in 1968 the authorized establishment of the Women's Section of the force was made up as follows-

Women Inspector	1
Women Sergeants	2
Women Constables	19
Total.	22

Mrs. Whitehurst

A Busy W.P.C.5 Doreen Whitehurst (nee Gribble)
taken about 1950

The policewomen of the City had come along way since Miss Broadhead and Miss Cowley first walked the street of the Potteries in 1924. They now rode motor scooters about the City, and served with the C.I.D.

OFFICERS AWARDED CORONATION AND JUBILEE MEDALS.

The following members of the force received the George the V Coronation Medal in 1911:-

Superintendent (Deputy Chief Constable)	William WILLIAMS
Superintendent	Charles HICKSON
Chief Inspector	George H. MIDDLETON
Chief Inspector	Percy L. BARRY
Inspector	Joseph HALL
Inspector	Thomas DAVIES
Sergeant	William BATEMAN
Sergeant	Joseph TURNER
Constable	Thomas DAY

The following members of the force were awarded the George the V Silver Jubilee Medal in 1935:-

Chief Constable	Mr. Roger J. CARTER
Superintendent	Charles Henry BOWLER
Det. Chief Inspector	Charles John DIGGLE
Inspector	George RYE
Sergeant	Thomas FLOWER
Sergeant	Ernest James TENNANT
Constable (80)	Dennis DILLON
Constable (102)	Thomas WARDLE
Constable (160)	James William BRANDRICK
Constable (73)	Joseph Charles HORLSETON

Constable (183)	George William WALSH
Constable (94)	George Ralph HARVEY
Special Inspector	Ernest SHIPMAN

The following members of the force received the George the VI Coronation Medal in 1937

Chief Constable	Mr. Frank L. BUNN
Superintendent	Arthur Lawton CLARKE
Chief Inspector	Harry Hadfield MARSHALL
Inspector	Gerald Frank GOODMAN
Det. Inspector	Edward TILL
Sergeant	Alfred Edward GODDEN
Constable	Albert Ellis NUNNS
Constable	Leonard Baden GAMBLE
Constable	Walter Edward BLANCHARD
Special Inspector	Warwick SAVAGE.

The following members of the force received the Queen Elizabeth the II Coronation Medal in 1953:-

Chief Constable	Mr. F L. BUNN, O.B.E.
Superintendent (Deputy Chief Constable)	L. WOODHOUSE
Superintendent	C. CARTWRIGHT
Det. Superintendent	P.COOKE
Chief Inspector	W.E.BLANCHARD
Chief Inspector	A. RUDDICK
Inspector	C.H. HOLLAND

Inspector	A.E. FAWCETT
Inspector	C.H. MIDDLETON
Inspector	I. SARGEANT
Det. Inspector	H. RIMMER
Sergeant	C.A.M. TOMLINSON
Sergeant	J.L. BOOTON
Det. Sergeant	G.H. CURRAN
Det. Sergeant	R. THRONTHWAITE
Constable	J.E. HARRISON
Constable	H.O. FRANCIS
Constable	W.J. HANCOCK
Det. Constable	TURNER.

SPECIAL CONSTABLES

Divisional Commandant	J.W. MOXON
Divisional Commandant	0. HAWLEY
Special Chief Inspector	M. FRIEDER
Special Inspector	W.C.F. GRIFFITHS
Special Inspector	E. STRAFFORD
Special Inspector	E.B. HAMMERSLEY

MEN IN COMMAND

Chief Constables of Stoke-on-Trent

Roger James CARTER.   1st April, 1910 - 13th April, 1936.

Born Kendal, Westmorland, December, 1866, was Educated at Kendal Grammar School, then served in his father's business (builders and timber merchant). He joined Kendal Borough Police in 1887. He served in Rochdale Borough Police from 1890 to 1898 rising to the rank of Inspector. Appointed Chief Constable of Windsor Borough on 31st August, 1898. He was then appointed Chief Constable of Hanley Borough Police on 31 August, 1901, becoming Chief Constable of Stoke-on-Trent on the Federation on 1st April, 1910. Mr. Carter died whilst still serving at the age of 70 years on 13th April, 1936. He was a member of the Royal Victorian Order which he was granted in 1913 for his previous service to Queen Victoria whilst Chief Constable of Windsor. He was later awarded the King's Police Medal.

Frank Leonard BUNN. 1st September, 1936 - 31st May, 1955.

Born at Great Yarmouth, Norfolk in 1888, joined the Regular Army in 1906, serving in India. In 1911 he joined the Great Eastern Railway Company Police. Joined the Norfolk Constabulary in October, 1912 until 1919. Served in the First World War 1914 to 1916. From 1919 until 1921, he served as a Sergeant in King's Lynn Borough Police, when he transferred to St.Helens Borough Police in July, 1921, being promoted to the rank of Inspector in 1922. On the 1st January, 1925, transferred to Bacup Borough Police as Inspector and Deputy Chief Constable. Bacup Borough Police had a strength of 25 men. In November, 1930 he was appointed Chief Constable of Gravesend Borough Police. On 1st September, 1934, was appointed Chief Constable and Director of the Fire Brigade at Grimsby Borough. On 1st September, 1936, he was appointed Chief Constable of Stoke-on-Trent City Police. Mr. Bunn retired on 31st May, 1955, and died in 1972 aged 84 years. He had been awarded the Order of the British Empire in 1943, and had become a qualified Barrister at Law in 1945.

William Edward WATSON. 1st June, 1955 - 31st December, 1967.

Born Middleton-in-Teesdale, Co.Durham in 1908, receiving an education at a local grammar school, and was appointed as a clerk in February, 1924, with the London North Eastern Railway Company Limited. On the 20⁻ May, 1929, he joined Newcastle-upon-Tyne City Police, and at the time held a Certificate of Ambulance Work, and also Shorthand. He received promotion as follows: Acting Sergeant 5th April, 1935; Sergeant 12th November, 1937; Acting Inspector 29th August, 1939; Inspector 2nd February, 1940. Appointed Superintendent and Chief Clerk 3rd September, 1948, then Assistant Chief Constable 13th December, 1952. He was appointed Chief Constable of Stoke-on-Trent City Police on 1st June, 1955. On the amalgamation of the City and County forces on 1st January, 1968, Mr. Watson became

Deputy Chief Constable of the then Staffordshire County and Stoke-on-Trent Constabulary, retiring in 1973, with over 44 years service. He died at his home in Hanchurch on the 19th October, 1994, aged 86 years. Mr. Watson was President of the Hanley Division of the St.John's Ambulance Association. He held the Order of the British Empire, Order of St. John, the Queen's Police Medal, Coronation Medal, and Police Long Service Medal.

Assistant Chief Constables.

During it's existence the Stoke-on-Trent City Police only had two Assistant Chief Constables. Prior to this, the Senior Superintendent, and later the Chief Superintendent would hold the post of Deputy Chief Constable. The first person to hold the office of Assistant Chief Constable was Mr. L. Woodhouse, who was followed by Mr. H. Steele.

Leonard WOODHOUSE.

Born at Huddersfield, Yorkshire, October, 1900, his civilian occupation was a Clerk. He served in the Army for four months, then joining Stoke-on-Trent County Borough Police 4th May, 1922. He was promoted Sergeant on 1st February, 1937, Inspector in June, 1939. Appointed Chief Clerk 1942 and promoted Chief Inspector and Chief Clerk in 1948. He was promoted Superintendent on 1st February, 1950, and appointed Deputy Chief Constable on 1st April, 1950. He was promoted to the rank of Chief Superintendent and Deputy Chief Constable in 1954, and was then appointed Assistant Chief Constable in 1960. He retired from the force on the 31st December, 1965. Mr. Woodhouse became a Member of the British Empire in 1955.

Harry STEELE.

Born Astbury, Nr. Congleton, Cheshire, in 1916, he was educated at King's Grammar School, Macclesfield. His civilian occupation was Clerk. He joined Stoke-on-Trent City Police in November, 1936. He served in the Royal Navy from 1942 until 1946, when he returned to the City force being promoted to Sergeant in 1948. In 1957 he was promoted Detective Inspector, then Superintendent in charge of C.I.D. in 1960. He was appointed Assistant Chief Constable on 1st January, 1966. He retired from the Staffordshire County and Stoke-on-Trent Constabulary as Assistant Chief Constable in March, 1968.

Mr. H. Steele

Officers Promoted Chief Constable of other forces.

During the years quite a number of officers transferred from both the Hanley Borough force, and later the Stoke-on-Trent City Police on advancement to higher office.

William LLOYD.

Joined Newcastle-under-Lyme Borough Police in 1866, transferring to Henley Borough Police in 1870, where he rose to the rank of Inspector. Was appointed Chief Constable of Louth Borough Police, Lincolnshire in 1878. He died in office in 1886 aged 50 years.

Joseph OGDEN.

Appointed Inspector Hanley Borough Police in 1870. He was appointed Chief Constable of Great Yarmouth Borough Police in 1878. Retired on ill health in 1881.

Gerald Frank GOODMAN.

Born 27th April, 1899, his civilian occupation was Gardener. He served 5 years in the Army (South Lancashire Regiment and Grenadier Guards), then joining the Stoke-on-Trent County Borough Police on the 22nd April, 1922. He was promoted Sergeant on the 8th May, 1930, Inspector in 1936, then Chief Inspector in 1938. Appointed Chief Constable of Newark Police, Nottingham, 1st April, 1939, Chief Constable of Scarborough Police in October, 1941, then Chief Constable of Halifax Borough Police on the 1st April, 1944. He retired from Halifax Borough Police on the 30th September, 1968, when the force amalgamated. Died on the 9th February, 1981.

Mr. G. F. Goodman Chief Constable of Halifax
1st January 1944 to 30th September 1968

Mr. Jack Wild Halifax

Alfred Edward GODDEN.

Born on the 7th September, 1900, at Dover, Kent, was educated at Drax Grammar School, Selby, Yorkshire. His civilian occupation was a Mineral Driller. He served 2 years in the Army (Life Guards). Joined Stoke-on-Trent County Borough Police on the 3rd May, 1923, being promoted Sergeant in 1936, Inspector and Chief Clerk in 1938, and Superintendent in 1941. Appointed Chief Constable of Wakefield City Police on the 1st April, 1942, retiring from that office on the 31st August, 1965. He died on the 1st April, 1979.

Mr. Colin Jackson of Wakefield

Mr. A. E. Godden Chief Constable of Wakefield
1942 to 1965

Percy Lionel BARRY

Born in London in 1878, later serving with the Army b(Mounted Infantry). He joined Hanley Borough Police on the 29th October 1901. He was promoted to Sergeant and Chief Clerk in OCtober 1906. Inspector on 1st January 1909, then Chief Inspector on the 16th March 1911. He was appointed the first Chief Constable of Wallasey on the formation of the force on the 1st April 1913. He retired from that office in 1930 and died in 1933.

Mersyside Police

Percy Lionel Barry photograph taken when
Chief Constable of Wallasey

Stoke-on-Trent City Police transferring to Staffordshire County and Stoke-on-Trent Constabulary on amalgamation 1st January, 1968.

The information contained in this list has had to be obtained from various sources due to the fragmentation of original records over a period of time. Although it is believed to be a fairly comprehensive list of officers transferring from the former Stoke on Trent City Police Force to the combined Staffordshire County and Stoke on Trent Constabulary on 1st January, 1968. It is possible that the names of some officers may be missing and we apologise for this omission.

Chief Constable	William Edward WATSON	Sergeant	Arthur Norman John BIRT
Assistant Chief Constable	Harry STEELE	Sergeant 6	Derek Norman BOWERS
Superintendent	John. William. MOSS	Sergeant 21	Eric Stuart BOWMAN
Superintendent	Irwin. SARGENT	Sergeant 41	John BRANDRICK
Superintendent	Frank. SHEPHERD	Sergeant 28	John Whitehurst BRYAN
Superintendent	Leslie. John. GRIFFITHS	Sergeant 4	Norman BRIDGE
Detective Superintendent	George. Trevor. FROGGATT	Sergeant 46	Joseph Arthur BUCK
Chief Inspector	Ernest. Edwin. DAW	Sergeant 60	Harold Ernest BURTON
Chief Inspector	Frederick LAPPER	Sergeant 1	Ernest CADWALLANDER
Chief Inspector	Richard. George. MARRIOTT	Sergeant 53	Geoffrey CATTELL
Chief Inspector	Raymond. WARD	Sergeant 47	Peter COGGAN
Inspector	Ronald James BICKERTON	Sergeant 10	Charles Donald COOKE
Inspector	William Sydney BARRETT	Sergeant 17	Peter COOPER
Inspector	Douglas CLARKE	Sergeant 50	Robert Aynsley COOPER
Inspector	Geoffrey Noel CLARKE	Sergeant 61	John COPE
Inspector	Ivan George DEETH	Sergeant 32	Frederick William COXON
Inspector	Owen GILDER	Sergeant 62	Roy Thomas GREEN
Inspector	William HOLDCROFT	Sergeant 38	Leslie Donald GREER
Inspector	Colin JOHNSON	Sergeant 36	Colin Rodney GRIBBLE
Inspector	Arthur Edward KING	Sergeant	Ralph Frederick GRIBBLE
Inspector	Kenneth John KINGSBURY	Sergeant 33	Bernard HAMPTON
Inspector	William MACK	Sergeant 12	Kenneth William HAWKINS
Inspector	Ernest John MALLABONE	Sergeant 8	Leonard Allen HOBSON
Inspector	Tom PARTON	Sergeant 15	Horace Bertram JAMES
Inspector	Donald Joseph RALPHS	Sergeant 34	Graham Vincent JEFFRIES
Inspector	Richard John REED	Sergeant 27	Jack JOHNSON
Inspector	Frank SEABRIDGE	Sergeant 65	Douglas JONES
Inspector	Frank Edward WHALLEY	Sergeant 9	Frank JONES
Detective Inspector	Denis BILLINGTON	Sergeant 55	Raymond Harry JONES
Detective Inspector	Derek Ivan JOHNSON	Sergeant 63	Ian McMaster KILLICOAT
Detective Inspector	George William LESTER	Sergeant 29	Jeffrey LEADBEATER
Detective Inspector	Edward TURNER	Sergeant 45	Winston Cooke LEESE
Sergeant 5	Peter Charles ASTILL	Sergeant 3	Sydney Albert LUDWIG
Sergeant	William BANBURY	Sergeant 69	Thomas Douglas MATTHEWS
Sergeant	George BARLOW	Sergeant 51	Ronald MONTFORD
Sergeant 44	Anthony Edward BAYLEY	Sergeant 18	Peter PRESCOTT

Sergeant 16	John RYDER	Constable 61	Ian Frederick BARBER
Sergeant	John SANDALL	Constable 123	Clive Wilton BARNES
Sergeant 67	Harold STOKES	Constable 86	Colin William BARSTEAD
Sergeant 7	Thomas Carlton THWAYTES	Constable 190	John BAYLEY
Sergeant 14	Gordon John TOFT	Constable 249	Albert BEAUMONT
Sergeant 48	Vincent TURNER	Constable 6	Leslie Arthur BEECH
Sergeant 40	Thomas WHELAN	Constable 255	Alan Arthur. BENNETT
Sergeant 11	John WILLIAMS	Constable 82	Norman Percy BENNETT
Sergeant	James WINKLE	Constable 264	Brian Victor BENTLEY
Sergeant 68	Thomas WOOD	Constable	Samuel BENTLEY
Sergeant	Thomas David WOOD	Constable 91	Graham Andrew BETTANEY
Sergeant	George Roy WOOLRIDGE	Constable 21	Sidney Albert. BILLINGTON
Sergeant	Graham Edwin WOOTTON	Constable 150	Ronald John BLOOR
Detective Sergeant 58	Thomas ADAMS	Constable 25	Harry Baker. BOOTH
Detective Sergeant 57	Gerald Arthur ALLCOCK	Constable 56	J. Peter BOSTOCK
Detective Sergeant 52	Thomas BAILEY	Constable 164	Alfred BOTFIELD.
Detective Sergeant 49	William Roy BARNES	Constable 262	John BOULD
Detective Sergeant 30	Edwin Michael BILLS	Constable 46	John Edward BOULTON
Detective Sergeant 20	Howard Ernest BIRD	Constable 258	Keith John BOULTON
Detective Sergeant 42	William Thomas CARR	Constable 290	Charles BOWYER
Detective Sergeant 35	Ernest Rex DINS DALE	Constable 132	Henry Hughes BRACE
Detective Sergeant 54	John Thomas DODD	Constable 256	John Weston BRAGG
Detective Sergeant	Ernest John GOODWIN	Constable 351	Rodney BRAKER
Detective Sergeant 22	Anthony William GEORGE	Constable 11	Reginald BRAYFORD
Detective Sergeant 26	Sidney Daniel HARDY	Constable 50	Alan BREEZE
Detective Sergeant 39	John Stuart HOLLINS	Constable 126	Alan Arthur BRERETON
Detective Sergeant 37	Kenneth HOLLINS	Constable 182	Henry Clive BRIAN
Detective Sergeant 66	Ronald Eric LARGE	Constable 34	Dennis BROAHURST
Detective Sergeant 43	Eric John PALMER	Constable 35	Ernest Alan. BROOKSBANK
Constable 52	David Charles ABBERLEY	Constable 7	John BROUGH
Constable 120	Roy ADAMS	Constable 18	Harold J BROWN
Constable 315	Howard Alan ALCOCK	Constable 214	Spencer James Stanton BROWNING
Constable 263	John ALCOCK	Constable 196	Derek BRUFFELL
Constable 4	Cecil E ALLENDER	Constable 296	Kenneth William BUCKLEY
Constable 333	Kenneth ALLMAN	Constable 54	David BUFTON
Constable 85	Frederick George ADSHEAD	Constable 298	Robert James BURDEN
Constable 37	John ARNOLD	Constable 62	Frederick BURGESS
Constable 59	Anthony John ASTBURY	Constable 2	George William BURGESS
Constable 111	Barry John ASTBURY	Constable 130	John BURNHAM
Constable 121	Gilbert AUCOCK	Constable 131	James Thomas BYRNE
Constable 352	Brian Llewellyn BAILEY	Constable 102	Walter Alan CAPEWELL
Constable 116	John BAILEY	Constable 230	Anthony Gerald CAPPER
Constable 314	Graham Richard BAKER	Constable 222	Alan CARTLIDGE
Constable 9	Peter BAKER	Constable 16	William Terence CARTWRIGHT
Constable 74	Graham James BALL	Constable 241	Michael Dennis Patrick CAULKIN
Constable 68	Douglas Francis BANKS	Constable 58	Wilfred John CHADDOCK
Constable	Harold Joseph BADDELEY	Constable 291	James CHADWICK

Constable 167	Samuel Cyril CHADWICK	Constable 358	William Henry EDWARDS
Constable	Bruce Joseph CHALLINOR	Constable 348	Kenneth George EDWARDS
Constable 236	Anthony Arthur CHAPMAN	Constable 75	William EDWARDS
Constable 248	James CHAPPEL	Constable 13	Arthur Francis ELLIOTT
Constable 268	John CHATFIELD	Constable 311	John Roger ELLIOTT
Constable 303	Christopher John CHATTERTON	Constable 346	Anthony William EVANS
Constable 137	Douglas CHENEY	Constable 265	Ramon Laurence FARNSWORTH
Constable	Douglas CLAYTON	Constable	Charles Johnstone FINLEY
Constable 161	William McJimpsey CLEGG	Constable	Terence FOY
Constable 10	Brian CLIFFE	Constable	Michael FOX
Constable 299	Howard CLOUGH	Constable 383	Thomas Paul HAMMERSLEY - FENTON
Constable 24	Geoffrey Anthony CLIFFE	Constable 177	William Alan FERN
Constable 207	Roy CLOWES	Constable 313	William Bernard FIELD
Constable 40	Trevor CLOWES	Constable 43	Howard FINNEY
Constable 199	Alan William COOKE	Constable 103	Michael William FLANNIGAN
Constable 55	John COONEY	Constable 139	Frederick FORRESTER
Constable 29	William Arthur COOPER	Constable 321	Brian George FREEMAN
Constable 359	William COPE	Constable	Peter William FOWELL
Constable 105	Peter CORBISHLEY	Constable 94	Peter GALLAGHER
Constable 216	Keith Alfred COSSON	Constable 281	Kenneth GALLEY
Constable 274	Adrian John COTTERILL	Constable 316	Harold Charles GALLIMORE
Constable 286	Derek Thomas COWEN	Constable 140	Jonathan Paul GIBBONS
Constable 53	George Henry COWEN	Constable 76	Kevin Leslie GIBBS
Constable 100	Patrick William CROWE	Constable 226	Alfred GIMBERT
Constable 101	Joseph Henry DARBY	Constable 231	Alan Alfred GIMBERT
Constable 310	Peter Stuart Philip DAVEY	Constable 22	Donald Nigel GOOD
Constable 204	Roland DAVIES	Constable 367	John GREATBACH
Constable 42	John DAVY	Constable 80	Arthur Alfred GRINDLEY
Constable 178	Anthony DAY	Constable 292	Peter GROCOTT
Constable 301	John William DEAN	Constable 295	Anthony Maddock HALL
Constable 117	Michael Alan DEAN	Constable 194	Edward S. HALL
Constable 179	Frederick James DEAVILLE	Constable 33	Keith HALL
Constable 308	Graham John DEETH	Constable 186	Kenneth HALLAM
Constable 363	John James DEVANEY	Constable 344	Alan HANCOCK
Constable 165	Lance Neville DOBELL	Constable 95	John Graham HANCOCK
Constable 364	Anthony Joseph Peter DOBSON	Constable 337	John G HANCOCK
Constable 159	John Percy DODD	Constable 270	Gerald John HANKEY
Constable 135	Raymond DODD	Constable 201	Eric HARGREAVES
Constable 221	Michael Barry DOORBAR	Constable 166	Peter James George HARVEY
Constable 78	David DRAY	Constable 353	Timothy HASSALL
Constable 66	Gordon Edwin DUTTON	Constable 312	Gary HAWKINS
Constable 326	Clifford Graham DYER	Constable 45	Graham William HAYNES
Constable 32	Glyn Olwyn DYER	Constable 366	John Edward HEATH
Constable 266	Stephen John. EARDLEY	Constable	Kenneth HEATH.
Constable	Robert Ernest ECCLES	Constable 162	Harold Arthur HENSHALL
Constable 153	Peter EDGE	Constable 114	Gerald HERBERT
Constable 158	Charles Vaughan EDMONDSON	Constable 97	Peter Martin HERWARD

Constable 81	Thomas Reginald HEWITT	Constable 118	Leslie LYNCH
Constable	Rowland HIBBERT	Constable 39	Michael James LYTTLETON
Constable 181	Brian William HINES	Constable 71	Stanley Raymond MADDOX
Constable 305	Derek HODGKINSON	Constable 127	John Francis MANDLEY
Constable 124	John William HOLBROOK	Constable 355	Philip Newton MANION
Constable 380	Donald Arthur HOLFORD	Constable 81	Alan MANSELL
Constable 323	Terence HOLMES	Constable 154	Royston MARSH
Constable 70	John HOOD	Constable	Norman MASON
Constable 327	Philip Michael HOPKINS	Constable	Trevor Cyril MASSEY
Constable 217	Alfred John HOUGH	Constable 5	Roy Thomas MATTHIAS
Constable 269	Gerald Malcolm HUDSON	Constable 23	Colin MAYER
Constable 239	Roger HUDSON	Constable 370	Robert MCMILLAN
Constable 223	Frederick Henry HUGHES	Constable 233	Geoffrey Hugh MELLENCHIP
Constable	Henry Louraine HUMPHREYS	Constable 180	Frederick Lawrence MILLER
Constable 172	John E HURST	Constable 235	Allan MITCHELL
Constable 160	Anthony Graham HUXLEY	Constable 64	Michael Patrick MOLLOY
Constable 338	John William INSKIP	Constable 329	Frederick James MOORE
Constable 15	Lewis JEFFREY	Constable 108	David Party MORGAN
Constable 345	Graham JOHNSON	Constable 119	Graham Leslie MORGAN
Constable 278	Keith Anthony JOHNSON	Constable 69	Barry John MOTHERSHAW
Constable 354	Keith Michael JOHNSON	Constable 373	Kelvin Bernard MOTTERSHEAD
Constable 251	William Albert JOHNSON	Constable 145	Anthony William MYATT
Constable 252	Alfred Brian JONES	Constable 341	John William MYCOCK
Constable 228	Brian Reginald JONES	Constable 219	John NIXON
Constable 203	Neville JONES	Constable 293	David James OAKES
Constable 208	Norman JONES	Constable 371	Alan George OAKLEY
Constable	Raymond Harry JONES	Constable 99	John William OLDFIELD
Constable 155	William Lionel JONES	Constable 60	Roger John OWEN
Constable	Gordon David KELSALL	Constable 192	Dennis Samuel PARKES
Constable 1	James Francis Joseph KELLY	Constable 96	Thomas Norman PARR
Constable 187	James KENT	Constable 129	John Alfred PARRY
Constable 267	Edwin Raymond KINVIG	Constable 218	Ronald Frederick Charles PATTINSON
Constable 147	William David KNIGHT	Constable 28	Derek Leonard PEAKE
Constable 112	John David LAKIN	Constable 149	Richard Maurice PEMBERTON
Constable 328	Geoffrey LANGTON	Constable	Graham PEPPER
Constable 27	Anthony David LEA	Constable 134	Eric PHILLIPS
Constable 234	Clive Ryder LEESE	Constable 307	William Ronald Patrick PHILLIPS
Constable 122	Derek LEESE	Constable 106	Laurence POINTON
Constable 44	Eric Hubert F LEVIE	Constable 185	Wilfred POINTON
Constable 350	Keith LEWIS	Constable 342	Howard POOLE
Constable 107	Thomas Arthur LEWIS	Constable 213	Roy POOLE
Constable 238	Geoffrey LIGHTFOOT	Constable 4	Wilfred Derek POOLE
Constable 138	Reginald LOCKLEY	Constable 237	Harold RALPHS
Constable 188	Kenneth LODEY	Constable 324	Norman Derek RANKIN
Constable 368	John Michael LOFTUS	Constable 47	John REEVES
Constable 57	Arthur LOVATT	Constable 176	George REID
Constable 317	John Michael LOVATT	Constable 232	Alfred Michael REYNOLDS

Constable 205	Graham REYNOLDS	Constable 289	Harold Marshall THOMAS
Constable 151	Kenneth R. RIDGE	Constable 36	Dennis William THOMPSON
Constable 113	William RILEY	Constable 30	Edward Arthur TILL
Constable 133	Frank ROBINS	Constable 144	Frederick Neil TOMLINSON
Constable 294	John Stuart ROBINS	Constable 272	Francis Thomas TWEMLOW
Constable 88	Derek F ROPER	Constable 339	Jeffrey UNETT
Constable 198	Alan ROTCHELL	Constable 19	John Edward UPTON
Constable 282	James Barry ROTCHELL	Constable 318	Michael David VAUGHAN
Constable 276	Brian Peter ROWBOTHAM	Constable 320	Derek Robert VERNON
Constable 260	Michael Norman ROWE	Constable 90	Jeffrey VIRGO
Constable 332	John ROWLEY	Constable 279	Arthur Edward VITTA
Constable 297	Derek ROYLANCE	Constable 189	Stanley VYSE
Constable 240	Charles Patrick RUSHTON	Constable 257	Brian WALKER
Constable 520	Albert Kenneth RUSSELL	Constable 168	John Leonard WALKER
Constable	Roger Sidney RUSSELL	Constable 259	Leonard WALTON
Constable 250	Ian SALT	Constable 125	Brian Newton WALWYN
Constable 193	Colin SARGENT	Constable 347	Anthony Robert WARD
Constable 369	Timothy David SCRIVENS	Constable 152	Dennis Charles WARDLE
Constable 171	John Charles SEABRIDGE	Constable 331	Clive Terence WEBSTER
Constable 357	Frederick John SHARPLEY	Constable 375	Brian WESTON
Constable 246	Alan SHAW	Constable 220	Thomas WESTWELL
Constable 244	Brian Ernest SHAW	Constable 319	Alan Joseph WHITBY
Constable	David Albert SHANNON	Constable	Robert Charles Geoffrey WHITE
Constable 210	Dennis SHELDON	Constable 261	William Daniel WHITEHURST
Constable	Derek John SHENTON	Constable 273	Tomas Graham WILKES
Constable	Michael Ormison SIMPSON	Constable 376	Keith WILLIAMS
Constable	Donald George SIMMONDS	Constable	Frank WILSHAW
Constable 143	Peter SIMS	Constable	Alan William WILSON
Constable 197	Ronnie SINKER	Constable 309	Brian WINSTANLEY
Constable 104	Clive SMITH	Constable 275	Sidney John WITHERS
Constable 157	Cecil Gordon SMITH	Constable 304	John Thomas WITHINGTON
Constable 148	Joseph Henry SMITH	Constable 136	Vincent WOODCOCK
Constable 374	Leslie SMITH	Constable 336	Clive David WOOLLEY
Constable 215	William Charles SMITH	Constable 362	Alfred Joseph WORTHINGTON
Constable 349	John William SNAPE	Constable 287	Derek Marshall WYS
Constable 330	David SNEYD	Detective Constable 20	Peter Mark ADDISON
Constable 174	Michael SPRUCE	Detective Constable 38	Eric James AMISON
Constable 209	John STANYER	Detective Constable	Thomas Fairbairn ASHWORTH
Constable 340	Alan Peter STEELE	Detective Constable 306	Harold Edward BEECH
Constable 243	Joseph STEPHENS	Detective Constable 83	Derek BIRD
Constable 361	Alan Alfred STEVENSON	Detective Constable 65	Richard BURNS
Constable 356	John Lionel STUBBS	Detective Constable 163	Geoffrey Arnold CLAY
Constable 284	Derek George SUTTON	Detective Constable 280	Samuel Graham CLOWES
Constable 48	John Michael TARPEY	Detective Constable 227	Edward James COVENTRY
Constable 343	Patrick Victor TAYLOR	Detective Constable 49	Charles EDWARDS
Constable 31	Roy TAYLOR	Detective Constable 183	Alan William EARDLEY
Constable 225	Edwin TEALE	Detective Constable 245	Frederick John FLETCHER

Other Books published by THREE COUNTIES PUBLISHING (Books) LTD - TCP Books, and which are all available by mail order from the publishers are: -

Policing The Potteries	By Alf Tunstall & Jeff Cowdell ISBN 0-9535239-9-3	*Price £ 17.95*
Hanley Wakes	by Derrick Woodward ISBN 0 9535239 - 8 - 5	*Price £ 7.95*
Where Have all The Year Gone	by Reg. Harvey	*Price £ 9.95*
A History of Longton	by Prof. J. H. Y. Briggs ISBN 0 9535239 - 1 - 8	*Price £14.95*
The Spirit of the Place	by M. J. W. Rogers ISBN 0 9535239 - 3 - 4	*Price £16.95*
In Name Only	by C. W. Sheldon ISBN 0 9535239 - 5 - 0	*Price £ 13.95*
Gently Thru' Life	by David Whitmore ISBN 0 9535239 - 4 - 2	*Price £ 12.95*
'A Victorian Pottery	by Peter Beckett ISBN 0 9535239 - 6 - 9	*Price £ 8.95*
'In Search of Fenton Castle'	by Barbara Maddox ISBN 0 9535239 - 7 - 7	*Price £ 7.95*

If you do not wish to order any books but would like to be sent our twice yearly newsletter on new publications please complete the address panel below and send it to us marked NEWSLETTER PLEASE

POSTAGE - PLEASE NOTE:

ORDER ONE BOOK	POSTAGE & PACKAGE ADD £ 1.20
ORDER TWO BOOKS	POSTAGE & PACKAGE ADD £ 2.00
ORDER ANY THREE BOOKS OR MORE	POSTAGE & PACKAGE **FREE**

TOTAL REMITTANCE Incl. POSTAGE   £   .   p

Your Name ....

Address ....

....

Post Code .... Tel. No. ....(for use only if difficulty with delivery)

Cheques should be made payable to **Three Counties Publishing (Books) Ltd**
and sent to **P.O. Box 435, Leek, Staffs, ST13 5TB**
Please allow up to 10 - 21 days for delivery of books in stock.
This Order Form may be photocopied if you require more or would like to pass one to a friend